*Power and
Marxist Theory*

Power and Marxist Theory

A REALIST VIEW

Jeffrey C. Isaac

Cornell University Press

ITHACA AND LONDON

First published 1987 by Cornell University Press.

International Standard Book Number 0-8014-1934-4
Library of Congress Catalog Card Number 87-6690
Printed in the United States of America
Librarians: Library of Congress cataloging information
appears on the last page of the book.

The paper in this book is acid-free and meets the
guidelines for permanence and durability of the
Committee on Production Guidelines for
Book Longevity of the Council on Library Resources.

For Debra and Adam,
with love

Contents

Acknowledgments

During the time I have been working on this project I have incurred intellectual debts to many colleagues and friends.

Three individuals must be singled out. I owe a special debt to Robert Dahl. As my teacher and as the supervisor of my doctoral dissertation at Yale, Professor Dahl has been a source of great inspiration as well as constant encouragement. Though my book is in large part a straightforward critique of his own work, Professor Dahl has always been its staunchest supporter. He has approached my work with a spirit of open-mindedness and tolerance which is the hallmark of genuine scientific inquiry. At times I left his office in wonderment, having just spent hours discussing with him this writer named "Dahl" in the third person. I have learned many things from him, about the character of democratic states and about the character of democratic individuals.

My undergraduate philosophy teacher at Queens College and my good friend and colleague ever since, Peter Manicas has been the primary intellectual influence on this book. Peter first introduced me to realist philosophy of science when he mailed me an essay by Roy Bhaskar back in 1979; and Peter's own prolific writing has been quite central in shaping my thinking on philosophical and political matters. He has read each chapter of this book assiduously, and he has provided me with numerous helpful suggestions. We have spent many hours arguing about realism and about Marxism and, though we have not always agreed, I could not have written the book without his encouragement and his questioning.

I also gratefully acknowledge the influence of Raymond Franklin.

Ray first sparked my interest in political economy and Marxism. As an undergraduate at Queens College, I spent hours too numerous to count in his office, where I learned what real intellectual conversation and real intellectual kinship were about.

Other people have helped me in the course of my work. James Farr, Terence Ball, Alan Gilbert, Paul Thomas, G. William Domhoff, and Allen Graubard all read the entire manuscript and offered valuable comments and criticisms. (Special thanks go to Jim, who read it all twice.) Roy Bhaskar, David Cameron, David Johnston, Michael Krasner, Irving Leonard Markovitz, David Mayhew, Douglas Rae, Gerald Rosenberg, Ian Shapiro, David Sprintzen, Alexander Wendt, Robert Paul Wolff, Erik Olin Wright, and Burt Zweibach read parts of the manuscript and made helpful comments. Three friends and colleagues at Fordham, Patricia Clough, Barry Goldberg, and Robert Orsi, have provided me with many stimulating conversations during the writing of this book, and the insights gleaned from these have undoubtedly made their way into the final draft.

I also thank John Ackerman of Cornell University Press, editors Kay Scheuer and Lois Krieger, and Deborah Hause, who have helped turn my manuscript into a better book.

Finally, I thank my family for their help and support throughout the writing of this book. My parents, Sylvia and Hyman Isaac, and my brother, Gary Isaac, have always encouraged me. From my father, a linotype operator, I first learned of the nobility of work, and of its degradation under capitalism; and it was over the dinner table that I first learned the value of political argument. My wife, Debra Kent, a writer herself, has provided me with more support, emotional, intellectual, and financial, than any scholar has any right to expect. To her, and to our new son Adam, this book is dedicated.

JEFFREY C. ISAAC

Farmingdale, New York

Power and
Marxist Theory

On the Reason for Yet Another
Argument about the Concept of Power

Social theorists seem to have an unfailing inclination toward methodological controversy. Such argument fills the pages of professional journals, and it makes (and breaks?) careers. But there is, we suspect, more to it than this. And so we continue the argument.

Ever since Aristotle, it has seemed impossible to write about society without also writing about writing about society. Sheldon Wolin has suggested that there is a political point behind such a concern with method, that argument about method is also both argument about theory and argument about the good society.[1] If this is true in general, it would seem to be supremely true of contemporary social science. We live in an age of science and technology. And even if the environmental horrors of the past two decades have caused us to reassess their value, there can be no doubt that understandings of science, and claims to scientificity, have played a crucial role in the development of contemporary social theory.

This is particularly true of recent discussions of the concept of power, in which notions of causality and proper scientific explanation have, as I shall argue, structured debate within certain narrow limits. There is a justifiable inclination to circumvent all this discussion, to extricate oneself from the tangled conceptual webs that social scientists have spun, and simply to do actual research.

[1]See Sheldon S. Wolin, "Max Weber: Legitimacy, Method, and the Politics of Theory," *Political Theory* 9 (August 1981), 401–24.

The proof of the pudding, after all, is in the eating, isn't it? Unfortunately, things are not that easy, for the question of whether we are properly eating the pudding, and whether it is indeed pudding that we are eating, will not go away. The conceptual problems remain, and they determine our scholarly activity. What, after all, is "actual research"? And what is this thing called "power" that we are researching?

Pure meta-theoretical argument tends toward a hopeless abstractness, and despite the important contribution of the "linguistic turn" in contemporary philosophy, which has taught us that we cannot get outside of our language,[2] the utilitarian in us forces us to ask for the theoretical payoff—is there a point, or are we simply spinning conceptual webs? In spite of this danger, however, one suspects that the injunction simply to "do research" is based on an extremely naive view of what constitutes scholarly activity.[3]

Political science, like any science, is a social practice. It is an activity undertaken by human beings in certain definite relationships and governed by norms, rules, and understandings that make activity meaningful. This may seem like an incredibly obvious and trivial claim with which to begin a book. But it is only recently that this sort of claim has become an accepted piece of commonsense wisdom among social theorists. Social scientists, particularly in America and particularly since the 1930s, have until recently believed that their endeavors involved primarily the observation and logical interpretation of a set of unmediated "facts," given in experience and fundamentally unproblematical. It is not necessary to rehearse the development of this self-understanding, centrally informed by logical positivist philosophy, nor is it necessary to rehearse its demise. It is sufficient to note that theorists as different as Thomas Kuhn, Jürgen Habermas, W.V.O. Quine, and Michel Foucault have taught us that as social scientists our encounters

---

[2]See Richard Rorty, *Philosophy and the Mirror of Nature* (Princeton: Princeton University Press, 1979).

[3]For the most sophisticated but, in my view, flawed polemic against methodological analysis, see John G. Gunnell, "In Search of the Political Object: Beyond Methodology and Transcendentalism," in John S. Nelson, ed., *What Should Political Theory Be Now?* (Albany: State University of New York Press, 1983), pp. 25–52.

with "reality" are fundamentally constituted by the normative and conceptual frameworks within which we operate.[4]

This understanding is absolutely critical from an epistemological point of view. It means that our theories about society are complex webs of interrelated concepts, and that there can be no Archimedean point from which to "observe" the world and adjudicate the "Truth" of scientific theories. The importance of this point, however, extends beyond the now familiar recognitions that facts are theory-laden and truth is rule-bound and irreducibly judgmental. For the norms and preconceptions governing social scientific practice not only (partly) determine our substantive conception of the world, they also determine our very notions of the proper methods of studying the world and, more generally, our understanding of its ultimate constitution, its *ontology*.

In this book I am not primarily interested in analyzing the set of substantive concepts that constitutes the dominant theory about power in political science—pluralism. This task is, of course, a very important one, one to which many others who figure in this book have set themselves. William Connolly's *Political Science and Ideology* (1967) and *The Bias of Pluralism* (1969), for example, were early efforts to expose the complex descriptive and normative presuppositions of pluralist theorists and their critics. And Peter Bachrach and Morton Baratz, in their *Power and Poverty* (1970), emphasized these issues in their critique of pluralism. However, while much of this important work staked its claim on the terrain of epistemology, opening up space for the critique of pluralism by employing post-positivist notions of theory and its irreducibly interpretative dimension, it never really challenged the consensus on other methodological issues, particularly ontological ones.

Of course some of these questions, regarding the nature of social being, intersubjectivity, and human agency, were not wholly ignored by political science. As Richard Ashcraft has noted, they were taken up by those who extricated themselves from the methods of behavioralism and asserted their independence as political philosophers and political theorists rather than as political *scien-*

---

[4]See Richard J. Bernstein, *Beyond Objectivism and Relativism: Science, Hermeneutics, and Praxis* (Philadelphia: University of Pennsylvania Press, 1983).

tists.[5] Here, these inquiries became part of the discipline of textual hermeneutics, focused on the various issues surrounding the reading of the classic texts of the Western tradition. But even here, ironically, a certain consensus about the nature of science, regarding the nature of causality, was hardly challenged. Thus, a rough division of labor developed in political science. On the one hand were those political scientists involved in actual, empirical research who, regardless of their avowed epistemology, undertook to do "real science" by arriving at lawlike predictive generalizations about political behavior. On the other hand were those who, repelled by this scientism, virtually abandoned causal explanation in favor of historical, exegetical, and moral inquiry.

In this book I will analyze those methodological, or meta-theoretical, understandings that are shared by most political scientists, pluralist theorists *and* their critics. In doing so, I hope to suggest, implicitly, the folly of the division of labor between political science and political theory which has developed in political inquiry. My primary interest, however, is in showing how social scientific research is shaped not only by substantive theoretical differences—pluralism versus elitism versus Marxism versus feminism—but by more general norms regarding the nature of scientific inquiry. The so-called "three faces of power" controversy is a perfect example of the way social science is normatively constituted. All the contestants in this controversy share a set of understandings, which I will label empiricism; and these understandings have determined both the acceptable ways of thinking about social power and the unacceptable ways.

This specific issue is particularly germane because of the perdurance and the irresolution of the controversy. Both of these are marked by the publication of the second edition of Nelson Polsby's *Community Power and Political Theory* in 1980.[6] The reissue of Polsby's book is interesting because the volume constitutes both a

---

[5]Richard Ashcraft, "One Step Backward, Two Steps Forward: Reflections upon Contemporary Political Theory," in Nelson, ed., *What Should Political Theory Be Now?* pp. 515–48. See also my "After Empiricism: The Realist Alternative," in Terence Ball, ed., *Idioms of Inquiry: Critique and Renewal in Political Theory* (Albany: State University of New York Press, 1987).

[6]Nelson Polsby, *Community Power and Political Theory*, 2d ed. (New Haven: Yale University Press, 1980).

recognition of the theoretical sterility of the entire debate about power and a restatement of old themes. Polsby notes the bankruptcy of the controversy but attempts to fortify his own position within it. The relevance of debate concerning the concept of power, however, is hardly limited to questions of the organization of political science as an intellectual discipline. The concept of power is central to all social scientific inquiry. It figures in contemporary debates regarding class structure, gender relations, the nature of the state, nuclear arms, and the danger of what Edward Thompson calls "exterminism." To locate the sources of power in society is to locate the enablements and constraints that operate on all of us as ordinary individuals, and that operate as well on those C. Wright Mills referred to as "extraordinary" individuals, those particularly powerful persons whose activities so shape our own. To locate power is also to fix moral responsibility, both upon those who exercise power illegitimately and upon those social structures that make this power available. To locate power is thus an enterprise central to "normative" as well as "descriptive" inquiry, for to do so is to identify the causes of what John Dewey called our "public problems," as well as the barriers to the solution of these problems. As Mills wrote: "The interest of the social scientist in social structure is not due to any view that the future is structurally determined. We study the structural limits of human decision in order to find points of effective intervention . . . to find within them the ways in which they are and can be controlled. For only in this way can we come to know the limits and the meaning of human freedom."[7]

My own interest in the presuppositions underlying the conceptualization of power come out of my experiences, as a graduate student, in confronting the "power" of Polsby's arguments, which have had the manifest effect of delegitimizing any talk of "power structure" or "dominant class." As a student of critical bent, interested in Marxian theory, I read Polsby, and came up squarely against the question of what the notion of a "dominant class" could possibly mean if not that one group regularly and predictably prevails over another under definite conditions. This road block was produced mainly by a set of sincerely held beliefs—some spe-

[7]C. Wright Mills, *The Sociological Imagination* (Oxford: Oxford University Press, 1959), p. 174.

cific (and rather primitive) notions of linguistic meaning, and some more general understandings of the nature of scientific explanation—and not by a set of coercive sanctions. My search for an answer led me to the works of Bachrach and Baratz, and of Steven Lukes, commonly taken to be the "radical" critics of Dahl and Polsby; I read their work with great excitement, but quickly became dissatisfied. Lukes seemed right that the approach of Bachrach and Baratz was little different from that of Dahl and Polsby. But while he raised some stimulating questions, Lukes's discussion, particularly his treatment of the problem of "objective interests," generated as many problems as it attempted to resolve. This debate helped me neither to understand the concept of power better nor to ground my belief that Marxism was a genuine theory of power.

At the same time that I was dealing with these issues, I developed a growing interest in the body of work in philosophy and social theory dealing with the problems of the "received" view of social science. My absorption in this literature and my understanding of these issues, centrally informed by Roy Bhaskar's *A Realist Theory of Science* (1978),[8] led me to an insight into the three faces of power debate—that it centered around an empiricist view of causation and scientific explanation. Further inquiry led me to locate the limitations of this debate precisely in its empiricism, and to seek to formulate an alternative conceptualization of power.

For all the participants in the three faces of power debate, power is a behavioral concept that refers to the regular conjunction of the behaviors of two parties, such that "A has power over B" means that in some sense A's doing something gets B to do something. This view is doubly confused. First, it is limited to situations of "power over," and fails to see that "power over," or what I will call domination, is parasitic upon a "power to." Second, it fails to distinguish between the possession and the exercise of power. These confusions rest upon a refusal, characteristic of empiricism, to talk of the "capacities" and "intrinsic natures" of things. As Jack Nagel has put it, such talk has "objectionable metaphysical implications."[9] But as we shall see, the weaknesses of this debate are

[8]Roy Bhaskar, *A Realist Theory of Science*, 2d ed. (Atlantic Highlands, N.J.: Humanities Press, 1978).

[9]Jack Nagel, *The Descriptive Analysis of Power* (New Haven: Yale University Press, 1975), p. 36.

themselves the result of certain objectionable implications of empiricist metaphysics—namely, the belief that the social world is nothing more than a set of behavioral regularities. Realist philosophy of science provides a different understanding of the social world, according to which society is a complex of structured relationships. If for empiricism the task of social science is the discovery and prediction of empirical regularities of the form "whenever A...then B," for realism science analyzes those enduring mechanisms that cause the occurrence of empirical events. On this view a much more adequate concept of power, as socially structured capacity, is possible.

This version of realism is to be distinguished from two other views that are also conventionally labeled "realist." The first is the doctrine of Realpolitik of the Kissinger/Morgenthau variety, a praxis according to which hardheaded "practicality" in a world of incessant struggle is recommended.[10] Realist philosophy of science bears no necessary relationship to this doctrine. While the realist ontology I will articulate below shares with the doctrine of Realpolitik an emphasis on the constraints upon agents' choices, and while I will argue that power is a concept that marks this question of constraint, my version of philosophical realism in no way entails that aggrandizement and domination are transhistorical human imperatives. In fact, my version of realism insists upon the historical specificity of forms of social power and, in highlighting the possibility of the historical transformation of these forms, has critical implications for social practice which distinguish it from the generally conservative orientation of Realpolitik doctrines. The second version of realism is a view within the philosophy of science, which holds that scientific theories converge upon a rough correspondence with reality, and are thus progressively more realistic. This view is often associated with the view of realism developed in this book, and there are some genealogical affinities, particularly in the common criticism of positivism and idealism. This latter view of realism, however, in the view of many philosophers, occludes the significance of the social dimension of science and severely underestimates the complexity of scientific language and judgment and the discontinuity that characterizes the actual history of science.

[10]See R. N. Berki, *On Political Realism* (London: Dent, 1981).

The view developed here, then, recognizes the necessary tension between the real objects of scientific explanation and theoretical explanation itself, and it posits no necessary correspondence between our understanding of the world and the way the world really operates. Thus realism here is not an epistemological claim about the progressive truth value of theories, but an ontological claim about the nature of causality and the form causal theories should properly take.

This alternative, realist understanding of power is what is necessary to ground Marxian theory, whose own analyses of power are not assimilable to the empiricist view. Marxian theory represents a different kind of theorizing about power than that envisioned by empiricism, a kind of theorizing in which the realist language of causal necessity and social structure plays a crucial role. And in developing a realist view of power, I discovered that such a perspective illuminates some of the central concepts of Marxian theory: class domination, class capacities, class struggle, and the relative autonomy of the state.

Illuminating Marxian theory, however, involves more than simply joining it to the realist view of power I formulate. It involves an extensive exposition and elaboration of its characteristic claims. This is necessary in order to combat the interpretation of Marxism proffered by mainstream political scientists and well articulated by Dahl, who writes that "according to Marxist theory, in capitalist societies, the capitalist class unilaterally rules over the society. In this sense the class as a whole might be considered the prime mover. But the unilateral dominance of the capitalist class is more a theoretical postulate or hypothesis than a well verified description of contemporary non-socialist nation-states with 'democratic' governments."[11] On this view the Marxian theory of capitalism involves a global claim to the effect that capitalists unilaterally dominate, or are the prime mover—that is, they always get what they want. This, it should be noted, is the same view articulated by Karl Popper in his many critiques of Marxism—namely, that Marxism is a historicism, that it makes predictions about events (e.g., capitalists always prevail) without specifying the empirical

[11]Robert A. Dahl, *Modern Political Analysis*, 3d ed. (Englewood Cliffs, N.J.: Prentice-Hall, 1976), p. 41.

conditions under which these predicted events can be expected to occur. Because Marxian theory makes such categorical instead of conditional claims, because it talks about the nature of capitalism rather than a set of empirical uniformities, it is unscientific.[12]

This kind of rejection of Marxism involves two sorts of claim. First it involves a specific theory of science—empiricism—which maintains that a scientific theory is a set of empirical predictions capable of falsification by the occurrence of a counterinstance. Second, it involves a particular interpretation of Marxian theory, according to which the notion of a dominant class involves a global prediction about events to the effect that capitalists always and unilaterally get what they want. In arguing that Marxism represents a genuinely scientific theory of power, I will challenge both of these beliefs.

Part I of this book is a strictly meta-theoretical treatment of the questions of science, social science, and power. This section is a critique of the three faces of power debate. By critique I do not mean rejection, but rather a critical analysis that dissects a given reality (in this case, the reality of empiricist theory) and explains its weaknesses. My analysis is a critique in that it dissects the empiricist concept of power, explains its weaknesses in virtue of its empiricism, and offers an alternative conceptualization. I develop a realist understanding of social power, according to which power is implicated in the enduring structural relations that characterize a society and is exercised by intentional human agents who participate in these relations. This view of power, I argue, not only makes better sense of the concept; it also integrates an understanding of social structure and human agency in a way empiricist formulations cannot.

Part II is a discussion of Marxian theory, particularly in its contemporary form, in the light of this argument. Here I argue that Marxism as a general orientation represents a scientific theory of social power, and that recent Marxian analyses of the class structure and politics of capitalist society can be understood only in realist terms. This section is not a consideration of the many important gaps and lacunae in Marxian theory, nor is it a substantive

---

[12]See, for instance, Karl Popper, *Conjectures and Refutations: The Growth of Scientific Knowledge* (New York: Harper Torchbooks, 1965).

defense of Marxism as a correct theory. It is a defense of Marxism as a genuine theory that deserves to be examined and criticized on its own merits as a theory, and not simply discarded on strictly formal (and specious) grounds because it fails to conform to the canons of empiricist philosophy. There is within Marxism a dangerous strand of essentialism, particularly as regards the Marxian theory of history, historical materialism. This essentialism is often expressed in reductionist accounts of social relations and political events, which would explain everything with reference to class relations and class interests. It is often expressed in what Louis Althusser has called "historicism," according to which history is treated as a unilinear process with an unfolding meaning and a necessary end—socialism. This essentialist Marxism would view gender conflicts, for instance, as being "really" the expressions of class conflict. And it frequently issues global predictions of the necessary instability of capitalism and the ruptural "moment" of socialist transformation.

The version of Marxism I reconstruct here attempts to avoid these problems, by disavowing any necessary connection between the theory of capitalism and a theory of universal history, and by concentrating exclusively on the former. Even this maneuver does not, however, insulate Marxian theory and practice from a number of serious criticisms. The point I would make about these weaknesses in Marxism, however, is that they are not a function of it not being properly scientific. They are a function of it being an incomplete, an inadequate, and possibly an untrue science. The point of this book is simply to argue that whatever defects exist within Marxism, they are not the defects charged by empiricism. It is not the fact that Marxism fails to conform to the deductive-nomological view of scientific explanation that accounts for whatever problems confront it. It is not the fact that it employs a metaphysical language of structure, that it talks about the nature of capitalist society, and that it attempts to uncover causal mechanisms. If Marxism is an inadequate social theory, this is because it fails to specify the *proper* causal mechanisms.

I thus do not claim that Marxism is the only realist scientific theory of power. In fact, I conclude by suggesting that pluralism represents an alternative theory, although its epistemological and ontological grounding is not the grounding its empiricist defenders believe it to be. Once again, however, to say pluralism is a genuinely scientific theory is not to say that it is true. And so I also conclude by suggesting some of its deficiencies and by suggesting that, despite its limitations, Marxist theory is a necessary, if not a sufficient, condition of our understanding of contemporary society.

This book is thus a normative argument, in the same way that Polsby's *Community Power and Political Theory*, Lukes's *Power: A Radical View*, and Nagel's *The Descriptive Analysis of Power* were normative—it makes an argument about how power should be studied, and more specifically, it attempts to justify the scientific status of Marxian theory. In the course of the discussion I quite self-consciously issue such injunctions; and, in doing so, I differ from my predecessors in this debate only in my open recognition of the normative implications of such an inquiry. Like my predecessors, I too proceed from an understanding of scientific practice to a discussion of the possibility of social scientific theories of power. Unlike them, I proceed from a different understanding of science, with different implications for social scientific practice. Also unlike them, in recognizing the lack of innocence of such a project, I attempt to deal with my theoretical opponents as generously as I can, directing my efforts primarily toward the legitimation of Marxian theory rather than the disqualification of its competitors. For as Roy Bhaskar has written: "There is no way in which philosophy can legislate in advance for the transposition of particular scientific procedures."[13] In other words, ultimately substantive considerations and judgments, and not abstract conceptual inquiry about power, are the only arbiters of social scientific truth.

One more point is in order regarding the general intention underlying this book. The aspiration to scientific status has been an important regulative ideal of contemporary political theory. The rhetorical function of this book is to expose some of the problems with the dominant view of science and, in doing so, to argue how social scientific theories of power should more properly be framed. I accept the ideal of scientific explanation, but only once it is shorn of its positivistic and honorific connotations.

[13]Roy Bhaskar, *The Possibility of Naturalism: A Philosophical Critique of the Contemporary Human Sciences* (Atlantic Highlands, N.J.: Humanities Press, 1979), p. 41.

Science is not to be equated with the kind of exotic, highly formalized and rarefied knowledge idealized by positivism. Some of the natural sciences do approximate this ideal in the kind of precision attained under laboratory conditions. But I hold, with Aristotle, that no science can demand more precision than its objects allow. And the objects of social science, the practices and relations of human beings, are implicated in the ongoing flow of interaction; they are constantly changing, constantly being reinterpreted by their participants. Social scientific theory can never get away from the flesh-and-blood reality of social practice and historical process. This does not make our theories more impressionistic and less subject to critical scrutiny and empirical contestation. But it means that what we are studying is richly textured, and inherently meaningful and interpretative, in a way mere nature is not. This places limits on what social science can be. Its concepts necessarily draw upon lay concepts. And its theories are irremediably qualitative, referring to dimensions of social life that can not be closed off, measured, and predicted in the confines of a laboratory experiment.

Neither is science a privileged form of knowledge, guaranteeing access to a special form of truth. Scientific knowledge, like all forms of knowledge, is fallible. And science, like all other human activities, is sustained by a social community engaged in a set of relations with the wider society. These realities point to the perennial question of the relation between theory and practice, or, more accurately, between the theoretical practice of science and the other, nonscientific practices that society is comprised of. This book is premised on the belief that social science can produce theoretical knowledge about society, knowledge that may not be apparent to ordinary social agents. This knowledge, however, is not privileged. It cannot negate the tacit skills and ordinary knowledge possessed by human beings. Nor can this knowledge make any necessary claim upon those it presumes to know about. Social science is a relatively autonomous practice. And the truth claims of its knowledge are properly valid only within the community of its practitioners. The truths (with a small "t") of social science do not license any practical applications. The truths of Marxism do not license a dictatorship of a privileged party elite. And the truths of policy study do not license the bureaucratic implementation of policy.

Social science may have practical implications, but their practical application always requires the mediation of other forces and other considerations.

This is not an argument for value neutrality. Nor is it an argument for the kind of skeptical nihilism that seems to be so popular among many self-styled "postmodern" political theorists. It is the premise of this book that social science can uncover features of social life and properties of social relationships that are opaque to its participants. Social science thus has critical and emancipatory implications. This is what makes arguments about the concept of power and study about the structure of power so important. But we must recognize that the belief in the critical promise of social science is not a form of scientism, in which the truths of scientific inquiry run roughshod over all other considerations. In fact, this book, insofar as it is interested in power, is based on the diametrically opposed belief that social science must always come to terms with the social facts of power. For apologetic theorists this coming to terms is a very easy thing. For more critical theorists, the truths of their analysis must be expressed and articulated in such a way that they persuade those whom they propose to emancipate. The truths of social science never speak for themselves, or act by themselves, outside of the scientific community. They must be made practically relevant by nonscientific, political activity. In making our theories critically relevant in social and political affairs, we can do no better than to heed the words of C. Wright Mills:

> If we take the simple democratic view that what men are interested in is all that concerns us, then we are accepting the values that have been inculcated, often accidentally and often deliberately by vested interests....
>
> If we take the dogmatic view that what is to men's interests, whether they are interested in it or not, is all that need concern us morally, then we run the risk of violating democratic values. We may become manipulators or coercers, or both, rather than persuaders in a society in which men are trying to reason together and in which the value of reason is held in high esteem.[14]

In avoiding the Scylla of political quiescence, we must also avoid the Charybdis of a cynical Machiavellianism. The theoretical anal-

[14]Mills, p. 194.

ysis of power can play an emancipatory role. But if theory is to play this role it must be aware of its limits, and of the practical considerations that both make it relevant and temper its application.

PART I

EMPIRICISM, REALISM, AND POWER

There have been too many books and articles written by social scientists on the concept of power. What follows in Part I is yet another intervention in this discourse. But it is one distinguished by its serious attention to recent developments in the philosophy of the social sciences, which have made it possible both to understand better the limits of mainstream academic discourse and to propose a more plausible alternative. The first, and more widely recognized, of these developments is the growing academic acceptance of the various philosophies Anthony Giddens has usefully labeled "interpretative sociologies." This general perspective, which has gained a particularly wide currency among political theorists, has made it possible to recognize the deficiencies of social scientific empiricism, and it has placed the questions of human agency and human understanding at the heart of social and political inquiry. The second, and less widely known, development is the convergence of many philosophers and social inquirers upon a realist understanding of scientific practice. If the first development has opened an unbridgeable gap between social study and what has been commonly understood by empiricists to be scientific inquiry, the second has more directly challenged this empiricist understanding of science itself. Realism has important implications for social and political analysis, and one of the underlying intentions of Part I is to make some of these clear. But the primary intention is to articulate a coherent concept of power, one that incorporates the insights of interpretative sociology but that refuses to abandon the ideal of scientific and critical knowledge.

CHAPTER 1

Behavioralism and the
Three Faces of Power

Intrafamily disagreements sometimes take on the color of major conflicts, family members in the heat of conflict forgetting the commonalities binding them together. Often it is only when confronted by an outsider that families under stress become aware of their relatedness and begin to recognize that what seemed like a major disagreement was really a family squabble. The three faces of power controversy in social theory is like a family squabble. A good deal of recrimination has been expressed by the debaters, who have understood their positions to represent major differences. When exposed to an outside perspective, however, the similarities between the contestants far outweigh any differences.

Despite the differences between Dahl, Bachrach and Baratz, and Lukes, all three remain wedded to an empiricist understanding of science. They agree that power is a causal concept, but they understand causality as no more than a regular sequence of behaviors. This can be seen as the legacy of behavioralism in social science. The consequence of this legacy is that, while the "second" and "third" faces of power point to a structural conception, they are ultimately unable to sustain such a view.

Behavioralism and Empiricism

The "behavioral revolution" in Anglo-American political science was a revolution in the methodology of practicing the academic discipline of political science. In response to what was believed by some to be a wrongful preoccupation with historical, descriptive, and constitutional studies, behavioralism demanded a focus on the more "informal," nongovernmental political processes and a concern with greater "scientific rigor."[1] Behavioralism in political science has, not surprisingly, had important and long-term effects on the practice of political research. These effects, however, have been much less innocent than the revolutionary vanguard believed. Robert Dahl, in his famous "monument to a successful protest," wrote: "The behavioral approach is an attempt to improve our understanding of politics by seeking to explain the empirical aspects of political life by means of methods, theories, and criteria of proof that are acceptable according to the canons, conventions, and assumptions of modern empirical science."[2] This quote gives something of the flavor of the intellectual moment—optimistic, naively self-assured about the nature of the "scientific outlook" that was to be emulated. As Dahl un-self-consciously makes clear, however, the triumph of this "protest movement" represented in fact much less the triumph of scientific methods than an emerging hegemony of an empiricist view of science. Dahl quotes from an early prescriptive tract, which he presents as simply and matter-of-factly scientific: "[We favor] a decision to explore the feasibility of developing a new approach to the study of political behavior. Based upon the study of individuals in political situations, this approach calls for the examination of the political relationships of men . . . by disciplines which can throw light on the problems involved, with the object of formulating and testing hypotheses concerning uniformities of behavior."[3]

Dahl's essay makes clear that this emerging "scientific outlook," which hoped "to provide political science with empirical propo-

---

[1]For an overview, see Bernard Crick, *The American Science of Politics* (Berkeley: University of California Press, 1959); Raymond Seidelman and Edward J. Harpham, *Disenchanted Realists: Political Science and the American Crisis, 1884–1984* (Albany: State University of New York Press, 1985); Heinz Euleau, *The Behavioral Persuasion in Politics* (New York: Random House, 1963); and David Truman, "Disillusion and Regeneration: The Quest for a Discipline," *American Political Science Review* 59 (December 1965), 865–73.

[2]Robert A. Dahl, "The Behavioral Approach in Political Science: Epitaph for a Monument to a Successful Protest," *American Political Science Review* 58 (December 1961), 767.

[3]Ibid., p. 764.

sitions and theories of a systematic sort, tested by closer, more direct and rigorously controlled observations of political events," had strong political and bureaucratic determinants.[4] What is central for our present purposes, however, is that the view of scientific explanation as the documentation and prediction of empirical uniformities was a central tenet of behavioralism. David Easton has written that a theory is "any kind of generalization or proposition that asserts that two or more things, activities, or events, covary under specified conditions."[5] A more recent and influential book on scientific method in political research asserts: "Science is concerned with the explanation (and prediction) of specific events by means of statements which are invariantly true from one set of circumstances to another."[6]

This conception of science is not peculiar to political science methodologists. Until very recently it has been the standard view in the philosophy of science. As Ernest Nagel wrote in his authoritative *The Structure of Science*: "The sciences seek to discover and to formulate in general terms the conditions under which events of various sorts occur, the statements of such determining conditions being the explanations of the corresponding happenings."[7] Science, on this view, consists of the documentation and prediction of empirical regularities. Scientific explanation consists of the sub-

---

[4]Ibid., p. 766. Dahl rather un-self-consciously celebrates the new state interest in financing research after World War II, and the role that academic institutions like the American Political Science Association and the Social Science Research Council played in supporting behavioral research. For a less sanguine view, one might consult C. Wright Mills, *The Sociological Imagination* (Oxford: Oxford University Press, 1959), particularly chap. 5, "The Bureaucratic Ethos"; see also Douglas Rae's "Political Theory and the Division of Labor in Society: Asleep aboard the Titanic and Steaming into Halifax," *Political Theory* 9 (August 1981), 369–78.

[5]David Easton, *A Systems Analysis of Political Life* (New York: Wiley, 1965), p. 7; see also his *A Framework for Political Analysis* (Englewood Cliffs, N.J.: Prentice-Hall, 1965), and his "Alternative Strategies in Theoretical Research," in Easton, ed., *Varieties of Political Theory* (Englewood Cliffs, N.J.: Prentice-Hall, 1966).

[6]Adam Przeworski and Henry Teune, *The Logic of Comparative Social Inquiry* (New York: Wiley, 1970), p. 18. For a similar view of scientific theory, see Robert T. Holt and John E. Turner, eds., *The Methodology of Comparative Research* (New York: Free Press, 1970).

[7]Ernest Nagel, *The Structure of Science* (New York: Harcourt Brace Jovanovich, 1965), p. 4.

sumption of events under "covering laws." This is sometimes called the deductive-nomological (D-N) view of science: laws are understood as conditional empirical statements whereby, given a general law and the statement of appropriate initial conditions, events can be deduced from the law. It thus follows that on this view explanation and prediction are seen as "symmetrical"—to be able to predict an event is to have explained it by bringing it under a covering law; and to be able to explain an event is simply to employ "retrospective predictions."[8]

Following Rom Harré and Roy Bhaskar,[9] I label this understanding of science "empiricism" insofar as it takes the empirical world, the world of experienced occurrences, to be the object of scientific investigation, and it eschews any appeal to underlying causes and natural necessities as unscientific "metaphysics." It bears emphasis that this view extends beyond the positivistic view, now in utter disrepute, that theories are verifiable in experience and refer to unproblematic and unmediated observables.[10] Many early behavioralists were positivists, but although positivism is a form of empiricism, the converse is not necessarily the case. The view I label empiricism hinges primarily on an ontology, or theory of reality, which can be traced back to David Hume—namely, that there is nothing but a flux of events whose only relationship is one of contingent conjunction.

Hume contended that "all the objects of human reason or enquiry may naturally be divided into two kinds, to wit, Relations of ideas, and Matters of fact."[11] Relations of ideas, typified by mathematics

---

[8]See Carl Hempel, *Aspects of Scientific Explanation* (New York: Free Press, 1965), pp. 364–67. For a discussion of the bearing of this view on social explanation, see William H. Dray, ed., *Philosophical Analysis and History* (New York: Harper & Row, 1966).

[9]Cf. Rom Harré, *Principles of Scientific Thinking* (Oxford: Oxford University Press, 1970); and Roy Bhaskar, *A Realist Theory of Science*, 2d ed. (Atlantic Highlands, N.J.: Humanities Press, 1978). For a defense of this label, and the position it denotes, see Bas C. Van Fraassen, *The Scientific Image* (Oxford: Clarendon Press, 1980).

[10]For a good discussion of the decline of positivism, see Harold I. Brown, *Perception, Theory, and Commitment* (Chicago: University of Chicago Press, 1977).

[11]David Hume, "Enquiry Concerning Human Understanding," in L. A. Selby-Bigge, ed., *Enquiries Concerning Human Understanding and the Principles of Morals* (Oxford: Clarendon Press, 1975), p. 25.

and logic, are characterized by analycity, or demonstrable certainty. Matters of fact, on the other hand, are elementary statements (to use more modern language) based upon "the present testimony of our senses." They are grounded in sense-data and map out that part of the word they represent. According to Hume, the only necessity is logical necessity. Matters of fact, by contrast, represent discrete and contingent experiences. He writes: "The contrary of every matter of fact is still possible; because it can never imply a contradiction, and is conceived by the mind with the same facility and distinctness, as if ever so conformable with reality. That the sun will not rise tomorrow is no less intelligible a proposition, and implies no more contradiction, than the affirmation that it will rise. We should in vain, therefore, try to demonstrate its falsehood."[12] This is the core of Hume's critique of the doctrine of causality and of the concept of natural necessity. Logic cannot provide us with the knowledge that the sun will rise tomorrow, or that objects will fall according to the law of gravity. Therefore, "cause and effect are discoverable, not by reason, but by experience." Causal knowledge is not necessary, but contingent: it "arises entirely from experience, when we find that any particular objects are constantly conjoined with each other."[13]

This view of causality is widely accepted by philosophers and social scientists who are otherwise critics of Humean bedrock empiricism. Karl Popper, arguably the most important post-positivist philosopher of science, is most noted for his critique of Hume's sense-data epistemology. But he too subscribes to a Humean view of causality.

Popper believes that a sense-data epistemology and a verificationist theory of meaning, two fundamental theses of logical positivism deriving from Hume, are dogmas. They are both logically unsound and misunderstand the real grounds of the objectivity of science. Popper argues that science cannot be grounded in experience, because of the unbridgeable gap between subjective experience and objective statements. Popper thus displaces the positivist insistence on verification with his own "criterion of demarcation." It is not that science, unlike metaphysics, is based on experience

---

[12]Ibid., pp. 25–26.
[13]Ibid., p. 27.

and is therefore the only meaningful form of knowledge. Science is demarcated from metaphysics by its method, and by the relationships that obtain between scientific propositions.[14]

According to Popper, the distinctive feature of science is its deductive method.[15] Because inference from singular statements to general theories is logically inadmissible, no theory is ever conclusively verifiable. But theories are "falsifiable." They cannot be verified, but they can be refuted, by experience. Popper writes: "My proposal is based upon an asymmetry between verifiability and falsifiability, an asymmetry which results from the logical form of universal statements. For these are never derivable from singular statements, but can be contradicted by a singular statement. Consequently, it is possible to argue from the truth of singular statements to the falsity of universal statements."[16]

For Popper there are no ultimate statements, only falsifiable hypotheses. We can test these by deducing their consequences and seeing whether the predicted events occur. Of course, our tests themselves are not unmediated encounters with experience. They are describable only through scientific concepts that are themselves fallible and potentially subject to test. The "basic statements," which function as the jury in the trial of a theory, are thus not like the "protocol statements," which positivists believed could be verified through experience. They are distinguished by their logical form, not their origin.[17] They are, "in the material mode of speech, statements asserting that an observable event is occurring in an identifiable region of space and time."[18] In other words, they are singular statements, themselves fallible, which refer to specific events in time. Theories are thus tested empirically by deducing their consequences and comparing them with experience as articulated through basic statements. If the basic statements contradict the consequences that are deducible from the theory, then the prem-

---

[14]Karl R. Popper, *The Logic of Scientific Discovery* (New York: Harper Torchbooks, 1959), pp. 34–39; see also his "The Demarcation between Science and Metaphysics," in Karl R. Popper, *Conjectures and Refutations: The Growth of Scientific Knowledge* (New York: Harper Torchbooks, 1965).

[15]Popper, *Logic*, p. 42.

[16]Ibid., p. 41.

[17]Popper, *Conjectures*, pp. 50–51.

[18]Popper, *Logic*, p. 103.

ise of the deduction must be deficient and the theory falsified. Of course, since basic statements are themselves fallible, there are no incorrigible foundations of truth. "From a logical point of view," says Popper, "the testing of a theory depends upon basic statements whose acceptance or rejection, in its turn, depends upon our decisions. Thus it is decisions which settle the fate of theories."[19]

One major point of Popper's philosophy of science is to delegitimize those "pseudo-sciences" (Marxism and psychoanalysis) which always seem, according to Popper, to provide instances of verification, but cannot specify the conditions under which they would be falsified. Anything and everything can be explained, and any apparent inconsistencies explained away by means of ad hoc hypotheses (like the false consciousness of the proletariat or the resistance of the patient).[20] Falsification is an alternative to verification which is quite suited to the task of rejecting these theories. Science thus becomes seen as a process of "conjectures and refutations." Scientists conjure up hypotheses that are "the free creations of our own minds." They then logically deduce the consequences of these hypotheses and test them. While theories cannot be conclusively proved, they can be decisively disproved, or refuted. Science is a method of trial and error, of boldly proposing theories, of trying our best to show that these are erroneous, and of accepting them tentatively and skeptically if our critical efforts are unsuccessful.[21] While most working scientists would think of science as an enterprise of constructing knowledge about substantive objects of knowledge, for Popper it is a process of *destruction* of conjectures, guided by a commitment not to substantive knowledge but to logical procedures.[22] The hallmark of the truly scientific theory, then, is that it is falsifiable, and that it states in advance the conditions under which it may be considered invalid. Theories must consist of deductive laws capable of predicting empirical events and of testing these predictions.

Popper's philosophy represents an important departure from positivism in its decisive repudiation of any foundationalist theory

[19]Ibid., p. 108.
[20]Popper, *Conjectures*, pp. 33–39.
[21]Ibid., p. 51.
[22]See Jonathan Lieberson, "The 'Truth' of Karl Popper," *New York Review of Books*, November 18 and 25, 1982.

of knowledge. Popper has always insisted that "a science needs a point of view, and theoretical problems,"[23] and has himself identified his philosophy with that of Kant insofar as both philosophers emphasize that knowledge is partly constituted by the human mind, which is not simply a passive recipient of impressions.[24] This dimension of Popper's thought has opened up the debate about "criticism and the growth of knowledge" and has stimulated the work of Thomas Kuhn, Imre Lakatos, and Paul Feyerabend on the decisionistic features of scientific practice.[25] This perspective is indispensable in social science and should serve to silence those positivistic researchers who insist upon "observability" as a criterion of scientific meaning. And it has played an important role in the debate on power, enabling the critics of Dahl, for instance, to insist that no concept of power is without its presuppositions, its point of view.

What is important for our purposes, however, is that Popper's philosophy, like that of Kant, is exclusively a criticism of positivist epistemology. Popper quite clearly accepts Hume's ontology and his account of causality. "To give a causal explanation of an event," writes Popper, "means to deduce a statement which describes it using as premises of the deduction one or more universal laws, together with certain singular statements, the initial conditions. . . . The initial conditions describe what is usually called the 'cause' of the event in question."[26] On this view causality is nothing but the regular sequence of cause-and-effect events. For example, on Popper's view a causal explanation of the marching of a marine platoon would be: *general law*—whenever marine sergeants say "march" marine platoons march; *initial condition*—the marine sergeant said "march"; *deduction*—the platoon marched. Here the causal relation is nothing more than the regular conjunction of the sergeant's order and the platoon's marching, and the theoretical explanation nothing more than a generalization about this conjunction. (This is the ideal form of empiricist theories of power, and, I will suggest below, it is fundamentally deficient.)

[23]Popper, *Logic*, p. 106.
[24]Popper, *Conjectures*, pp. 189–93.
[25]See Imre Lakatos and Alan Musgrave, eds., *Criticism and the Growth of Knowledge* (London: Cambridge University Press, 1970).
[26]Popper, *Logic*, pp. 59–60.

Popper explicitly links himself with the Humean view, which denies that there are any necessary causal connections in nature. He quotes Wittgenstein paraphrasing Hume: "A necessity for one thing to happen because another has happened does not exist. There is only logical necessity."[27] Therefore "ultimate" explanations—which attempt to understand the essential properties of things, and make "existential" statements about their natures instead of "conditional" statements about their predictable behaviors—are rejected by Popper as unscientific. He writes, describing science as "methodological nominalism": "Methodological essentialism, i.e., the theory that it is the aim of science to reveal essences and to describe them by means of definitions, can be better understood when contrasted with its opposite, methodological nominalism. Instead of aiming to find out what a thing really is, and at defining its true nature, methodological nominalism aims at describing how a thing behaves under various circumstances, and especially, whether there are any regularities in its behavior."[28]

There is in Popper's remark more than a trace of the kind of scorn Hume heaped upon medieval scholasticism and a suggestion that any talk of causal necessities and essential natures is akin to scholastic references to occult powers and cosmic teleology. This is an extremely constricted view of science, but regardless of its philosophical limitations, it has been taken up with a vengeance by contemporary political scientists. This has been particularly significant for the understanding of power. Jack Nagel, in his *The Descriptive Analysis of Power* accurately expresses the consensus when he writes that any talk of necessary causal connections smacks of "objectionable metaphysical implications."[29]

The First Face of Power: Behavioral Compliance

The understanding of causality as constant conjunction, and ideal of scientific explanation as prediction, shaped a new and

---

[27]Ibid., p. 436.

[28]Karl R. Popper, *The Open Society and Its Enemies*, vol. 1 (Princeton: Princeton University Press, 1966), p. 32; see also *The Poverty of Historicism* (New York: Harper Torchbooks, 1960), pp. 26–36.

[29]Jack Nagel, *The Descriptive Analysis of Power* (New Haven: Yale University Press, 1975), p. 36.

rigorous effort to formalize the concept of power and to understand it as a causal relation between the behaviors of agents. Harold Laswell and Abraham Kaplan, in their influential *Power and Society*, wrote that power "is a process in time, constituted by experientially localized and observable acts."[30] A number of articles expressed a similarly behavioral view. Thus James March wrote: "We can say that two individuals are in an influence relation if their behaviors are linked causally."[31] And Herbert Simon wrote: "For the assertion, 'A has power over B,' we can substitute the assertion, 'A's behavior causes B's behavior.' "[32]

This approach was taken up by Robert Dahl, one of the most important figures in the three faces of power debate. Dahl, in a series of methodological articles, asserted the need for a definition of power amenable to the kind of empirical research envisioned by behavioralism. Thus he wrote: "Power terms in modern social science refer to subsets of relations among social units such that the behavior of one or more units (the response units, R) depend in some circumstances on the behavior of other units (the controlling units, C)."[33]

Power, then, is an empirical regularity whereby the behavior of one agent *causes* the behavior of another. (We might also note that Dahl's language of stimulus and response has obvious affinities with B. F. Skinner's behaviorist psychology.) Dahl is very explicit about this. He continues: "For the assertion 'C has power over R' we can substitute the assertion 'C's behavior causes R's behavior,' ...the language of cause, like the language of power, is used to interpret situations in which there is a possibility that some event will intervene to change the order of other events."[34] It seems obvious that this notion of power rests on a Newtonian analogy. We are all naturally at rest or at constant velocity, until our move-

[30]Harold Laswell and Abraham Kaplan, *Power and Society* (New Haven: Yale University Press, 1950), p. xiv.

[31]James G. March, "An Introduction to the Theory and Measurement of Influence," *American Political Science Review* 49 (1953), 47.

[32]Herbert A. Simon, "Notes on the Observation and Measurement of Power," *Journal of Politics* 15 (1953), 5. In the same vein, see Felix E. Oppenheim, "Degrees of Power and Freedom," *American Political Science Review* 54 (1960), 437–46.

[33]Robert A. Dahl, "Power," in *International Encyclopedia of the Social Sciences*, vol. 12 (New York: Macmillan, 1968), p. 407.

[34]Ibid., p. 418.

ment is altered by an external force. Power is that force whereby social agents alter the behavior of other agents or, as Dahl puts it, get them to do what they would not otherwise do.[35] And true to his empiricism, Dahl insists that there are no necessary relationships between the behaviors of agents. He writes in his essay "Cause and Effect in the Study of Politics": "The only meaning that is strictly causal in the notion of power is one of regular sequence: that is, a regular sequence such that whenever A does something, what follows, or what probably follows, is an action by B."[36]

These remarks may sound unexceptionable, but their force must be emphasized. Dahl is making a positive statement about the meaning of the concept of power. But he is also making a negative statement, about what power does not mean. He is insisting that his concept of power does not smack of metaphysics, that it involves asserting nothing that is not empirically evident. This causal view of power forms the basis of the entire three faces of power debate. All of the contestants agree that power is an empirical relation of cause and effect, and none of them conceives of power as involving any necessary connections, or what I will later call structural relationships. This is not to say that the reason for this is that subsequent participants in the debate consciously wished to endorse the Humean view of causality. It is, rather, simply that they failed to challenge it, most likely because they failed to recognize it—an interesting example of the power of a view that is neither asserted nor recognized as such, and that is sustained by virtue of its misrecognition as a simple fact of life.

The controversy over power does not revolve around this major, Humean, premise. It revolves, rather, around the question "How do we identify those instances in which A gets B to do what B would not have done otherwise?" As Lukes points out, this question hinges on the question of a counterfactual—what would B have done otherwise? Dahl's answer to this is that B's revealed preferences indicate what B would have done.[37] Thus, "A has power over B" means that A's behavior regularly and predictably causes B to

---

[35]Robert A. Dahl, "The Concept of Power," *Behavioral Science* 12 (July 1957), 203–204.

[36]Robert A. Dahl, "Cause and Effect in the Study of Politics," in Daniel Lerner, ed., *Cause and Effect* (New York: Free Press, 1965), p. 94.

[37]Dahl, "Concept," pp. 203–204.

do something B does not want to do. This has been called the "first face of power" insofar as it involves instances of manifest conflict and compliance. And it has been called the "decisionist" view insofar as it limits itself to instances of actual decision making, or choice, in action.

Dahl

It is on the basis of this interpretation of the counterfactual that Dahl and his student, Nelson Polsby, insisted that any "scientific" claims about power must focus on instances of manifest conflict and demonstrate constant conjunctions of cause-and-effect behaviors. In so insisting, they employed their understanding of scientific method in order to delegitimize radical critics of American society who wrote about power and employed the language of power structure without referring to sequences of the sort just mentioned. Thus Polsby, in his influential and recently reissued *Community Power and Political Theory*, chastised what he called "categorialism," or categorical claims like "A has power over B," which fail to specify the empirical conditions, the causal behaviors, under which B can be predicted to act. (Note the similarity of this criticism to Popper's invidious distinction between methodological nominalism and methodological essentialism.) Polsby writes about the claim that there is a dominant class in a particular society: "For this latter statement to mean anything in a scientific sense, we must, according to the formal requirements postulated above, make reference to specific decisions in which particular outcomes are affected by members of the classes into which we divide the population, and secondly, we must state the conditions under which we can take it as demonstrated that the upper class does not have more power than the lower class."[38]

Ascriptions of power, then, are conditional statements of regularity, falsifiable predictions about the "stimulii" of the powerful and the "responses" of the weak, which always refer to the "actual behavior" of the agents in question.[39] Similarly, Dahl, in his now classic "Critique of the Ruling Elite Model," criticized C. Wright Mills by asserting: "I do not see how anyone can suppose that he has established the dominance of a specific group in a community

[38]Nelson Polsby, *Community Power and Political Theory* (New Haven: Yale University Press, 1963; 2d ed., 1980), pp. 5–6.
[39]Ibid., p. 121.

or nation without basing his analysis on the careful examination of a series of concrete decisions."[40]

It is important to see what these sorts of criticisms accomplished, and doing so will clarify more precisely what this book sets out to challenge. On the one hand, some very sensible and plausible points are made regarding the importance of empirical evidence and the possibility of theoretical criticism. This is one way of reading a claim like Polsby's, that any assertion about power "must be put in such a form that in principle it is directly or indirectly subject to disproof by an appeal to evidence." On the other hand, the whip hand of science is being deployed in order to question the very meaning and reference of claims about power not conformable to Dahl's "decisionist" interpretation. Thus, Polsby's claim is not simply a sensible and innocent remark about evidence and criticism, but also a claim about the formal structure of properly scientific explanation, namely, that it must conform to some variant of the D-N model and must refer to empirical events and their uniformities. Part of the reason for the widespread influence of Polsby's critique is the conflation of these two very different sorts of claim. And part is, undoubtedly, due to the widespread acceptance of empiricism as second nature among social scientists. It is not Dahl's and Polsby's emphasis on the importance of empirical evidence, but their reliance on *empiricism*, on the Hume/Popper view of causality and scientific explanation, that is the problem with their view of power. And the dislodgement of empirical research from the confines of philosophical empiricism is one of the major tasks of the present analysis.

The Second Face of Power: Variations on the Same Theme

This view, and its theoretical deployment, were immediately challenged by Bachrach and Baratz, who introduced the notion of a "second face of power."[41] Their criticism of the formulations of

[40]Robert A. Dahl, "A Critique of the Ruling Elite Model," *American Political Science Review* 52 (1958), 463–64.

[41]Peter Bachrach and Morton Baratz, "The Two Faces of Power," *American Political Science Review* 56 (1962), 942–52, and "Decisions and Nondecisions: An Analytic Framework," *American Political Science Review* 57 (1963), 632–42.

Dahl rested on two basic points. The first, important but for our purposes secondary, was that Dahl and Polsby sometimes write in a naively positivistic vein, as if the analysis of power is self-evident, and the location of power unproblematic, simply a question of observation. Bachrach and Baratz insist that this is a mistake, that all science involves the making of judgments of significance deriving from the scientist's theoretical perspective. Here they draw upon post-positivist philosophy of science in order defend research into those aspects of political life that are covert and "nonobvious." The second point is that Dahl's formulation misses a crucial feature of what we ordinarily think of as power—the suppression of conflict. In criticizing Dahl's decisionist focus on actual conflict, they introduce the concept of the "nondecision," which they define as "a decision that results in suppression or thwarting of a latent or manifest challenge to the values or interests of the decision-maker."[42]

The point of this argument is to conceptualize not simply interaction, but limitations on interaction, as features of power. Their own formulation, however, is crucially ambiguous, opening them up to the charge that it is little different from Dahl's. They gesture at a structural formulation, conceiving power as implicated in institutionalized practices, but are ultimately unable to sustain this conceptualization.

It is in gesturing toward a structural view that they invoke E. E. Schattschneider's concept of the "mobilization of bias." Schattschneider wrote: "All forms of political organization have a bias in favor of some kinds of conflict and the suppression of others because *organization is the mobilization of bias*. Some issues are organized into politics while others are organized out."[43] Bachrach and Baratz argue that the way issues get "organized" in and out of social interaction has everything to do with power, and yet these features are ignored by an exclusive focus on actual behavioral conflict. They write: "Political systems and sub-systems develop a 'mobilization of bias,' a set of predominant values, beliefs, rituals,

---

These essays are reprinted in the authors' *Power and Poverty* (New York: Oxford University Press, 1970).

[42]Bachrach and Baratz, *Power and Poverty*, pp. 43–44.

[43]E. E. Schattschneider, *The Semi-Sovereign People* (Hinsdale, Ill.: Dryden Press, 1960), p. 71.

and institutional procedures ('rules of the game') that operate systematically and consistently to the benefit of certain groups and persons at the expense of others. Those who benefit are placed in a preferred position to defend and promote their vested interests."[44] This formulation comes dangerously close to postulating underlying structural relations determining behavior, risking the essentialism so scorned by properly trained, "scientific" theorists. Polsby writes: "The central problem is this: Even if we can show that a given status quo benefits some people disproportionately (as I think we can for any real world status quo), such a demonstration falls short of showing that the beneficiaries *created* the status quo, *act* in any meaningful way to maintain it, or could, in the future, *act* effectively to deter changes in it" [italics mine].[45] Once again, the mark of scientificity is the examination of behavior; "a given status quo," in and of itself, holds no interest for the theorist of power. Bachrach and Baratz seem to find this sort of criticism compelling.

And so Bachrach and Baratz sacrifice their interest in structure in the interest of "science." They explicitly state that power involves actual compliance, going so far as to assert that "it cannot be possessed," only exercised.[46] They admit that "although it is true that a nondecision is not visible to the naked eye, a latent issue is and so is the mobilization of bias . . . the nondecision-making process is indeed subject to observation and analysis."[47] And conceding to behavioralism, they hold that "although absence of conflict may be a non-event, a decision which results in prevention of conflict is very much an event—and an observable one to boot."[48]

In making these concessions, they confirm a point made by Geoffrey Debnam—that implicit in their formulation is an important distinction between power as nondecision and power as mobili-

---

[44]Bachrach and Baratz, *Power and Poverty*, pp. 43–44.

[45]Polsby, *Community Power*, p. 208. See also Raymond Wolfinger, "Nondecisions and the Study of Local Politics," *American Political Science Review* 65 (1971), 1063–80 for a similar criticism. For an interesting critique of the positivism that Polsby and Wolfinger fall into, and a defense of inquiry into covert decisions of Bachrach and Baratz's sort, see Frederick Frey, "Comment: On Issues and Nonissues in the Study of Power." *American Political Science Review* 65 (1971), 1081–1101.

[46]Bachrach and Baratz, *Power and Poverty*, p. 19.

[47]Bachrach and Baratz, "Decisions and Nondecisions," p. 641.

[48]Bachrach and Baratz, *Power and Poverty*, p. 46.

zation of bias. The former refers to actual decisions, or actions, which involve behavioral causation, differing from the "first face" only insofar as it includes covert instances of suppression as well as overt instances of compliance.[49] The latter is an unexplicated and ultimately nonbehavioral phenomenon. Polsby's criticism is thus decisive: "How to study this second face of power? To what manifestations of social reality might the mobilization of bias refer? Are phenomena of this sort in principle amenable to empirical investigation?"[50] Bachrach and Baratz never explicitly answer this question. Instead, they sacrifice their insight about the institutional basis of power to the scholarly "mobilization of bias" which we have labeled empiricism.

Bachrach and Baratz's contribution to the debate was nonetheless important. Even if they did not get beyond a behavioral understanding of power, they opened up scholarly debate in two significant ways. First, in the course of making their argument about nondecisions, they introduced some interesting, if generally unrecognized, phenomenological questions into the debate regarding the rationality and intentions held by parties to a power relationship.[51] As I argue in Chapter 3, these questions regarding social ontology are crucial to thinking about social power. Dahl's language of stimulus and response is simply not adequate to the understanding of social power, and Bachrach and Baratz open up the possibility of making norms and ideologies central to thinking about power. Second, Bachrach and Baratz insist that all social research begins with presuppositions and is never simply a question of observation. Ironically, this insight was lost to them in their own discussion of the concept of power; if it had not been, they might have recognized the Humean presuppositions they shared with their antagonists. Nonetheless, however limited their discussion of power, this insight into the social production of knowledge played an important role in the critique of the dominant theory of power in American political science—pluralism. It stimulated inquiries, like William Connolly's *The Bias of Pluralism*,[52] into the implicit presuppositions

[49]Geoffrey Debnam, "Nondecisions and Power: The Two Faces of Bachrach and Baratz," *American Political Science Review* 69 (September 1975), 889–999.

[50]Polsby, *Community Power*, p. 190.

[51]Bachrach and Baratz, *Power and Poverty*, pp. 17–38.

[52]William E. Connolly, *Political Science and Ideology* (New York: Atherton

of pluralism as a substantive theory; and it thus opened up the possibility of inquiry into features of political life which, while not necessarily apparent to common sense, were nonetheless available to investigation.[53] Despite these contributions, however, Bachrach and Baratz did not get beyond the empiricist foundations of the discussion of power. In failing in this regard, they also failed to remove the stigma of "metaphysics" from the language of "power structure," failing as well to conceptualize the conditions of interaction as key dimensions of social power.

critique of B & B

The Third Face of Power

Steven Lukes, in his important *Power: A Radical View* picks up where Bachrach and Baratz left off. He calls their "two dimensional view" of power an advance over Dahl's "one dimensional" insistence that power involves only behavioral relations of compliance. He agrees that the study of power involves interpretative questions about which kinds of phenomena to study, but he also believes that Bachrach and Baratz have not probed deeply enough into the way collective action and social institutions shape power. He writes of their formulation:

> In the first place, its critique of behaviorism is too qualified, or, to put it another way, it is still committed to behaviorism—that is, to the study of overt, "actual behavior," of which "concrete decisions" in situations of conflict are seen as paradigmatic. In trying to assimilate all cases of exclusion of potential issues from the political agenda to the paradigm of a decision, it gives a misleading picture of the ways in which individuals and, above all, groups and institutions, succeed in excluding potential issues from the political process. Decisions are choices consciously and intentionally made by individuals between alternatives, whereas the bias of the system can be mobilized, recreated, and reinforced in ways that are neither consciously chosen nor the intended result of particular individuals' choices. . . . Moreover, the bias of the system is not simply sustained by a series of

---

Press, 1967); William E. Connolly, ed., *The Bias of Pluralism* (New York: Atherton Press, 1969).

[53]See Frey, "Nondecisions."

individually chosen acts, but also, more importantly, by the socially structured and culturally patterned behavior of groups, and practices of institutions which may indeed be manifested by individuals' inaction.[54]

Lukes thus proposes that, if the concept of power is to take account of the way in which interaction is itself shaped and limited, then it cannot limit itself only to instances of behavioral compliance, as would the one- and two-dimensional views. He writes elsewhere: "Is not the supreme exercise of power to avert conflict and grievance by influencing, shaping, and determining the perceptions and preferences of others?"[55]

Lukes submits that his view of power, and those of Dahl and Bachrach and Baratz, "can be seen as alternative interpretations and applications of one and the same underlying concept of power, according to which A exercises power over B when A affects B in a manner contrary to B's interests."[56] It is actually Lukes who makes the concept of interest central to the debate, but it is important to see how much similarity underlies his differences with his predecessors. Lukes agrees that power is a causal concept denoting behavioral regularities. To refer to our earlier example, he agrees that "A has power over B" means that A's behavior causes B to do something that B would not otherwise do. As Lukes puts it, "Any attribution of the exercise of power ... always implies a relevant counterfactual."[57] In the cases of the first two faces of power, the counterfactual was provided by the existence of empirical conflict between the revealed preferences of A and B. Lukes's formulation differs from these views in insisting that preferences can themselves be the effect of the exercise of power. He thus insists that what B would otherwise do cannot be properly gauged by B's preferences, but rather by B's *interest*. Lukes then defines power as: "A exercises power over B when A affects B contrary to B's

---

[54]Steven Lukes, *Power: A Radical View* (London: Macmillan, 1974), pp. 22–23.
    [55]Steven Lukes, "Power and Authority," in Tom Bottomore and Robert Nisbet, eds., *A History of Sociological Analysis* (New York: Basic Books, 1978), p. 669.
    [56]Lukes, *Power*, p. 27.
    [57]Ibid., p. 41.

interest."[58] The concept of power can thus refer to relations between A and B even in the absence of empirical conflict.

Lukes contends that this view captures the essence of power as an empirical relation between A and B, and that the sole difference between this view and those articulated by his antagonists is that "those holding the three different views of power I have set out offer different interpretations of what are to count as interests and how they may be adversely affected."[59] Lukes's own view is that the concept of interest, or what has been called "objective interest," has to do with what an agent would do under ideal democratic circumstances. It thus follows that if it can be argued plausibly that A affects B in a manner that limits B from doing what B would do under ideal conditions, then it properly can be said that A exercises power over B.[60]

This notion of objective interest has been subjected to a great deal of criticism, some of which we will discuss below. But regardless of the merits of Lukes's notion of interest, the importance of the concept for him is grounded in his commitment to viewing power as an empirical regularity. Despite his differences with his antagonists, he explicitly states that he is merely interpreting a shared concept. Insofar as this is the case, Lukes's formulation (like that of Bachrach and Baratz) is ambiguous regarding those "socially structured and culturally patterned" dimensions of power he referred to in his critique of Bachrach and Baratz.

A later essay, "Power and Structure," is intended to clarify this.

---

[58]Ibid., pp. 22–25.

[59]Ibid., p. 27.

[60]Ibid., pp. 34–35. This view of interest, as Lukes acknowledges, is drawn from William E. Connolly, "On 'Interests' in Politics," *Politics and Society* 2 (Summer 1972), 459–77. This conception owes much to the work of Jürgen Habermas, particularly his *Knowledge and Human Interests* (Boston: Beacon, 1968). Lukes explicitly links himself to the idiom of critical theory in a later paper, "On the Relativity of Power," in S. C. Brown, ed., *Philosophical Disputes in the Social Sciences* (Atlantic Highlands, N.J.: Humanities, 1979), p. 267. It is therefore curious that in a more recent paper Lukes rejects Habermas's (and his own earlier) transcendental conception of objective interest, opting instead for a Weberian subjectivism in many ways akin to Polsby's view. See Steven Lukes, "Of Gods and Demons: Habermas and Practical Reason," in John B. Thompson and David Held, eds., *Habermas: Critical Debates* (Cambridge, Mass.: MIT Press, 1982). This is an issue on which Lukes shows some confusion. For a critique, see Michael Bloch, Brian Heading, and Phillip Lawrence, "Power in Social Theory: A Non-Relative View," in Brown, *Philosophical Disputes*, pp. 243–60.

Here Lukes argues that there must be a synthesis of structural and empirical orientations, suggesting that there is a "dialectic of power and structure."[61] Social structure limits action, and power, being an eventlike phenomenon, is discernible empirically. Power, he proposes, is an "agency" concept, not a "structural" one. Yet it "is held and exercised by agents (individual or collective) within systems and structural determinants."[62] This is a clarification of the relation between power and structure—social structure provides the limits within which power is exercised. But it also leaves unanswered the problem posed by Lukes's earlier discussion, in *Power: A Radical View*, of power in structural terms. In other words, what is the nature of these structural determinants of power? How determining are they? If power is an agency concept rather than a structural one, and if it denotes behavioral regularities, then what precisely is the difference between Lukes's third face of power and the Bachrach and Baratz view he criticizes? Is it simply a focus on a different class of events, those involving the transgression of objective interest rather than simply compliance? If Lukes's view is different, his analytic bifurcation of power and structure doesn't go far in showing us how. In short, Lukes is unable to articulate the structural nature of social power that, he rightly notices, is so important.

This is because, while he has made an important contribution to the discussion of power by introducing the concepts of structure and agency into the debate, his discussion of these issues reveals some serious confusion. As we have seen, Lukes polarizes the concepts of structure and agency and insists that power is an agency category. In a recent defense of his views he writes: "Whether power is a form of structural determination or a concept tied to the notion of human agency (whether individual or collective) hinges on whether the alleged holder of power is correctly claimed to be able to act otherwise than he does."[63] Lukes's emphasis on the question of human agency is meritorious, as is his more general concern with questions of social ontology—language, interpretation, being—which bear upon the nature of a specifically social

---

[61]Steven Lukes, "Power and Structure," in Steven Lukes, *Essays in Social Theory* (London: Macmillan, 1977).

[62]Lukes, "Power and Authority," p. 635; "On the Relativity," pp. 263–64.

[63]Lukes, "On the Relativity," p. 264.

(versus natural) science. Lukes's reasoning, however, suffers from two difficulties. The first is that he fails to see, even though he cites Anthony Giddens's *New Rules of Sociological Method* (see Chapter 2), that the bifurcation of structure and agency is misplaced. In short, to think of human agency as structured is not to deny its significance or efficacy in any way.[64] Power can be structurally determined *and* exercised by intentional human agents who can always "do otherwise." This requires a view of determination different from the empiricist view, in which determination is understood as one thing regularly following another. And it requires a more elaborate conceptualization of structure and agency. As we will see in the next chapter, contemporary developments in realist philosophy of social science make such an understanding possible. But it is surprising that Lukes, who is one of the foremost social theorists in the contemporary Anglo-American tradition, simply takes for granted conventional understandings of structure and determination, especially given the literature he cites.

If Lukes's first difficulty involves his polarization of structure and agency in favor of an agency approach, his second involves his inability to recognize who the real determinists are. In "On the Relativity of Power," Lukes associates proponents of a structural concept of power with the behaviorist psychology of B. F. Skinner. He claims that they both are interested in systems of "causal or statistical connections," and in this regard have a "cognitive interest in technical control."[65] This claim is so remarkable because the intellectual cousins of B. F. Skinner are none other than the behavioralists with whom Lukes aligns himself. None of the contemporary structuralist theorists whom Lukes mentions—Louis Althusser and Nicos Poulantzas in particular—have ever advocated deductive-nomological or statistical theory. In fact they are all, in one way or another, committed to the kind of theoretical abstrac-

[64]Anthony Giddens, *New Rules of Sociological Method: A Critique of Interpretative Sociologies* (New York: Basic Books, 1976). Giddens has noted: "In representing structure as placing limitations or constraints on the activities of agents ... Lukes tends to repeat the dualism of agency and structure that I have spoken of in earlier papers" (Anthony Giddens, *Central Problems in Social Theory: Action, Structure, and Contradiction in Social Analysis* [Berkeley: University of California Press, 1979], p. 91).

[65]Lukes, "On the Relativity," pp. 266–68; Bloch et al., p. 251, also make this mistake.

tion about hypothesized structural relations that Lukes's behavioralist predecessors attempted to discredit. It is Dahl, however, who writes about stimulus and control. Strangely, in the same breath in which Lukes defends an agency approach, he also asserts in a footnote that Jack Nagel's *The Descriptive Analysis of Power* is a "fine book," which outlines a methodology compatible with Lukes's own "three dimensional view."[66] Yet Nagel is exclusively concerned with operationalizing the concept of power, and with a positivistic zeal that would make even Skinner blush, in order to formulate predictive laws of statistical regularity.

Lukes's problem here is that, though he is sensitive to the importance of agency in social theory, he fails to see that behavioralism, while nominally concerned with actual behavior, inadequately conceptualizes it. As we shall see in the next chapter, a concern with structure, far from negating, complements an adequate understanding of human agency. Lukes, in his aversion to what he regards as the determinism of structural analysis, remains wedded to the regularity determinism of behavioralism.

In the end Lukes leans toward a view of power differing little from that of his predecessors in the debate. Like them, he views power in terms of behavioral regularities rather than their structural determinants. And like them he conflates the possession with the *exercise* of power, insisting that power is an agency concept rather than a structural one. Lukes is explicit in his rejection of the locution "power to," and instead accepts an exclusive emphasis on "power over." For him power is exhausted in interaction, in the regularity with which A can get B to do something, thus having power over B, and his formulation leaves no room for consideration of the enduring powers to act possessed by A and B, and brought to bear in interaction. He justifies inattention to the locution "power to" by arguing that it is "out of line with the central meaning of power as traditionally understood and with the concerns that have always preoccupied students of power."[67] But it is precisely this traditional idiom that I question. An adequate formulation of the concept of power must recognize that the power one agent exercises "over" another agent in interaction is parasitic upon the relatively enduring powers to act that the agents possess.

[66]Lukes, "On the Relativity," pp. 273–74n.
[67]Lukes, *Power*, p. 31.

Beyond the Three Faces of Power

The purpose of this discussion has been to demonstrate the root similarities between the contestants of the three faces of power controversy and to point out that what is usually taken to be the contours within which the concept of power can be discussed is in fact a controversy within rather narrow parameters. Nonetheless, within these parameters, some serious problems are left unresolved. And while the irresolution of conflict is not always a signal of something awry, in this case it may indicate the need to broaden the parameters of debate and in fact to jettison the discussion from its behavioralist foundations.

The major unresolved difficulty of the debate concerns the problem of the limits within which interaction occurs, or what I have called the structural nature of power. As I have attempted to suggest, this problem has proven inarticulable within the confines of the debate, by virtue of the shared premise, established by the behavioral revolution, that power is the empirical causation of one actor's behavior by that of another actor.

Both Bachrach and Baratz, and Lukes, have failed to develop the structural dimension of power they rightly point to. This is not a problem for Dahl, who never raises the question of a structural dimension of power. In this sense, it may very well be true that Dahl's view, which March has called a "simple force" model, is the most consistent.[68] Its consistency is purchased at a price, however—its inability to conceptualize the way power is implicated in the constitution of the conditions of interaction. Dahl's critics insist, rightly, that A can have power over B without it being the case that B resists in any way, in fact by virtue of B's quiescence. The critics, however, have not been able to formulate a clear alternative conception. To take an example, it seems reasonable to claim that the Soviet Communist Party apparatus has power over the Soviet workers and peasants even though it clearly does not prevail over

---

[68]James March, "The Power of Power," in Easton, ed., *Varieties of Political Theory*, pp. 67–68. He writes: "The measurement of power is useful primarily in systems that conform to some variant of the force model [i.e., behavioral compliance—J.I.]. . . . If I interpret recent research correctly, the class of social-choice situations in which power is a significantly useful concept is much smaller than I previously believed."

the masses in situations of actual conflict of revealed preferences; yet Dahl's view would prevent us from claiming this. (I do not mean, and do not believe, that Dahl would deny this, only that the logic of his articles about power would deny it.)[69] And yet is it necessary to argue about the "objective class interests" of the workers and peasants in order to say this? I should think not.

Of course there is another possibility, one that appears startlingly commonsensical but that violates the basic premise of the three faces debate. That is, that the CPSU has power over the Soviet masses by virtue of the structure of Soviet society, in which political power is monopolized by a single party. This claim about power, however, is clearly essentialist in Popper's sense, in that it is interested in the nature of Soviet society rather than in the search for behavioral uniformities. Such theoretical interests, therefore, require more than going beyond the three faces of power controversy; they require the rejection of the empiricism that is the controversy's foundation.

[69]Dahl himself has on one occasion asserted that his view of power is applicable only to democratic systems. He writes in defense of his method: "It might be objected that the test I have proposed would not work in the most obvious of all cases of ruling elites, namely in the totalitarian dictatorships. For the control of the elite over the expression of opinion is so great that overtly there is no disagreement; hence no cases on which to base a judgement arise. The objection is a fair one. But we not concerned here with totalitarian systems. We are concerned with the application of the techniques of modern investigation to American communities" (Dahl, "A Critique," p. 468). This is a peculiar qualification to make about a meta-theoretical position. One is tempted to ask Dahl on what *basis* he knows that elites have such control in totalitarian systems, and that power does not operate in similar ways in American communities. But this remark does indicate something I will suggest later in this book—that Dahl's theory of pluralism is *not* a consequence of the application of his method.

CHAPTER 2

Realism and Social
Scientific Theory

It is widely claimed that we live in a post-positivist era. The positivist ideal of a perfectly formal and deductive science, tied indubitably to sensory perception through "correspondence rules," has been abandoned by the philosophical mainstream. Social scientists are well aware of this and therefore exhibit much less optimism about the possibility of such "ideal" explanations. It is common knowledge among social scientists that our investigations are shaped by our theoretical questions, that, as Popper has insisted, "a science needs a point of view, and questions."[1]

The abandonment of positivism, and with it the naive (and self-righteous) optimism of behavioralism, has been an important achievement. Indeed, it has liberated social scientists from a frustrating and impossible ideal. But as is all too often the case in political struggle, the beneficiaries of hard-fought victory forget the battle, losing sight as well of the need to extend the struggle. So, while most contemporary social theorists are well aware of the demise of positivism, they all too often take the critique of positivism for granted. In doing so they risk failing to recognize the limits of their post-positivism. It is ironic that many of these theorists are the first to heap scorn on "another critique of positivism," mistakenly believing that its distorting legacy has been effectively dislodged.

As we pointed out in the last chapter, empiricism is a doctrine

---

[1]Karl R. Popper, *The Logic of Scientific Discovery* (New York: Harper Torchbooks, 1959), p. 106.

more inclusive than positivism; and, further, many post-positivists are in fact empiricists. Many social theorists have not seen this, a fact that can be attributed to the strong hold Humean notions of causality and theoretical explanation have on us. They have thus not recognized the necessity of extending the criticism of positivism into a more general criticism of empiricism and its effects upon social scientific investigation.

In the last chapter we examined some of the consequences of empiricism for the conceptualization of power. In this chapter we will outline an increasingly accepted "realist" alternative to empiricism and suggest its relevance to social and political analysis. As we will see, realism builds upon the epistemological insight of post-positivism—that scientific analysis requires a theoretical framework. But realism goes further, subjecting to criticism the Humean understanding of causality and explanation as well.

Realism, Post-Positivism, and Scientific Theory

Popper's rejection of foundationalism, and his belief that science is a process of critique rather than induction from experience, is an important source of post-positivist philosophy. There is, however, one crucial respect in which Popper fails to break with positivism: his commitment to a *logical* analysis of scientific practice. He has written on many occasions that "logic is the organon of criticism."[2] His own critique of positivism was based in large part on his analysis of the logic (or rather illogic) of induction. And it is the logical certainty of Popper's deductive theory of science that provides its appeal for him. While Popper has always insisted that ultimately the falsification of a theory involves a scientific decision, a judgment, he has also insisted that in order for a theory to be properly scientific, it must be judged according to an invariable, formal decision rule. Of his method of falsification he writes: "Deduction, I contend, is not valid because we choose or decide to adopt its rules as a standard, or decree that they shall be accepted;

---

[2]Karl R. Popper, "The Logic of Social Science," in Theodor Adorno, ed., *The Positivist Dispute in German Sociology* (New York: Harper Torchbooks, 1971), p. 98.

rather, it is valid because it adopts, and incorporates, the rules by which truth is transmitted from (logically stronger) premises to (logically weaker) conclusions, and by which falsity is retransmitted from conclusions to premises (this re-transmission of falsity makes formal logic the Organon of rational criticism—that is, of refutation)."[3] It is this commitment to formal logic as the basis of scientific method, and the belief that to reject it is to ground science on arbitrary decrees and pure decisions—a kind of scientific Hobbesianism—which has generated the now famous controversy over scientific rationality and the growth of knowledge.

Kuhn's concept of a "paradigm," Lakatos's concept of a "methodology of research programmes," and Feyerabend's "theoretical anarchism" all represent attempts to articulate the nature of scientific decision making.[4] While there are important differences between these authors, they share in common a "conventionalist" view of science—they all view science as a social practice, defined by a set of conventions, and undertaken by socially and historically situated practitioners. All of them have questioned what Lakatos has called Popper's "naive falsificationism"—the belief that a counterinstance constitutes sufficient grounds for the refutation of a scientific theory. In different ways all three have emphasized the fact that the practical-experimental and conceptual elements of scientific theory are always in the process of being worked out by scientists, and that no simple, logical canon can govern scientific decision making and determine the appropriateness or validity of a given theory. The adequacy of a theory is always determined by

[3]Karl R. Popper, *Conjectures and Refutations: The Growth of Scientific Knowledge* (New York: Harper Torchbooks, 1965), p. 64. See also Popper's *Objective Knowledge* (Oxford: Clarendon Press, 1972).

[4]See Thomas Kuhn, *The Structure of Scientific Revolutions* (Chicago: University of Chicago Press, 1962), and *The Essential Tension: Selected Studies in Scientific Tradition and Change* (Chicago: University of Chicago Press, 1977); Imre Lakatos, "Falsification and the Methodology of Scientific Research Programmes," in Imre Lakatos and Alan Musgrave, eds., *Criticism and the Growth of Knowledge* (London: Cambridge University Press, 1970). All of the essays in this volume are excellent and indispensable, particularly Kuhn's "Reflections on My Critics" and Paul Feyerabend's "Consolations for the Specialist"; and Paul Feyerabend, *Against Method* (London: Verso, 1978). On conventionalism, see Russell Keat and John Urry, *Social Theory as Science* (London: Routledge & Kegan Paul, 1975), pp. 46–66. For a recent critical summary of this approach, see Richard J. Bernstein, *Beyond Objectivism and Relativism* (Philadelphia: University of Pennsylvania Press, 1983).

the considered judgments of members of scientific communities, by comparing it with other theories. In short, theories are *underdetermined* by the facts they explain.

This conventionalist view of science captures many of the most characteristic features of scientific practice—the messiness of theoretical belief systems, which are not formally and deductively organized,[5] the reasoning by analogy and by iconic representation, which plays such a crucial role in scientific discovery,[6] and the controversy, and discontinuity, which tends to accompany scientific change.[7] Like Popper himself, however, his followers remain neo-Kantian with regard to the critique of Humean empiricism. While they have all emphasized the irreducibly human and social basis of theoretical knowledge, none of them has questioned the understanding of natural laws as empirical invariances and causality as constant conjunction. Like Kant, their critique has been exclusively epistemological—if Humean causality is to be possible, then certain things must be true about the human production of knowledge of it.[8]

Contemporary realism in the philosophy of science accepts the analysis of post-positivism—that science is a social practice, that scientific language and concepts do not correspond with something immediately given in experience but are socially produced, and that their meaning is constituted through their use. Realism, as it is developed here, joins with post-positivism in rejecting any notion that science necessarily converges upon a true representation of reality, and in insisting that scientific encounters with reality are necessarily mediated by language and interpretation.[9] On the realist

[5]See W. V. O. Quine, "Two Dogmas of Empiricism," in W. V. O. Quine, *From a Logical Point of View: Logico-Philosophical Essays* (New York: Harper Torchbooks, 1953).

[6]See Mary Hesse, *Models and Analogies in Science* (Notre Dame, Ind.: University of Notre Dame Press, 1966), and "The Explanatory Function of Metaphor," in Mary Hesse, *Revolutions and Reconstructions in the Philosophy of Science* (Bloomington: Indiana University Press, 1980); Rom Harré, *Principles of Scientific Thinking* (Oxford: Oxford University Press, 1970); and Norwood Russell Hanson, *Patterns of Discovery* (Cambridge: Cambridge University Press, 1958).

[7]See John Krige, *Science, Revolution, and Discontinuity* (Atlantic Highlands, N.J.: Humanities Press, 1980).

[8]See Roy Bhaskar, *A Realist Theory of Science* (Atlantic Highlands, N.J.: Humanities Press, 1978), p. 261.

[9]The version of realism developed here differs from that which offers a "realistic"

view, however, scientific practice is aimed at the development of models that explain *real causal mechanisms*.[10] Realism is primarily an ontological doctrine, which rejects the Humean view of causality and causal explanation and insists that the world consists of a complex of mechanisms which causes the phenomena of experience.

In the realist view, things are not simply real in the weak, ep-istemological sense of existing independently of the knower. They are real in a strong, *ontological* sense, in that they are not neces-sarily isomorphic with experience at all. This point needs to be emphasized and clarified, because very few philosophers, empiri-cists included, would deny that there are "real things" that exist.[11] The positivist Moritz Schlick, in the classic and influential 1932 essay "Positivism and Realism," clearly articulates the prevailing empiricist view of "reality": "I must confess that I should repudiate and consider absurd any philosophical system that involved the assertion that clouds and stars, mountains and sea were unreal, that the chair by the wall ceased to exist whenever I turned my back."[12] He continues: "If one understood by positivism a view which denies the reality of bodies I must declare positivism to be simply absurd." In rejecting idealism, however, Schlick defines "reality" as: "When we say of any object or event—which must

---

interpretation of theories as corresponding to reality and converging upon truth. For this realistic realism, see Hilary Putnam, *Meaning and the Moral Sciences* (Boston: Routledge & Kegan Paul, 1978). Mary Hesse writes: "A feature of this type of realism is that it retains the logical presuppositions of empiricism, namely the accurate applicability of logic and an ideal scientific language to the world.... In a wider perspective this realist problematic looks parochial and over-intellec-tualized. It has not only underestimated the challenge to empiricist presuppositions arising from modern history and philosophy of science, but it also bypasses two other features of the general philosophical scene"—hermeneutics and the sociology of knowledge ("Introduction," in Hesse, *Revolutions*, p. xiii).

[10]See Harré, *Principles*; Bhaskar, *Realist Theory*; Keat and Urry, *Social Theory*; Ted Benton, *Philosophical Foundations of the Three Sociologies* (London: Rou-tledge & Kegan Paul, 1977); Andrew Sayer, "Abstraction: A Realist Interpreta-tion," *Radical Philosophy* (Summer 1981), 6–15; Peter T. Manicas, "Reduction, Epigenesis, and Explanation," *Journal for the Theory of Social Behaviour* 13 (October 1983), 321–54.

[11]See Karl Popper's *Realism and the Aim of Science* (Totowa: Rowman and Littlefield, 1982).

[12]Moritz Schlick, "Positivism and Realism," in A. J. Ayer, ed., *Logical Posi-tivism* (New York: Free Press, 1959), p. 97.

be designated by a description—that it is *real* this means that there exists a very definite connection between perception or other experiences, that under certain conditions certain data appear."[13] In other words, of course there are things that are real; but to say that X is real is to say that X is an event we have experienced or can experience, or as Schlick puts it: "To be real always means to stand in a definite relationship to the given."[14] This view of the real, which Schlick labels "empirical realism," is the prevailing view. On it one doesn't deny reality; one insists that what is real is what is experienceable. Nelson Polsby, whose views of causality and explanation we have already encountered, is representative when he writes: "My idea of theory, a widely held but evidently not universally shared view, is that it exists primarily for the purpose of facilitating the storage of information about *objects of empirical inquiry*, and for producing knowledge ... about a world that has some existence independent and apart from the language in which scholars palaver" (italics mine).[15]

Realism is based upon a more substantial view of what is entailed by the independence of the world from the observation of the world. Schlick considered it absurd that the chair by the wall ceased to exist whenever he turned his back. On the realist view, it is not enough to say that the chair exists whether I look at it or not; the fact that the chair exists, whether I look at it or not, means that there is no reason we should suppose that the ontological reality of the chair is nothing more than those (possible) experiences of it through which I can come to know it. For realism, the real is not simply the events we experience. However much we require experience in order to know about the world, and however much we can only experience events, the appearances of the world and the reality of the world should not be conflated. On this view science is precisely the use of reason to figure out what real mechanisms are causally responsible for the phenomena of experience.

Realism thus rejects the understanding of causality as constant conjunction and scientific explanation as the prediction of empirical regularities. It defends the concept of "natural necessity," that nat-

---

[13]Ibid.

[14]Ibid., p. 99.

[15]Nelson Polsby, *Community Power and Political Theory*, 2d ed. (New Haven: Yale University Press, 1980), p. 233.

ural (scientific) laws explain the properties and dispositions of things that are not reducible to their effects. For example, the physical properties of copper—malleability, fusibility, ductility, electrical conductivity—are not contingent effects caused by antecedent events; they are the enduring properties of copper as a metal, which can be accounted for by its atomic structure. On this view causality is understood as the actualization of the properties of real entities with "causal powers."[16] Scientists develop theories explaining the phenomena of experience (e.g., the fact that copper conducts electricity and string doesn't) via appeal to the structures which generate them. It is these structures, and the effects they tend to produce, which are the primary objects of scientific investigation.

Rom Harré and E. H. Madden, in their *Causal Powers*, provide an example. The earth possesses the power of gravitational attraction, although the barn won't collapse unless the center beam is removed. Physical theory, however, is not about whether or not the center beam will be removed and the barn collapse, an event that is purely contingent; it is about gravity and the gravitational properties of various masses. Similarly, fire has the power to burn human beings. Of course, whether I get burned by fire is purely contingent; I may never encounter a fire, or I may do so wearing an asbestos suit. But science tells us about the *enduring properties* of the world. As long as fire is fire and has the properties of fire (i.e., the production of heat), and as long as humans are humans and are so biochemically constituted, fire has the capacity to burn humans, whether or not it will do so on any particular occasions. The actualization of causal powers is contingent. But causal powers are naturally necessary—they are the way the things of the world tend to operate in virtue of what they are.[17]

On the realist view, the world is not constituted such that it can be explained by subsuming events under "covering laws" of the form "whenever A, then B." Rather, it is composed of a complex of what Harré has called "powerful particulars," or causal mechanisms, which operate in an unpredictable, but not undetermined, manner. Roy Bhaskar writes in his *A Realist Theory of Science*:

[16]Rom Harré and E. H. Madden, *Causal Powers* (Totowa: Rowman and Littlefield, 1975).
[17]Ibid., chap. 1.

The world consists of things, not events.... On this conception of science it is concerned essentially with what kinds of things there are and with what they tend to do; it is only derivatively concerned with predicting what is actually going to happen. It is only rarely, and normally under conditions which are artificially produced and controlled, that scientists can do the latter. And when they do, its significance lies precisely in the light that it casts on the enduring natures and ways of acting of independently existing and transfactually active things.[18]

This understanding of science does not eschew empirical evidence. But it construes this evidence as the means by which scientists come to explain underlying causes that are not apparent in experience. Bhaskar, in fact, argues that it is only such a view that can make sense of the role of evidence and experiment in natural science. Bhaskar argues, through a "transcendental argument," that if science as we know it is to be possible, then the world must be characterized by natural necessity, and to put it negatively, empiricism must be wrong. Bhaskar's argument hinges on an analysis of experimentation in theoretical science. The scientist, making use of the skills, tools, and knowledge produced by the scientific community, closes the world through experiment so that knowledge of nature is possible. Under conditions of experimental closure, scientists isolate theoretically relevant phenomena and produce empirical regularities. These regularities are the evidence for the laws discovered by science. But, Bhaskar argues, if the universality of the laws is to be sustained, and the practice of experiment made intelligible, then the laws discovered and validated through experimental closure must be applicable outside their conditions of identification.[19] In short, scientists *identify* natural laws by producing regularities through experiment. But clearly the practice of experiment would make no sense if these laws were considered real only under experimental conditions. Scientists produce empirical regularities in order to identify how things tend to behave even in the absence of experimental conditions. Experiments are necessary because causal mechanisms do not always produce their natural ef-

[18]Bhaskar, *Realist Theory*, p. 51.
[19]Ibid., pp. 63–127.

fects in the open world outside of experimentally closed conditions, and when they do, they are often interfered with by other effects of other mechanisms. But experiments are intelligible only if we suppose that laws apply even in the absence of experimentally produced regularities, and if we view documenting the regularities not as the aim of science, but as the means of discovering and isolating the enduring causal mechanisms which produce them.

Events in the world, on this view, are usually complexly caused by the conjunction of a variety of mechanisms.[20] If we want to explain, for example, why my pipes broke on December 12, 1986, we must have recourse to certain explanatory theories that tell us about the properties of things like water (H_2O tends to freeze and expand at certain temperatures), copper piping, and so on. We must also have knowledge of more specific circumstances not built into the theories (e.g., the heater in my basement, which had prevented the pipes from freezing all winter long but broke on December 11). No general theory can have built into it enough specific information to enable us to deduce that the pipes will break in my basement, because the set of events (and decisions—why did I not replace that old heater last autumn?) pertinent to that occurrence are both idiographic and contingent. But given our theoretical knowledge and a more historical account filling in the specific circumstances in question, we can explain the breaking of the pipes (the temperature was below zero, water tends to free at below-zero temperatures, copper piping tends to expand but these pipes were defective, etc.).

In the realist view theoretical science is about the properties of enduring mechanisms—like H_2O—which are ascertained under experimentally produced circumstances. Given our knowledge of the various natural necessities in question, we can understand why, if the specific set of entirely unpredictable circumstances that occurred in my basement obtained, my pipes would break. But the circumstances themselves were not necessary. For realism the natural necessity of causal mechanisms is associated with the *contin-*

[20]This example, and the more general analysis of explanation, is drawn from Peter T. Manicas, "Structure and Explanation" (unpublished manuscript, Department of Philosophy, Queens College).

gency of particular outcomes. Realism understands there to be determinants—the tendencies of real entities. But it is not deterministic.[21]

It bears emphasizing that realism as a philosophy of science is not an esoteric or a priori doctrine, but is based on an analysis of the actual practice of science. For realism, the ontology of natural necessity is presupposed by what scientists do, in their classificatory schemas, in their experimentation, and in their development of causal concepts. Stephen Toulmin has written of the scientist: "He begins with the conviction that things are not just happening (not even just happening regularly) but rather that some fixed set of laws or patterns or mechanisms accounts for Nature's following the course that it does, and that his understanding of these should guide his expectations. Furthermore, he has the beginnings of an idea what these laws and mechanisms are . . . [and] he is looking for evidence which will show him how to trim and shape his ideas further. . . . This is what makes 'phenomena' important for him."[22]

Science is thus essentialist and metaphysical in Popper's (and Polsby's) invidious sense. It is interested in how things happen, primarily as a means of understanding *why* things happen, what mechanisms cause things to happen, and what their causal powers are. But it does not therefore presume any immutability or teleology about the world, nor does it presume that the world can be unproblematically and rationally perceived. Rather, it presumes that the natural world exists independently of human experience, that it has certain enduring properties, and that science, through the development and criticism of theoretical explanations, can come to have some (however imperfect) knowledge of it. No greater testimony can be provided on behalf of this view than that of Albert Einstein, who in a 1931 letter to Moritz Schlick wrote: "In general your presentation fails to correspond to my conceptual style insofar as I find your whole orientation so to speak much too positivistic. . . . I tell you straight out: Physics is the attempt at the conceptual

---

[21]Bhaskar, *Realist Theory*, p. 106–107. See also Roy Bhaskar, "Emergence, Explanation, and Emancipation," in Paul Secord, ed., *Conceptual Issues in the Human Sciences* (Beverly Hills: Sage, 1981); and Michael Polanyi, "Emergence," in his *The Tacit Dimension* (New York: Doubleday/Anchor, 1967).

[22]Stephen Toulmin, *Foresight and Understanding* (New York: Harper Torchbooks, 1961), p. 75.

construction of a model of the real world and its lawful structure. ... In short, I suffer under the (unsharp) separation of Reality of Experience and Reality of Being. ... You will be astonished about the 'metaphysicist' Einstein. But every four- and two-legged animal is de facto this metaphysicist."[23]

Realism, Human Agency, and Social Practice

In the realist view social science should be similarly concerned with the construction of models of the social world and its lawful structure.[24] Not behavioral regularities, but the enduring social relationships that structure interaction, would be the primary object of theoretical analysis. In proposing this, however, realists do not advocate a form of hyperdeterminism that reifies social structure. Rather, in criticizing empiricism in social study, they have drawn on those critics of social science who, harkening back to the nineteenth-century German *Methodenstreit*, maintain that social study requires a different mode of understanding (*verstehen*).[25] Realism thus maintains that society is in important respects different from nature, and that empiricism has failed to take account of this. However, realism also insists that this stands as an indictment of social scientific empiricism, not the project of social science per se.

The Humean view of explanation and ontology has never gone uncontested in social theory. Giddens has usefully labeled the critics of the Humean view "interpretative sociologists."[26] They have argued that: (1) the social world, unlike the world of nature, must be understood as the skilled creation of active human subjects; (2) the constitution of this world as meaningful depends on language, regarded not simply as a system of signs but as a medium of practical and intentional activity; and (3) generating descriptions of

[23]Quoted in Gerald Holton, "Mach, Einstein, and the Search for Reality," *Daedelus* 67 (1968), 636–73.

[24]See my "Realism and Social Scientific Theory," *Journal for the Theory of Social Behaviour* 13 (October 1983), 301–8.

[25]See William Outhwaite, *Understanding Social Life* (London: Allen & Unwin, 1975), for a historical discussion of this approach. See also Richard Palmer, *Hermeneutics* (Evanston, Ill.: Northwestern University Press, 1969).

[26]Anthony Giddens, *New Rules of Sociological Method: A Critique of Interpretative Sociologies* (New York: Basic Books, 1976).

social conduct depends on the hermeneutic task of "penetrating the frames of meaning which lay actors themselves draw upon in constituting and reconstituting the social world."[27] Unlike post-positivist philosophy of natural science, "interpretative sociology" is an ontological doctrine—it is concerned with the nature of social being itself. And it insists that the differences between natural and human science should properly reflect real differences between nature and society. While natural science aims at the documentation of empirical regularities and the subsumption of events under predictive covering laws, human action is purposive and can only be understood by grasping the rules, norms, and concepts that are essentially (not contingently) related to action.[28] To understand the human world is to understand the purposes of human agents, and the conventions within which these are articulated. Perhaps the classic modern statement of this position is Peter Winch's *The Idea of a Social Science*. Here Winch insists that while natural scientists investigate causal regularities, social conduct is rule-governed and not causal. Social study, therefore, is radically unlike the study of nature.[29]

This approach has attained a certain prominence among political theorists and has become something of a new counterorthodoxy in political science, particularly among those who consider themselves theorists but who reject the implications of behavioralist scientific theory. This explains the preoccupation of contemporary political theory with questions regarding the nature of language and subjectivity and the history of political concepts and speech.[30] John Dunn summarizes this preoccupation: "The great strength of the hermeneutic approach is that it takes consciousness and action as the core subject matter of the human sciences and treats them

---

[27]Ibid., p. 153.

[28]See Quentin Skinner, "Social Meaning and the Explanation of Social Action," in P. Laslett, W. G. Runciman, and Q. Skinner, eds., *Philosophy, Politics, and Society*, 4th ser. (Oxford: Blackwell, 1972). Skinner's analysis here draws heavily upon J. L. Austin's *How to Do Things with Words* (Cambridge, Mass.: Harvard University Press, 1962).

[29]Peter Winch, *The Idea of a Social Science* (London: Routledge & Kegan Paul, 1959).

[30]See my "After Empiricism: The Realist Alternative," in Terence Ball, ed., *Idioms of Inquiry: Critique and Renewal in Political Theory* (Albany: State University of New York Press, 1987).

as essentially linguistic phenomena, the possibility of characterising which in language is constitutive of them in a sense in which it is not in the case of non-human nature."[31]

Perhaps the most influential proponent of this hermeneutic in political science is Charles Taylor. In a number of essays and books Taylor has argued that to understand society is to understand the norms and vocabularies constituting its practices.[32] In his now classic "Interpretation and the Sciences of Man," Taylor subjects to criticism the behavioralist project of "public opinion research," which is concerned with formulating cross-cultural empirical generalizations about the correlation of various opinions and behaviors.[33] He argues that political actions presuppose a normative, "institutional" context. To meaningfully say that one has political opinions and performs political activities, we must first grasp the social understandings that constitute these. One can only vote if one participates in certain activities and possesses *concepts* about the meaning and rightness of these activities. Taylor writes:

> The point is that the objects of public experience—rite, festival, election, etc.—are not like facts of nature. For they are not entirely separable from the experience they give rise to. They are partly constituted by the ideas and interpretations which underly them. A given social practice, like voting in the ecclesia, or in a modern election, is what it is because of a set of commonly understood ideas and meanings, by which the depositing of stones in an urn, or the marking of bits of paper, counts as the making of a social decision. These ideas about what is going on are essential to define the institution. They are essential if there is to be voting here, and not some other activity which could be carried on by putting stones in urns.[34]

[31]John Dunn, "Practicing History and Social Science on 'Realist' Assumptions," in C. Hookway and P. Pettit, eds., *Action and Interpretation: Studies in the Philosophy of the Social Sciences* (Cambridge: Cambridge University Press, 1978), pp. 159–60. I should point out that by "realism" here Dunn is referring to the reality of an agent's intentionality, not to the reality of social structure.

[32]Charles Taylor, *Philosophical Papers*, 2 vols. (Cambridge: Cambridge University Press, 1985).

[33]Charles Taylor, "Interpretation and the Sciences of Man," *Review of Metaphysics* 25 (1971), 1–45.

[34]Charles Taylor, *Hegel and Modern Society* (Cambridge: Cambridge University Press, 1979), p. 88.

Taylor thus contends that the explanation of human action must be in terms of the practical understandings, norms, and purposes of human agents. This kind of explanation, for Taylor, is radically different from the explanation of nature because, unlike nature, the object of human science is itself normatively constituted.

Interpretative theory thus sees the social world as consisting of normatively governed practices rather than of contingently caused behaviors.[35] This is a very important distinction, one that is lost, for instance, on Lukes, who mistakenly believes that the only way to make sense of human agency is through the lens of behavioralism. The rejection of empiricist views of human action does not mean that there are no behavioral regularities in society. It simply means that these regularities or patterns are not mechanistically or contingently connected. They are, rather, the ways in which activities are practiced, are purposively done according to certain social rules and self-understandings. Most things are done rather routinely in the course of everyday life and lack the quality of "events."[36] Moreover, they are not done simply as a matter of course, but in a variety of ways within normative limits. Thus, if we want to understand why children go to school in the morning, we would not formulate a law of the form "whenever it is 8:30 A.M., children go to school," or "whenever parents say so, children go to school." Rather, we would attempt to understand the social concepts and norms that make school going a meaningful activity routinely undertaken by children (e.g., respect for authority, belief in merit, obedience to parents).

These norms are not, however, apodictic; they do not deterministically cause people to act in the manner in which a cue ball causes another billiard ball to move upon contact. Rather, they are both enabling and constraining, within limits; they are the materials that make possible what Stuart Hampshire has called "practical

[35]See Richard J. Bernstein, *Praxis and Action: Contemporary Philosophies of Human Activity* (Philadelphia: University of Pennsylvania Press, 1976), and *The Restructuring of Social and Political Theory* (Philadelphia: University of Pennsylvania Press, 1978); and Anthony Giddens, *Central Problems in Social Theory: Action, Structure, and Contradiction in Social Analysis* (Berkeley: University of California Press, 1979).

[36]See K. W. Kim, "The Limits of Behavioral Explanation in Politics," in Charles A. McCoy and John Playford, eds., *Apolitical Politics: A Critique of Behavioralism* (New York: Crowell, 1967), pp. 47–50.

reasoning"[37]—"the clarification of one's intentions and purposes," the "considered decisions" grounded in values and reasons, which are the stuff of human activity. Michael Oakeshott has observed: "All activity springs up within an already existing idiom of activity."[38] Practices can be thought of as idiomatic activities rather than as mechanistic behavioral regularities.

The notion that society is constituted by the norms and concepts of its participants, and that interpretation and intentionality are distinctive properties of the human world, is a crucial one. As Anthony Giddens has pointed out, however, this insight is often wedded to philosophically idealist positions, which ignore: (1) the practical involvements of human life in material activity; (2) the causal conditions of human activity; (3) asymmetries of power and divisions of interest in society; and (4) the possibility of false consciousness and systematic mystification.[39] To explain why I go to school requires recourse to my understandings and purposes (as well as my *unconscious* motives). But it also involves analyzing what are such things as schools, which are (both logically and historically) pregiven, which do not exist simply in virtue of my own beliefs about and reasons for attending them, and which may in fact have properties that remain unacknowledged by me as I participate in them.

It should be obvious at this point that interpretative theory's antiscientific approach is based upon the implicit acceptance of an empiricist view of science and causality. Winch is representative here. He does not question the Humean account of causality as constant conjunction; he questions whether, given the nature of science, society can be scientifically studied.[40] Interpretative theory has properly rejected the empiricist ideal of social study. But it has

---

[37]Stuart Hampshire, "Freedom and Explanation, or Seeing Double," in Alan Ryan, ed., *The Idea of Freedom: Essays in Honor of Isaiah Berlin* (Oxford: Oxford University Press, 1979).

[38]Michael Oakeshott, *Rationalism and Politics* (New York: Free Press, 1962).

[39]Giddens, *New Rules*, p. 155. On mystification, see Ernest Gellner, "Concepts and Society," and Alasdair MacIntyre, "The Idea of a Social Science," and "Is Understanding Religion Compatible with Believing?" in Bryan Wilson, ed., *Rationality* (Oxford: Blackwell, 1970).

[40]See Roy Bhaskar, *The Possibility of Naturalism: A Philosophical Critique of the Contemporary Human Sciences* (Atlantic Highlands, N.J.: Humanities Press, 1979), pp. 169–95.

improperly rejected the project of a causal and explanatory social theory. A realist understanding of science is capable of appreciating the specificity of the human world and of agreeing, with Taylor, that social science must study the concepts and values of societies. It is capable, however, of recognizing the purposeful nature of human conduct *and* of seeing it as determined by causal mechanisms. These mechanisms, though, will be understood not as antecedent events but as the enduring, structural relations which enable and constrain human conduct.

Realism and Social Structure

The concept of social structure recently developed by realists is based on a categorical rejection of the bifurcation of structure and human agency. Anthony Giddens argues that there is a "duality of structure."[41] He proposes that social structures are both the medium and the effect of human action. As such, they do not exist apart from the activities they govern and human agents' conceptions of these activities, but they are also a material condition of these activities. Giddens uses the analogy of language to illustrate this: there would be no language without speakers speaking, and yet language is at the same time the medium of speech. Language has structural properties that agents draw upon in order to perform communicative acts. Giddens draws this notion of the sui generis, pregiven nature of society, which provides the conditions for human conduct, from Emile Durkheim's classic formulation:

> When I fulfill my obligations as brother, husband, or citizen, when I execute my contracts, I perform duties which are defined, externally to myself and my acts, in law and in custom. . . . The system of signs I use to express my thought, the system of currency I employ to pay my debts, the instruments of credit I utilize in my commercial relations, the practices followed in my profession, etc,. function independently of my own use of them. . . . Even when I free myself from these rules and violate them successfully I am always compelled to struggle with them.[42]

[41]Giddens, *New Rules*, p. 121.
[42]Emile Durkheim, *Rules of Sociological Method* (New York: Free Press, 1966), pp. 1–3.

Pace Durkheim, however, for Giddens society does not exert a "coercive force" on individuals such that they simply "internalize" its dictates. Society not only constrains, but it *enables* purposive human action. Those social roles available in society constitute the basis of human identity. Stripped of these roles, and of the activities associated with them, the individual would be nothing but a cipher. These roles, however, are also sustained by their continued performance by intentional human agents. Society is thus both the condition and the product of human action.

The major point of this realist approach is that human agency has social-structural preconditions. On this view social structures consist of those relatively enduring social relations between agents in the performance of definite social practices. The family, for example, is a social structure, composed of enduring relations between its members (husbands/wives, parents/children) in the performance of specific social practices (child rearing, maintenance of the household, etc.).[43] There are, of course, many different kinds of relations in society. The relation between two cyclists crossing paths is different from the more enduring, structural relation between a teacher and a student. The latter is what Bhaskar calls an internal relation. He writes: "A relation R_{AB} may be defined as *internal* if and only if A would not be what it *essentially* is unless B is related to it in the way that it is."[44] Social structures are enduring, internal relations. At the intersection of various socially structured relations are the chance encounters that play a not insignificant part in everyday life. Interaction, however, is social by virtue of the persistence of the ties binding action together. Thus, even the chance encounter between cyclists is made possible by more enduring relationships—citizenship, for example—which provide a common ground of interaction (the street) and a common set of signals, symbols, and expectations (glances, words) which constitute spatio-temporal proximity as interaction.[45]

Bhaskar proposes that this realist view of social structure corresponds to a "transformationalist" view of human agency: human activity is understood as the purposive *transformation* of material

[43]See Peter T. Manicas, "On the Concept of Social Structure," *Journal for the Theory of Social Behaviour* 10 (1980), 65–82.

[44]Bhaskar, *Possibility*, p. 54.

[45]See Giddens, *Central Problems*, pp. 198–233.

(social) causes by human agents. People, in the course of their everyday lives, participate in social practices and relations, and draw upon their rules and resources, in order to achieve their own specific goals. Bhaskar summarizes this perspective:

> The conception I am proposing is that people, in their conscious activity, for the most part unconsciously reproduce (and occasionally transform) the structures governing their substantive activities of production. Thus people do not marry to reproduce the nuclear family or work to sustain the capitalist economy. Yet it is nevertheless the unintended consequence (and inexorable result) of, as it is also a necessary condition for, their activity. Moreover, when social forms change, the explanation will not normally lie in the desires of agents to change them that way, though as a very important theoretical and practical limit it *may* do so.[46]

Society, understood as an ensemble of enduring relations and practices, is thus reproduced and transformed through the intentional activity of concrete individuals and groups. Giddens argues that the concept of the structuring of social life is tied to the concept of *structuration*—the ongoing processes of action and interaction whereby structures are sustained or changed. "To study the structuration of a social system," he writes, "is to study the ways in which that system, via the application of generative rules and resources, and in the context of unintended outcomes, is produced and reproduced in interaction."[47] E. P. Thompson has similarly argued that this process should be seen as a process of *eventuation*, where human beings, in their "unmastered practice," make their own history, realizing certain historical possibilities.[48]

Corresponding to this methodological distinction between social structure and intentional activity is a distinction between social scientific and historical explanation. Theoretical social science explains the general characteristics of enduring social relations that

---

[46]Bhaskar, *Possibility*, p. 44.

[47]Anthony Giddens, *A Contemporary Critique of Historical Materialism* (Berkeley: University of California Press, 1981), p. 27. See also Giddens, "On the Theory of Structuration," in his *Studies in Social and Political Theory* (New York: Basic Books, 1977).

[48]E. P. Thompson, *The Poverty of Theory and Other Essays* (New York: Monthly Review Press, 1978), pp. 45–50.

exist, as it were, "out of time" for particular agents. As Giddens puts it: "Structures exist in time-space only as moments recursively involved in the production and reproduction of social systems. Structures have only a 'virtual' existence."[49] History tells us about the actions, events, and processes that actually occur in the concrete world, in specific times and places. Historical analysis is thus properly thought of as *conjunctural*—it involves the analysis of complex historical events that have many causes, including a set of structural conditions and the irreducible effectivity of individual and collective activity.

This distinction, however, should not be reified. Social structures are real determinants of what happens in social life. But so are the intentions and purposes of concrete agents. Social structures exist "out of time" for specific agents, insofar as they are enduring, and usually unacknowledged, conditions of activity. But they are only *relatively* enduring. They govern action in time, they are reproduced in the process of interaction, and they are subject to historical transformation. They are, in short, *historically specific*. This has two important implications. The first is ontological—it must be made clear that when we undertake theoretical analyses of social structures (like capitalism or pluralist democracy) we are performing what Giddens has called a "methodological epoché."[50] That is, we are abstracting from the concrete processes of social interaction in specific times and places, in order to understand the general structural properties governing these interactions. In doing so, we recognize that these structures are no more or less than the ways in which historically situated human practices are done. Our "epoché" is in no way intended to undermine the theoretical or moral significance of human agency in process. The second implication is epistemological—as Mills argued, history is the shank of social science.[51] We cannot spin general theories of society from our heads. The analysis of social structure necessarily relies on historical and empirical knowledge, without which it is impossible to construct adequate theories. As Mills demonstrates in *The Sociological*

---

[49]Giddens, *Contemporary Critique*, p. 26.
[50]Giddens, *Central Problems*, p. 80.
[51]C. Wright Mills, *The Sociological Imagination* (Oxford: Oxford University Press, 1959), pp. 143–64.

Imagination, the refusal to properly ground theoretical explanation results in a hopelessly vacuous "grand theory."

In avoiding this danger, however, we should not fall into its obverse, the pitfall of "abstract empiricism," in any of its forms. The historian Quentin Skinner, in properly objecting to deductive-nomological accounts of historical events, once suggested that "the [political analyst's] primary aim should not be to explain, but only in the fullest detail to describe."[52] It is tempting to heed this suggestion and to believe that only concrete human activity is real. This too has its dangers though. On the realist view developed above, social structures are real determinants of the social world, despite their being nonempirical conditions of activity. If this is true, no matter how necessary historical and empirical knowledge is to theoretical analysis, it can never be sufficient. It is, in explanatory theory, the "raw material" that requires, as Althusser insists, theoretical labor in order to produce social explanations.[53]

As Giddens points out, then, "in respect of sociology, the crucial task of nomological [i.e., general-theoretical] analysis is to be found in the explanation of the properties of structures."[54] This requires the work of theoretical abstraction. But Giddens also insists that "the identification of structures can in no sense be regarded as the only aim of sociological investigation. The instantiation of structures in the reproduction of social systems, as its medium and outcome, is the proper focus of sociological analysis."[55] In other words, there is a complementarity between the two basic tasks of social and political theory, on the one hand analyzing the characteristics of specific social structures (e.g., capitalism), on the other investigating the way these structures are instantiated in the concrete events of the social world.

---

[52]Quentin Skinner, "The Limits of Historical Explanations," *Philosophy* 41 (1966), 214.

[53]Louis Althusser, "From Capital to Marx's Philosophy," in Louis Althusser and Etienne Balibar, *Reading Capital* (London: New Left Books, 1970). For critical discussion, see Andrew Collier, "In Defense of Epistemology," in John Mepham and David-Hillel Ruben, eds., *Issues in Marxist Philosophy,* vol. 3 (Brighton, Sussex: Harvester Press, 1979), and Ted Benton, *The Rise and Fall of Structural Marxism: Althusser and His Influence* (New York: St. Martin's, 1984), esp. pp. 35–51.

[54]Giddens, *New Rules,* p. 160.

[55]Giddens, *Central Problems,* p. 106.

Lukes, in one of his discussions of power as an "agency" category,[56] invokes Stephen Cohen's *Bukharin and the Bolshevik Revolution*[57] as an example of a political analysis sensitive to the efficacy of agency and the relevance of choice to the question of power. But Cohen's book makes clear that this sensitivity hardly negates the importance of structural analysis. The Revolution of October 1917, for example, was a complex of events, of which Lenin's return to Petrograd by way of the Finland Station was crucial. An account of the Revolution that left out the story of such events and processes would be hopelessly inadequate (one of the great virtues of Cohen's account is that it teaches us how complex the process was and how many other events were necessary components of it). In this sense historical analysis must be narrative and concrete. If we are to understand the Revolution, however, we must also understand how Lenin's return (along with other occurrences, of course) could have precipitated a revolutionary upheaval. In order to do this, we must undertake an analysis of the structures and contradictions of Russian society, the international system and the balance of forces, the effects of World War I on these, and more. To understand all this is not simply to analyze the choices of individuals and groups; it is also to analyze the enduring relationships that characterized Russian society and the way they were instantiated in the Revolution as the medium of the revolutionary process and as the transformed product of the revolution.[58]

It should be clear that on the view suggested here there are different levels of analysis and abstraction which must be combined in order to understand the concrete social world, and that these levels of analysis are not reducible to one another.[59] *First*, we must have theories of social structures—the family, the economy, the state (these examples are here purely illustrative; realism is agnostic about how to theoretically describe and interpret social structures).

[56]Steven Lukes, "Power and Structure," in his *Essays in Social Theory* (London: Macmillan, 1977).

[57]Stephen Cohen, *Bukharin and the Bolshevik Revolution* (Oxford: Oxford University Press, 1976).

[58]I draw here upon Peter T. Manicas, "Review Essay: States and Social Revolutions," *History and Theory* 20 (1981), 204–18.

[59]See Althusser and Balibar, *Reading Capital*; and Nicos Poulantzas, *Political Power and Social Classes* (London: New Left Books, 1973), pp. 11–33.

These theories are abstract, and they make reference to hypothetical entities that, although determinants of empirical phenomena, are not themselves empirical. Capitalism, for example, is a historically specific social structure. But to speak of capitalism is not to speak of its instantiation in specific locales. It is to refer to its properties as a real structure that always exists in complex relation to other structures in the concrete world, and that we can come to know through theoretical abstraction. *Second*, we must have theories of concrete societies, or what Althusser has called "social formations." At this level of abstraction we are not simply interested in understanding capitalism, but French (or British or American or Brazilian) capitalism. Here particular national and historical traditions, and the specific relationship between social structures in particular societies, come into play (e.g., the importance of the family enterprise in French capitalism, or the connection between the authoritarian state and capitalism in Brazil). *Finally*, we must have interpretations of the historical moment—France in 1986, or New Haven in 1953. At this level of analysis, we apply theoretical knowledge of structures and social formations to specific events and processes, in order to provide theoretical explanations of historical conjunctures. Of course, at this level we must relax our methodological epoché; the ways in which participants define their situation, the networks of interaction, and the feints and jabs of strategic maneuvering are all relevant to the working out of events and the transformation of structures. But we must already have some structural theory if we are to understand how concrete agents in a specific time and place are shaped by and are shaping their society.

Thus, for instance, Walter Dean Burnham's *The Current Crisis in American Politics*[60] provides an analysis of the current moment in American politics which integrates (1) a theoretical understanding of the way capitalism in general operates; (2) an analysis of the American social formation, with particular emphasis on the connection between class relationships, political party alignments, and electoral participation; and (3) a concrete analysis of the politics of Reaganism and its ascendancy. Burnham's analysis views

[60]Walter Dean Burnham, *The Current Crisis in American Politics* (Oxford: Oxford University Press, 1982).

current political history as a process of structuration, viewing events with an eye toward their significance in the reshaping of political and economic relationships. How participants define their situations and organize to effect them are not mere epiphenomena. But their significance can only be grasped by understanding the structural context that is both the cause and the product of their activity.

Criticism and Social Scientific Knowledge

The major point of this chapter is that realism is an ontological doctrine regarding the nature of causality and scientific explanation, and that this perspective makes intelligible the theoretical analysis of the properties of social structures. No such discussion could be complete, however, without some remarks on more properly epistemological issues. Without such a discussion, this book could easily fall prey to the criticism of empiricists of various stripes, who will express wonderment about the rationalistic implications of the realist understanding of theoretical abstraction and worry about the dogmatism that seems to be its consequence.

One might note again Karl Popper's insistence that "a science needs a point of view, and theoretical problems," and note further his observation that "it is decisions which settle the fate of theories." As we noted, however, Popper never reconciles this view with his own insistence on the scientific necessity of the deductive-nomological method.[61] The real burden of the realist argument here falls on the question of falsification. Popper's method, despite its inapplicability to the actual history of science, has always seemed to empirically minded researchers to be a clear means of scientific testing, of separating the scientific wheat from the chaff. Realism builds upon the arguments of Kuhn, Feyerabend, and Lakatos, namely that Popper's empirical falsification cannot be a sufficient basis of theory choice. Realism insists, further, that empirical prediction is not even a *necessary* condition of scientific knowledge. But if scientific explanation does not involve empirical prediction,

[61]See James Farr, "Popper's Hermeneutics," *Philosophy of the Social Sciences* (1983).

then how can theories be falsified? And if they cannot be falsified, then how are they properly scientific as opposed to, say, religious?

The key word here is *falsification*. In the realist view scientific theories are most definitely susceptible to falsification, if we mean by this susceptible to criticism and refutation. Popper's great contribution to philosophy of science is his insistence that it is not "verificationism," but criticism, that is the hallmark of scientific practice. It is not this insight, but his own narrow interpretation of what scientific explanation and criticism entails, which realists reject.

Before I proceed to a discussion of how theories can be constructed and evaluated, I should state that I do not believe there can be a blueprint for scientific activity, nor can there be an extra-practical formula for the evaluation of scientific theories. I do believe, however, that science is a rational endeavor in the specific sense that it involves the construction of arguments and the deployment of evidence, and the judgment of these on the basis of their cognitive adequacy. In this sense there are certain very general considerations relevant to the construction and evaluation of theories.

In the first section of this chapter we discussed Bhaskar's analysis of the nature of natural scientific experimentation. In his view scientists experimentally close off the world in order to isolate certain of its causal mechanisms. The empirical regularities that are experimentally produced are not, however, the aim of scientific investigation; they are only the means of isolating causes and of (predictively) testing theories. Now, it is a specific feature of society that experimental closure is a methodological impossibility. Experimental psychology is, of course, capable of designing small group experiments, through which some kinds of knowledge about the properties of human individuals is possible.[62] But social science is primarily concerned with the production of knowledge about

---

[62]See Peter T. Manicas, "The Human Sciences: A Radical Separation of Psychology and the Social Sciences," in Paul F. Secord, ed., *Explaining Human Behavior* (Beverly Hills: Sage, 1982); and Peter T. Manicas and Paul F. Secord, "Implications for Psychology of the New Philosophy of Science," *American Psychologist* 39 (April 1983) 399–413. On the episodic nature of social life and the impossibility of experimental closure, see Rom Harré and Paul F. Secord, *The Explanation of Social Behaviour* (Oxford: Blackwell, 1972).

social structures, those enduring relationships that are complexly instantiated in human practice. To "observe" these practices is necessarily to examine them in particular and highly localized conditions, and moreover in circumstances in which no specific relationship is hermetically sealed. It is impossible to separate the typical behaviors of capitalists and workers in a factory, for instance, from the idiosyncratic behaviors of the people who occupy these roles; and it is further impossible to separate the effect of class relations on their conduct from, for example, the effect of gender or of citizenship. To even begin to do so would require a prior theoretical identification of these relationships. But even armed with our theoretical apparatus, we would still be unable to test our theories in the same way natural scientists can.

Two important methodological implications follow from this. The first is that we cannot come to know about social structures by examining them in their "pure," isolated form. Second, we cannot decisively test social scientific theories as we can in natural science. Empirical prediction, which is only germane to natural science under situations of closure, cannot be a decisive epistemological feature of social scientific explanation. I will discuss each of these two points in turn.

All science involves the development of theoretical abstractions in order to explain real objects presumed to exist independently of our theoretical inquiries. In natural science we can come to know about causal mechanisms by using our pregiven theories in order to set up experiments. Our observations, always through the lens of our theories, enable us to isolate causal mechanisms in their pure form. An experimental situation can thus enable us to experience the effects of a magnetic field in isolation from other causal processes operating outside of experimental conditions, and thus to develop and test relatively precise theories about magnetic fields per se. In social science we cannot have analogous access to social structures, and we thus cannot experience their specific effects in isolation from other causal processes. But as Giddens points out, this difference between nature and society—the fact that social structures are necessarily instantiated in the ongoing flow of interaction—provides us with another, specific means of identifying social structural relations. Social structures, unlike natural structures, are already partially constituted and differentiated by the concepts participants have about them. Social science involves the development of theories that, at least in part, draw upon and transform the concepts of everyday life. This point decisively refutes naively positivistic versions of social science, with their talk of preconceptual "observation." We cannot simply observe interest groups, voting behavior, or political conflicts in unmediated form. As Taylor insists, we can only identify such phenomena because we possess concepts of them, concepts of what is involved in practicing such activities. The social scientific concept of "voting behavior," for instance, does not denote certain observable behaviors physicalistically or otherwise understood, but rather certain practices that are what they are partly by virtue of people's beliefs about them. Voting behavior is a social scientific concept parasitic upon, and derivative of, the notions people in liberal democratic societies have about electoral politics.

This important epistemological point takes on added significance in light of the fact that not only *how* we know, but that which we know *about*, is determined at least partially by the concepts of everyday life. This is what Anthony Giddens has called the *double hermeneutic* of social science.[63] Like natural science, social inquiry involves the further development of an interpretative schema; but unlike natural science, it involves developing a hermeneutic framework about a reality that is already preinterpreted by its participants. Social scientific theory construction always involves, then, the penetration and working up of everyday practical concepts, and the scientific differentiation of social phenomena is parasitic upon the lay identification of social practices. On the basis of these identifications (e.g., economy, money, marriage, voting, government) social scientists develop theoretical abstractions (e.g., unemployment equilibrium, surplus value, patriarchy, pluralist democracy). This process of theoretical abstraction involves not only a working up of lay concepts, but a dialectic, a dialogue with and a critique of other theories as well. In short, theory construction never takes place in a vacuum. Just like all other social practices, it involves the transformation of preexisting materials. If social scientific concepts have an epistemic origin, then, it lies in the

---

[63]Giddens, *New Rules*, pp. 148–54.

practical concepts of ordinary social practice, and not in some unmediated experience.[64]

Once we have constructed a theory of a hypothetically real social structure (like "pluralist democracy" or "capitalist democracy," two different theoretical identifications of hypothetical character- istics of our political process), we are still left with the problem of how to evaluate and test it. Of course these are not, as Popper would have it, two separate and discrete processes, the spinning of a theory (which Popper calls the "free creations of our own minds") and then the testing of a theory after it is spun (which Popper insists is governed by strict canons of deductive logic).[65] To a very large extent, both processes necessarily occur simulta- neously, the development of an explanation at once being a con- sideration of prior theoretical difficulties and possible future objections, the evaluation of a theory being at once the reworking and fortification of it. These processes, however, are methodolog- ically distinct, as they must be. This is because the problem of testing and evaluation is *really* the problem of the grounds on which a theory is submitted to its opponents for evaluation and debate. While there may not be any simple, logical procedure governing such determinations, which are chronic features of scientific prac- tice, realism insists that there is a necessary tension between the explanatory aspirations of theory and the elusiveness of reality. Theories may be underdetermined by facts, but they are not *un*- determined by them. The problem of theoretical criticism will thus not go away, and it cannot be made to so so by insisting that we cannot get outside of our theories. For while it is true that we cannot get outside of *some* interpretative framework, this does not license any particular framework.

In thinking about this problem, it is important to keep in mind that a scientific explanation is not the documentation of an em- pirical regularity, but a model of those enduring mechanisms that cause the phenomena of experience. Even natural scientific theories

[64]For criticisms of Schutz's "postulate of adequacy"—the view that social ex- planations must be adequate to the understandings of social agents—see Giddens, *New Rules*, pp. 27–33, and Bhaskar, *Possibility*, pp. 59–64.

[65]See Jonathan Lieberson, "The 'Truth' of Karl Popper," *New York Review of Books*, November 18 and 25, 1982.

are not predictions; it is just that we can test them, under certain conditions, through prediction. The problem for social science is thus not the ontological one of "to what do your theories refer if not to empirical events?" but the epistemological one of how to establish the validity of theories without falling into an invidious rationalism. This is a crucial problem, but it is a problem of testing, not of the meaning of claims about nonempirical entities.

This problem is significantly lessened by the fact that we are usually confronted not with a single theory, but with competing theories. As Lakatos points out, theory choice is never the result of a simple "measuring" of a theory against reality. Rather, it involves deciding which of a number of theories has explanatory power; we compare competing theories about reality rather than comparing a single theory to an unmediated reality. We can outline in the most general terms three criteria governing such determinations.[66] The first is *exhaustiveness*: a superior (or adequate) theory must be able to account for known phenomena and anticipate new phenomena by providing a fruitful research program. This, of course, involves the making of scientific judgments about the relevance of those things a theory can explain and about the future promise of its projected lines of inquiry.

The second is *independence*: a theoretical explanation of a range of phenomena must postulate a model of a hypothesized mechanism that would account for those phenomena, the phenomena being explained not being a part of the explanation. Norwood Hanson points out that the hypothesis that the color and odor of chlorine are explained by the presence of atoms with this color and odor is debarred by this criterion.[67] The explanation of the phenomenon must appeal to a deeper level, to an underlying cause, and not simply reiterate the phenomenon itself. This does not mean that we must view the empirical qualities of chlorine as contingently related to an antecedent cause. It is quite proper to view them as the necessary effects of the causal properties of chlorine in virtue of its atomic structure. But the explanation must make independent reference to the atomic structure of chlorine such that it causes these empirical effects.

[66]For discussion, see Derek Sayer, *Marx's Method: Ideology, Science, and Critique in 'Capital'* (Atlantic Highlands, N.J.: Humanities Press, 1979), pp. 115–17.
[67]Hanson, pp. 86–88.

The third criterion is *consistency*: a theory must be internally and logically consistent. This should not be understood as the unrealistic requirement that theories be organized as rigidly deductive systems of propositions, and that they be falsifiable in Popper's sense. As W. V. O. Quine points out, theoretical systems involve much more complicated networks of beliefs:

> The totality of our so-called knowledge or beliefs, from the most casual matters of geography and history to the profoundist laws of atomic physics or even of pure mathematics and logic, is a manmade fabric which impinges on experience only along the edges... [it] is like a field of force whose boundary conditions are experience. A conflict with experience at the periphery occasions readjustments in the interior of the field. Truth values have to be redistributed over some of our statements. Reevaluation of some statements entails reevaluation of others, because of their logical interconnections—the logical laws being in turn simply further statements of the system, certain further elements of the field. Having reevaluated one statement we must reevaluate some others....But the total field is so underdetermined by its boundary conditions, experience, that there is much latitude of choice as to what statements to reevaluate in the light of any single contrary experience. No particular experiences are linked with any particular statements in the interior of the field, except indirectly through considerations of equilibrium affecting the field as a whole.[68]

The point is that logic imposes constraints upon theories by compelling redefinitions and readjustments of our beliefs. It is oftensupposed, for instance, that Marx's theory of the tendency of the rate of profit to fall has been conclusively disconfirmed by empirical evidence, calling into question the entire edifice of his economic theory.[69] As Quine's comment would suggest, however,this belief about the rate of profit is connected to many other beliefs—about the class relations of capitalism, about the abstract understanding of the operation of markets, and more. No amount of empirical evidence about the rate of profit can, therefore, conclusively refute Marxian economics. But the constraint of logical consistency re-

---

[68]Quine, pp. 42–43.
[69]For a discussion of these issues, see Ian Steedman et al., *The Value Controversy* (London: Verso, 1981).

quires that this theory equilibrate itself in the face of the evidence, using its basic concepts to invoke causes—counter tendencies, contingent empirical occurrences—to restore its integrity. This does not mean that any old ad hoc explanation will do, as, for instance, Popper fears. Basic terms of the theory must be mobilized to preserve "equilibrium." And in so doing, theorists will also be simultaneously making judgments regarding the satisfaction of the other two criteria, exhaustiveness and independence. It maybe, for instance, that another theory can better explain empirical trends regarding profit rates, accounting for the phenomena explained by Marxism and explaining other things besides. It does mean that theoretical practice, and the dialectic between competing theories, is a protracted process of contestation and reasoned judgment in which there can be no Archimedean point of scientific certainty.[70]

I would suggest, then, that while there are certain conditions of argumentative adequacy that any social scientific theory must satisfy, there are no extra-scientific considerations that can simpliciter ground theoretical decisions and judgments. Substantive questions will ultimately ground theoretical commitments. This troubles those empiricists who remain wedded to an objectivist view of knowledge as correspondence with something given in experience, and of epistemology as the general, logical requirements of all valid knowledge. This is, however, the only possible way to do science, and the way it *is* done, even by social scientists who believe otherwise. Theoretical disputes in "democratic theory" revolve not around the falsification of regularity statements (of which there are few, if any), but around the ability of different theories to account for a range of phenomena—social inequalities, political conflict, and more.[71] Disputes in contemporary theory of the state involve arguments about what the state is and how various theories can account for different forms of state, wars, and revolutions.[72] If the

---

[70]See Peter T. Manicas and Alan Rosenberg, "Naturalism, Epistemological Individualism, and the 'Strong Programme' in the Sociology of Knowledge," *Journal for the Theory of Social Behaviour* 15 (March 1985), 76–101.

[71]See David Greenstone, "Group Theories," in Fred I. Greenstein and Nelson Polsby, eds., *Handbook of Political Science* (Reading, Mass.: Addison-Wesley, 1975), pp. 243–318.

[72]See Martin Carnoy, *The State and Political Theory* (Princeton: Princeton University Press, 1984).

remainder of this book is correct, and there is no theory of power conforming to the canons of empiricism *and* Marxism represents a realist theory of social power, then contemporary disagreements about the distribution of power are similarly to be resolved by arguments possessing not apodictic, but simply persuasive force.

For realism, then, while empirical facts and evidence are absolutely indispensable components of theoretical inquiry, it is not facts, but judgments about the way theories explain a range of facts, which alone can determine the adequacy of theories. This epistemological perspective is not peculiar to realism; as we have seen, it is accepted by a number of important post-positivist philosophers. What distinguishes realism is its insistence that the aim of social science is to explain causal mechanisms that are not reducible to their empirical effects, which are, so to speak, real but not empirical. Realism thus claims that the adequacy of theories is grounded in judgments regarding their ability to explain a world that exists independently of our theoretical inquiries, and that defies the regulative ideal of deductive-nomological explanation.

As Paul Feyerabend points out, any apodictic, extra-scientific criterion of theoretical choice can only be a conservative dogma— it can never provide sufficient reasons for choosing, only establish formal canons requiring institutional sanctions for their force.[73] It would not be too cynical to suspect that this is the way empiricism has functioned as a hegemonic method in contemporary social science. As we shall see in the next chapter, the contestation of power is not the same thing as its negation, and so despite the growing skepticism about social scientific empiricism, it would not be wrong to consider it the dominant perspective in social science. In proposing its abandonment, I do not mean to imply that one intellectual straitjacket be replaced by another. The great virtue of realism is that, in recognizing the necessary limits of any methodological approach, it can shift social inquiry from a concern with specious canons of scientificity to a concern with substantive explanation.

[73]Feyerabend, pp. 196–99.

CHAPTER 3

The Concept of
Power Revisited

We are now in a better position to appreciate the basic weakness of the three faces of power debate and to reformulate the concept of power. The behavioralist foundations of the debate constrained its participants from conceiving of power as anything more than a behavioral regularity and prevented them from seeing it as an enduring capacity. To do so, of course, risks presupposing what Jack Nagel has called "objectionable metaphysical implications." But as we have seen, on another view of science—realism—such presuppositions about the enduring natures of causal mechanisms are the essence of actual scientific practice. It is only at great cost that the discussants of power have eschewed such premises.

In this chapter I will outline a realist analysis of the concept of power and its role in social and political inquiry. I will argue that a power is an enduring capacity to act, which may or may not be exercised on any particular occasion. And I will suggest that social power is implicated in social structure and is a necessary feature of human agency. In advancing this argument, I will challenge the behavioralist focus of the three faces debate, as well as its view that the concept of "power structure" is a metaphysical construct at odds with properly social scientific analysis. A realist view of power, we shall see, allows discussion of a number of features of power ignored in the three faces debate—domination, reciprocity, and ideology.

Power as Capacity

Possibly the most glaring deficiency of the three faces debate is its failure to discuss what power is, instead stipulating in the most general way what "power terms" in social science have traditionally meant. Like all words, *power* can be used in a variety of contexts. As Hannah Pitkin has pointed out, empiricist theorists of power have flagrantly abused language by their inattention to linguistic complexities and to questions of meaning.[1] Witness, for example, Nagel's observation: "Words, as Humpty Dumpty observed, can mean anything we choose them to mean. Why bother to dispute definitions? I do so precisely because definitions are merely arbitrary, whereas hypotheses are potentially subject to agreement producing tests. Therefore, the most useful definitions are those which direct efforts to empirical research."[2] This was, as we have seen, the attitude of the behavioralist innovators regarding the concept of power—that the concept should acquire a formal definition amenable to their understanding of scientific explanation and falsification. This effort was a striking failure in its own terms. If the most useful definitions are those that direct efforts toward empirical research, then the three faces of power debate must be judged useless, as it has generated a dearth of research actually conforming to the methods it prescribed. This attitude is frivolously mistaken, however, and in a way that sheds light on the theoretical sterility of the debate.

Words can be used only in the context of their previous usage. The empiricist theorists of power have confined themselves to one particular locution, "power over," corresponding to their belief that a proper social science is a science of behavioral regularities. What is crucial is that they have all quite carelessly failed to provide a real definition of power, substituting instead an operational definition of the form "A has power over B means that whenever A does Y, B does Z." Power, a "potential" word, becomes redefined to describe contingent regularities. As Pitkin has observed, however, such an operationalist attitude toward language is self-

[1] Hannah Feneichel Pitkin, *Wittgenstein and Justice* (Berkeley: University of California Press, 1972), pp. 264–86.

[2] Jack Nagel, *The Descriptive Analysis of Power* (New Haven: Yale University Press, 1975), p. 175.

defeating: "Operational definitions ultimately are useful if they come close to the real definition; if our operational definition of 'power' is not related to the meaning of 'power' then the results of any study we conduct with it will not yield information about power."[3] It is thus not surprising that the three faces of power controversy remains unresolved, and that the parameters of the debate prevent us from saying many things about power we should want to say.

The word *power* derives from the Latin *potere*, meaning "to be able." It is generally used to designate a property, capacity, or the wherewithal to effect things.[4] The attribution of properties or capacities is a common feature of everyday life (e.g., "that fire is hot," "this car is fast," "your friend is smart"). This does not mean that ordinary ascriptions constitute valid scientific explanations, but it does indicate the congruence of the ordinary sense of the term with the arguments we are developing. According to the realist philosophy of science outlined above, powers are a central subject matter of natural science. Harré writes: "To ascribe a power to a thing or material is to say something about what it will or can do . . . in virtue of its intrinsic nature."[5] Power is, then, a *causal* concept; but it is causal in the realist sense, as it refers to necessary properties, not contingent effects. To use an earlier example, to assert that conductivity is a power of copper is to claim that copper possesses the enduring capacity to conduct electricity, in virtue of its intrinsic nature, in this case its atomic structure.

Social science should be similarly concerned with the ascription of powers to social agents, and with the explanatory reference of these powers to agents' intrinsic natures. By the intrinsic natures of social agents I mean not their unique characteristics as individ-

[3]Pitkin, p. 275. On real definitions, see Peter T. Manicas and Arthur N. Kruger, *Logic: The Essentials* (New York: McGraw-Hill, 1976), pp. 34–38.

[4]See "Power," *Oxford English Dictionary* (Oxford: Clarendon Press, 1933), p. 1213. See also Pitkin, pp. 274–79; Quentin Gibson, "Power," *Philosophy of the Social Sciences* (1971), 101–12; and Stuart Clegg, "Power, Theorizing, and Nihilism," *Theory and Society* 3 (Spring 1976), 65–85. In what follows I am building on Terence Ball's "Power, Causation, and Explanation," *Polity* 8 (Winter 1975), 189–214, and his "Models of Power: Past and Present," *Journal of the History of the Behavioral Sciences* (July 1975), 211–22.

[5]Rom Harré, "Powers," *British Journal of the Philosophy of Science* 21 (1970), 85.

uals, but their social identities as participants in enduring, socially structured relationships. Theories of power, then, should be conceived as interpretative models, developed by social scientists as submitted to the rigors of critical consideration, about the social structures which shape human action and distribute the capacities to act among social agents. And at the level of epistemology, to speak of the social structures that account for power is no different from speaking of the atomic structure that accounts for conductivity. Both sorts of claims are equally fallible, equally subject to theoretical and empirical criticism, and equally about underlying and nonobservable causal mechanisms (the important differences between nature and society we have discussed above notwithstanding).

Power and Agency

As we will recall, Steven Lukes identifies the empiricist view of power with an "agency approach," insisting that to think of power in structural terms is to reify human activity. It is true that on the empiricist view power is exhausted in interaction, as behavioral regularity, and thus the empiricist formulation recognized no distinction between the possession and the exercise of power. It would thus seem to have the merit of placing agency at the center of social analysis. A few clarifications of the relationship between power and agency, however, will show that Lukes's claim is highly deceptive.

First, on the realist view of power as capacity, power is not a specific kind of practice; it is implicated in all social practice, as a logically necessary feature of activity. For empiricism the exercise of power is a specific kind of act, one in which an actor gets another actor to do something that would not otherwise be done. This is a restrictive view of power, which fails to see that all human action entails the capacity to perform the activity in question. Power is implicated no more or less in my typing of this page, or my lecturing to my class, than it is in my getting my employer to comply with my demands for a raise. Giddens writes: "The relation between the concepts of action and power, on the level of strategic conduct, can be set out as follows. Action involves intervention in events in

the world, thus producing definite outcomes. . . . Power as transformative capacity can then be taken to refer to agents' capabilities
of reaching such outcomes."[6] Not only does the realist view place
agency at the center of power, as the exercise of power; it also
places power at the center of agency, as a property of human agents
that makes their activity possible.

Second, not only does the empiricist view fail to recognize that
power is a necessary feature of action, it also misconceives the nature of action. We have seen that, for empiricism, the aim of social
science is the discovery of behavioral regularities and the formulation of predictive generalizations. As interpretative critics have observed, this explanatory ideal fails to countenance the idiographic
dimension of social life, which, constituted by the specific meanings
and purposes of agents, defies predictive generalization. In short,
empiricist theorists of power have failed to make the distinction be
tween behavior and practice we noted in Chapter 2. Robert Dahl's
language of stimulus and response is only the extreme form this inattention to the specificity of human agency has taken.

On the realist view, power is implicated in all social life as the
capacity to perform intentional activities and to engage in normatively constituted practices. To speak of the power of an agent
is thus to speak of the things an agent can do, where *doing* is
understood not as behaving in response to an antecedent cause,
but as performing a practical activity according to certain understandings and reasons. These understandings and teleologies, or
ends toward which activity is directed, are not incidental but essential dimensions of action and of power. Thus, instead of asking
about the regularity with which teachers gets their students to do
homework, an interest in practice would direct our attention to
the practice of education itself, to those norms defining the activities
of its participants and those capacities entailed by these activities.
As we saw in Chapter 2, this view of activity as rule-governed is
tied to a view of activity as rule-*interpreting*. There is thus an
inherent *indeterminacy* in social life, the future being caused in part
by the definitions of reality of social agents. This is different from

---

[6]Anthony Giddens, *Central Problems in Social Theory: Action, Structure, and
Contradiction in Social Analysis* (Berkeley: University of California Press, 1979),
p. 88.

saying, as for instance Dahl does, that theories of power are necessarily incomplete, because there are "an indefinite number of critical links in the chain of causation and therefore an indefinite number of 'faces' of power."[7] Dahl's point is an epistemological one—the world is complex, and knowledge of it hard to come by. Our point is an ontological one—the world is open, and it is crucially determined by the purposive choices of social agents. Causality is thus not conceived as a chain in which particular behaviors are but "critical links." It is thought of as an intricate web of determinants, structural and purposive, which complexly cause social interaction.

Peter Winch has similarly noted the failure of social scientific empiricism to appreciate the hermeneutic dimension of power:

> An event's character as an act of obedience is *intrinsic* to it in a way which is not true of an event's character as a clap of thunder, and this is in general true of human acts as opposed to natural events. ... There existed electrical storms and thunder long before there were human beings to form concepts of them. ... But it does not make much sense to suppose that human beings might have been issuing commands and obeying them before they came to form the concept of command and obedience. For their performance of such acts is itself the chief manifestation of their possession of those concepts. An act of obedience itself contains, as an essential element, a recognition of what went before it as an order.[8]

Winch rightly insists that the exercise of power presupposes a normative and institutional context. A command presumes some mode of mutual understanding, and obedience some "uptake" of the command. My instructions to my class to read Machiavelli, and their obeying of these instructions, presuppose a set of shared concepts (teacher/student, homework/grades) and norms (regarding school, the value of learning, the value of good grades). The outcome of classroom interaction depends on these concepts, *and how they are interpreted by teachers and students.* (We will return to

[7]Robert A. Dahl, *Modern Political Analysis*, 3d ed. (Englewood Cliffs, N.J.: Prentice-Hall, 1976), pp. 39–40.
[8]Peter Winch, "The Idea of a Social Science," in Bryan Wilson, ed., *Rationality* (Oxford: Blackwell, 1970), pp. 9–10.

the question of the negotiation of power below.) But while the exercise of power certainly presupposes some social concepts, this does not necessarily mean that it presupposes the concept of the exercise of power. In fact, although social relationships of power involve some element of mutual recognition on the part of their participants, most such relationships do not involve the full recognition of the character of the relationship itself. Most relationships of power, in short, are not recognized as such. The subordination of slaves, for example, certainly involves some concept on their part of "master" and some notion of "obedience." But it also typically involves other beliefs—about God, natural inferiority—which obscure and mystify this relationship.

As we saw in Chapter 2, the great strength of interpretative theory is its insistence upon the hermeneutic character of social life. We also saw, however, that social life is only partly constituted by the concepts of its participants. It is also constituted by a set of enduring structural relationships that are likely opaque to their participants. Ernest Gellner, for instance, discusses the example of *igurramen*, the privileged elite of Moroccan Berber tribal society, who are believed to possess *baraka*, a magical power of plenitude bestowed by God. While the elite is in fact recruited through a complicated process of patronage and election, the concepts of *baraka* and *igurramen* are constitutive of this process, providing it with both meaning and justification; as Gellner points out, "There is here a crucial divergence between concept and reality, a divergence which moreover is quite essential for the working of the social system." He thus argues that a purely hermeneutic social analysis, which takes social concepts as exhaustive of social reality, "blinds us to the possibility of, for instance, social control through the employment of absurd, ambiguous, inconsistent or unintelligible doctrines ... we can sometimes only make sense of the society in question by seeing how the manipulation of concepts and the violation of categorial boundaries help it to work."[9]

This observation is also the basis of Jürgen Habermas's critique of hermeneutics. For Habermas the hermeneutic grasp of the self-

---

[9]Ernest Gellner, "Concepts and Society," in Wilson, *Rationality*, pp. 43–47. See also Alasdair MacIntyre, "Is Understanding Religion Compatible with Believing?" in Wilson, *Rationality*.

understandings embedded in social praxis is an absolutely necessary moment of social analysis, but it is not sufficient. For it is also necessary to produce general knowledge about institutional relations—social power—and in so doing to remain sensitive to "when they express ideologically frozen relations of dependence that can in principle be transformed."[10] Social agents necessarily possess some concepts of their power relationships. But they do not therefore necessarily possess all of the concepts sufficient to fully understand the determinants of their activity. An understanding of social power, then, must extend beyond a concern with shared concepts to a concern with structural relations. Such a mode of analysis is not only necessary to generate adequate knowledge; it also contains, as Habermas emphasizes, a critical promise, serving to potentially demystify social reality and releasing agents from "hypostatized powers."

Social Power and Social Structure

Social power must be understood relationally. By relationally I do not mean, as in empiricism, in terms of contingent behavioral regularities, but rather in terms of the *real* underlying social relations that structure behavioral interaction. The relation between teacher and student, for example, is not a contingent relation between two parties who happen to encounter one another. It is a historically enduring relation, the nature of which is precisely that teachers have students and vice versa; it is the nature of these social identities to be in relation to one another. And, as such, it is their nature to possess certain powers, powers that simply cannot be conceived as contingent regularities between the behaviors of teacher and student. The teacher possesses the power to design the syllabus, to speak in front of the class and direct classroom activities, and to give and grade assignments; the student possesses the power to attend class, to do the schoolwork, and to earn academic credit for his or her work. The capacities to perform these activities

[10]Jürgen Habermas, *Knowledge and Human Interests* (Boston: Beacon, 1971), p. 310. See also Anthony Giddens, "Habermas's Critique of Hermeneutics," in his *Studies in Social and Political Theory* (New York: Basic Books, 1977), pp. 135–64.

are part of the nature of the relationship; and their performance involves the drawing upon and the exercise of powers. The possession of these powers is a necessary feature of the structure of education; but the successful exercise of these powers is contingent. To be a teacher is to possess the power to direct the classroom, but teacher A may not succeed in directing her classroom, and the class may be unruly. Her power as a teacher, however, is not nullified by this particular failure. A particular teacher's consistent failure to direct the classroom is a different story, and it may well nullify her power. We would then likely say that she was a bad teacher, unsuited to the role of teacher and personally unable to exercise the social powers required by the role. And, more generally, the persistent inability of teachers *in general* to successfully direct their classrooms may very well indicate that the teacher-student relationship is in crisis and that students are exercising *their* powers to contest the structure of the relationship.

I will thus define social power as *those capacities to act possessed by social agents in virtue of the enduring relations in which they participate.* Giddens distinguishes between a broad sense of power, the capability of an actor to intervene, and a narrower sense, "the capability to secure outcomes where the realization of these outcomes depends on the agency of others."[11] What I have defined as social power refers to the more restricted sense. Thus, while the word *power* is properly used to describe many circumstances—for instance, my neighbor's persuasive ability, which resides in his .45 Magnum—the phrase "social power" is intended to call attention to the way capacities to act are distributed by generalized and enduring social relationships (is my persuasive neighbor also a policeman?).

I am not proposing to univocally define the meaning of power, nor to stipulate a single acceptable use of the concept in social analysis.[12] What I am suggesting is that a generalizing social science takes as its primary object of study those enduring social relationships that distribute power to social agents. Individuals certainly

[11]Giddens, *Central Problems*, p. 93.

[12]For a discussion of the different uses, and "grammars" of "power," see Peter Morriss, "The Essentially Uncontestable Concepts of Power," in Michael Freeman and David Robertson, eds., *The Frontiers of Political Theory: Essays in a Revitalized Discipline* (New York: St. Martin's, 1980), pp. 198–232.

possess idiosyncratic powers. But what makes these socially significant is the way they are implicated in more enduring relationships. It makes perfect sense to claim that "David Rockefeller is a powerful man." But a social theory of power must explain what kinds of social relations exist and how power is distributed by these relations, such that it is possible for David Rockefeller to have the power that he has. To do this is not to deny that it is *he* who possesses this power, nor to deny those personal attributes determining the particular manner in which he exercises it. It is simply to insist that the power individuals possess has social conditions of existence, and that it is these conditions that should be the primary focus of theoretical analysis.

To propose such a structural understanding of social power is not to detach the concept of power from human agency. As we have seen in Chapter 2, the understanding of social structure I rely on rejects any bifurcation of structure and agency. As we have defined it, social power refers to the capacities to act possessed by agents in virtue of their social relations. And what are these relations but idioms of human conduct? To say that teachers and students are in a structural relationship is only to say that there are people called teachers and students who characteristically do the things the relationship involves, who characteristically *exercise* those powers distributed by their roles. A social power that is never exercised can hardly be said to exist. But its exercise is always shaped and constrained by pregiven relations. I am going to school this afternoon to give a lecture on Machiavelli; and in doing so, however unintentionally, I am exercising the power of a teacher. It is this power that enables me to give a lecture to a class full of students rather than to an empty room (imagine how quickly campus security guards would cart away someone off the street who, claiming to know about Machiavelli, walked into a classroom full of students waiting to hear their teacher's lecture), and also constrains me from doing otherwise (I would really much prefer to sit in the fields beneath an oak tree, reflecting upon virtue with a group of dedicated students).

The sorts of structurally distributed powers of which we speak are chronically exercised in the course of everyday life, at home, at work, at school, at the tax collector's office. And the successful exercise of them is always contingent. Bosses by nature have the power to supervise production, but tomorrow the workers may strike. Teachers by nature have the power to conduct class lessons, but tomorrow the students may boycott class and conduct their own teach-in. It is a real, necessary feature of the currently existing structure of education that teachers possess certain supervisory powers. But the exercise of these powers, the way the teacher-student relationship is worked out in practice, is contingent, determined by the way particular individuals and groups choose to deal with their circumstances. Thus, as Ted Benton has characterized the realist view: "The advocated position is systematically determinist and causal, but at the same time it does not reduce agency to a mere 'bearer' of the activity of extrinsic structures."[13]

The relational concept of power we have outlined above is defended by Terence Ball in an important essay.[14] Ball argues that the empiricist view of power as a contingent behavioral relation is impossible if certain social scientific concepts are to be taken seriously. This is because the meanings of these concepts entail certain relations of power. Ball, drawing heavily upon Hegel, insists that certain terms are necessarily relational. The terms of the relation between master and slave, which is the paradigm of all power relations, are a case in point. Ball writes: "Since (as Hegel certainly recognized) A would not even *be* A without B, then the relationship between them is conceptual and not contingent... is not part of the *meaning* of being a 'master' to have a 'slave' to do your bidding? ... to *be* a master *means* to be able (or in a position) to command and be obeyed. That, after all, was the point of Hegel's excursis on lordship and bondage: the master's very *identity* as master is (logically) dependent upon the slave's continued subservience."[15] Because the master-slave relationship is not contingent but conceptually necessary, Ball concludes, on the empiricist view it is not a relation of power. The empiricist concept of power is thus, as Ball writes, "reduced to absurdity."[16]

Ball, in line with post-positivist philosophy, makes a convincing

---

[13]Ted Benton, "Objective Interests and the Sociology of Power," *Sociology* 15 (May 1981), 179.

[14]Terence Ball, "Two Concepts of Coercion," *Theory and Society* 15 (January 1978), 97–112.

[15]Ibid., pp. 106–109.

[16]Ibid., p. 108.

case for the theory-ladenness and mutual implication of theoretical terms. The concept of master entails the concept of slave, and the relation between these concepts is thus necessary. It is very important to insist that our theoretical language for talking about social power fails to conform to Humean canons. We must, however, push this argument a bit further. Power is not just conceptually necessary in the above sense; it is *really* necessary. The concept of master entails power over slave. But the real master, to whom this concept refers, does not have power because the concept of master means that he does; he has power because he is an element of a real, structural relationship with real slaves. The conceptual necessity Ball exposes is grounded in the real social necessity of the master-slave relationship. Ball in fact comes close to asserting this when he writes that the relationship between master A and slave B, being conceptually necessary, is not for empiricism a relation of power because it fails to "qualify as *causal in the contingent Humean sense.*"[17] Ball is satisfied to perform a reductio ad absurdum, demonstrating the incompatibility of empiricist notions with commonly accepted social scientific terms. But he also suggests the possibility that the master-slave relationship, while not causal in the Humean sense, is causal in another, realist sense.

Power and Domination

The concept of domination does not figure in the three faces of power controversy. Instead, all power is assimilated to "power over," which is construed as a behavioral regularity. This view of "power over" suffers from two basic deficiencies that the realist view avoids. It deprives the notion of "power over"—domination— of its specific significance, and it also provides a misleading picture of domination as a causal relation.

In the realist view power, as those capacities implicated in ongoing social practices, is a necessary feature of social interaction; where there is society there is social power. However, "power over," or domination, is *not* therefore a necessary feature of society. Following Giddens, I define domination as *the asymmetrical dis-*

[17]Ibid.

tribution of social power.[18] Relations of domination and subordination comprise a subset of power relations, where the capacities to act are not distributed symmetrically to all parties to the relationship. The term *domination* comes from the Latin *dominus*, or lord; and it has obvious connections with the mastery of the household, as it does with the desmegne/dominion/domain of the feudal lord (the concept of domain here designating the necessary connection between a social space and a social prerogative). It means, variously, mastery, control, command, or prevalence.[19] The general sense of its meaning is clear. By asymmetry we do not simply mean social interdependence or a division of labor. Medieval butchers and bakers, for instance, perform different occupations and are mutually dependent on one another; but they are symmetrically related by mutual need. They possess equivalent powers of self-employment. And factory workers on an assembly line are similarly dependent on one another, but they too are symmetrically related by mutual need and the shared possession of the capacity to work. These are relations of *difference*, but not necessarily of domination. But the Roman lord does not simply perform a different set of activities from those of his wife and his slaves; he directs the household, thereby directing and controlling the conditions under which his wife and slaves perform their activities. Similarly, as we shall see, the capitalist directs the labor process, controlling the conditions under which wage laborers labor.

The concept of domination thus refers neither to a contingent regularity nor to mere social difference; it refers to a structurally asymmetrical relationship, whereby one element of the relationship has power over another in virtue of its structural power to direct the practices of the other. This is what Max Weber seems to have meant when he defined domination as the "authoritarian power of command." He writes "To be more specific, *domination* will thus mean the situation in which the manifested will (*command*) of the *ruler* or rulers is meant to influence the conduct of one or more others (*the ruled*) and actually does influence it in such a way

[18]Giddens, *Central Problems*, p. 93; Anthony Giddens, *A Contemporary Critique of Historical Materialism* (Berkeley: University of California Press, 1981), pp. 50–52.
[19]See "Domination," *Oxford English Dictionary*, vol. 2 (Oxford: Clarendon, 1933).

that their conduct to a socially relevant degree occurs as if the ruled had made the content of the command the maxim of their conduct for its very own sake. Looked upon from the other end, this situation will be called *obedience*."[20]

Weber's conceptualization of domination was an early causality of behavioralism in political science, having been co-opted into the attempt to "operationalize" the concept of power.[21] This is understandable insofar as Weber, operating within the tradition of methodological individualism, emphasizes the dimension of will and intentionality or, in Lukes's terms, action. Moreover, when Weber writes of "the causal chain extending from the command to the actual fact of compliance,"[22] he offers what appears to be an unmistakably Humean formulation. But his definition also suggests a structural dimension, conceiving of domination as a situation or condition rather than an event. He makes this clear by treating modern bureaucracy as the paradigm of domination, and by providing as further examples the village chief, the banker, the judge, the craftsman—socially positioned roles that, by their nature, possess certain powers over subordinates. The language he uses—command and obedience, ruler and ruled—is equally suggestive of a structural approach.

A realist view is not simply able to appreciate the structural nature of "power over" which is occluded by empiricism; it also provides a more plausible account of what kind of causal relation is involved in relations of domination. On the empiricist view to say that master has power over slave, or dominates slave, means that the behavior of the master causes the behavior of the slave, that is, it regularly antecedes it. According to the realist position it is not the behavior of the slave that is caused by the behavior of the master; rather, the master-slave relationship is the material

---

[20]Max Weber, *Economy and Society*, vol. 2, ed. Guenther Roth and Claus Wittich (Berkeley: University of California Press, 1978), p. 946.

[21]See, e.g., Robert A. Dahl, "Power," *International Encyclopedia of the Social Sciences*, vol. 12 (New York: Macmillan, 1968). We should not overlook Talcott Parsons's notorious translation of Weber's *herrschaft* as "imperative coordination" rather than domination. For a good discussion of this issue, see Randall Collins, "A Comparative Approach to Political Sociology," in Reinhard Bendix et al., eds., *State and Society: A Reader in Comparative Political Sociology* (Berkeley: University of California Press, 1973).

[22]Weber, *Economy*, p. 946.

cause of the behavior of both the master *and* the slave, and the specific way the master and the slave (an equally purposive agent) choose to act out the relationship is the efficient cause. For empiricism there are only efficient causes; but the consequence of this is an inability to explain both the mutual identities and the capabilities available to parties to social relationships. On my view the master, while dominant, operates under constraints just as the slave does. And the slave, though subordinate, is also causally effective in determining the outcomes of his encounters with his master.

Nicos Poulantzas makes a similar point in discussing the class relations of capitalism: "The field of power is strictly relational. ... The place of each class, and hence its power, is delimited (i.e., at once designated and limited) by the place of other classes. Power is not attached to a 'class in itself' understood as a collection of agents, but depends upon, and spring from, a relational system of material places occupied by particular agents."[23] Poulantzas, and the Althusserian tradition more generally, emphasizes the determinacy of the "relational system of material places" at the expense (though not to the exclusion) of the effectivity of the agents who exercise their structurally given powers (See Part II). What is pertinent here, though, is his insistence on the structural constitution of all power, including the power of dominant groups.

There are a number of important consequences of the realist view. Whereas the empiricist concept of power metaphorically represents domination as a lateral relation between the behaviors of social agents, realism views domination as a vertical relation between the agents themselves. This view takes much more seriously the realities of command and obedience as enduring features of social life differing in kind from the more contingent encounters of everyday life. It also refuses to conflate power and domination. While power is a necessary feature of social existence, domination is not. And while it may very well be true that human history is a history of structures of domination, it does not follow that this is the way it has to be. To think of power as a causal concept is not necessarily to imagine that there will always be some people possessing power over others.

Finally, on the realist view the practical outcomes of relations

---

[23]Nicos Poulantzas, *State, Power, Socialism* (London: Verso, 1980), p. 147.

of domination are open-ended, determined both by the structural powers accruing to social agents and the particular ways they exercise these powers. It is to this issue that we now turn.

Reciprocity and the Negotiation of Power

While on the empiricist view power is a one-way relationship of behavioral causation, on the realist view we have developed relationships of power necessarily involve reciprocity. Giddens writes: "However wide the asymmetrical distribution of resources involved, all power relations manifest autonomy and dependence 'in both directions.' "[24] Thus even the power of a slaveowner is circumscribed by the structure of the master-slave relationship, more specifically its basis in slave labor and all of the normative and cultural elements surrounding this. The power the slaveowner has to buy and sell slaves, to control the conditions of their activity, and to direct and exploit their labor is articulated with the minimal powers slaves possess over their bodies so that they can perform those services defined by their relation to the master.

Roderick Martin, in *The Sociology of Power*, takes antebellum American slavery to be an extreme example of the one-sided character of power, based upon the "total power" of the master. In support he produces an interesting text, a Virginia slave code of 1669 legalizing the killing of slaves by masters: "It cannot be presumed that the propensed malice (which alone makes murder felony) should induce any man to destroy his own estate."[25] Martin, however, seems to miss the point of this code, which can only be ascertained by inquiring into the relation between the laws and the practices of slavery. The *legal right* to violently punish slaves seems here quite explicitly articulated with the *real function* slaves performed. As real property, as exploited labor, there was no reason to assume that a master would simply murder a slave for no good reason (keep in mind, of course, that the master's reasons need not be our reasons; as C. Wright Mills pointed out long ago, social

---

[24]Giddens, *Central Problems*, p. 149.
[25]Roderick Martin, *The Sociology of Power* (London: Routledge & Kegan Paul, 1977), pp. 59–63.

rationalities are not necessarily truly reasonable). The rationality of slavery involved the requirement of a reproduced slave labor force. Of course, the fact that the master possessed legally unlimited powers of violence is crucial and serves to highlight that slavery is a relationship based on extreme asymmetries of power. But even here the actual role of violence, as a social practice, was determined by the structure of the master-slave relationship and the distribution of powers to masters and slaves.

This is not to deny the brutality of slavery, and it is certainly not to offer a substantive historical analysis of its modes of operation. In fact, it is quite possible that some masters did wantonly kill their slaves. The point is simply that, in doing so, they would have accomplished the same thing that capitalists accomplish when they squander their capital—undermined the very basis of their position of domination. What Marx writes about capitalism could just have easily been said about slavery by substituting *slave* for *capital* and *worker* and *master* for *capitalist*: "Capital in its being-for-itself is the capitalist....I may well separate capital from a given individual capitalist, and it can be transferred to another. But in losing capital, he loses the quality of being a capitalist. The capital is indeed separable from the individual capitalist, but not from the capitalist, who as such confronts the worker."[26]

To be a master is to have certain powers in relation to slaves, and vice versa. Just as the imperatives of capitalism place limits on what any typical capitalist can do with his or her capital, the imperatives of slavery, and its basis in slave labor, place limits upon what any rational master can do. It is possible, of course, for particular masters to overstep these bounds, to abuse a power that, in its "normal" operations, is violent and dehumanizing enough.[27] But in doing so, they would be, so to speak, consuming their power through its exercise; a power that, under the conditions of slave society, while separable from this particular master, is inseparable from the master as such.

The structural limits of power are important both because they define the specific nature of power relations (e.g., master-slave ver-

[26]Karl Marx, *Grundrisse*, trans. Martin Nicolaus (New York: Vintage, 1973), p. 303.
[27]On the dehumanizing character of slavery, see Orlando Patterson, *Slavery and Social Death* (Cambridge, Mass.: Harvard University Press, 1979).

sus official-citizen versus capitalist-worker), and because they shape the contours of the life chances of agents, of social conflict, and of the possibilities for social change. To emphasize that power relations always involve some element of reciprocity is not to deny the salience of domination. It is to recognize that domination is always of a specific sort, and, moreover, that it involves the mutual performance of activities. This recognition also enables us to incorporate directly into the conceptualization of power the chronic *negotiation* attending its exercise. Giddens calls this the "dialectic of control." He writes: "However wide-ranging the control which actors may have over others, the weak nevertheless always have some capabilities of turning back resources against the strong."[28]

This emphasis on the mutuality of power relations, and on the genuine agency of the subordinate, is an important theme within the phenomenological tradition. Thus in Hegel's famous chapter "Lordship and Bondage" in *The Phenomenology of Mind*, while the slave appears to the master as "inessential," a wholly dependent instrument of the master's will, it becomes "evident that this object does not correspond to its notion"—that it is the master who is dependent on the slave's activity. (Of course, in Hegel this insight is incorporated within a philosophy of history, and thus for him "just as lordship showed its essential nature to be the reverse of what it wants to be, so, too, bondage will, when completed, pass into the opposite of what it immediately is: being a consciousness repressed within itself, it will enter into itself, and change around into a real and true independence.")[29] Georg Simmel also insists on the effectivity of the subordinate. He writes:

Nobody, in general, wishes that his influence completely determine the other individual. He rather wants this influence, this determination of the other, to act back upon him. Even the abstract will-to-dominate, therefore, is a case of interaction. This will draws its

[28]Giddens, *Contemporary Critique*, p. 63.
[29]G.W.F. Hegel, *The Phenomenology of Mind*, trans. J. B. Baillie (New York: Harper Torchbooks, 1967), pp. 229–40. For discussion, see Alexandre Kojève, *Introduction to the Reading of Hegel*, trans. Allan Bloom (New York: Basic Books 1969), chap. 1; and Jean Hyppolite, *Genesis and Structure of Hegel's Phenomenology of Spirit* (Evanston, Ill.: Northwestern University Press, 1974). For a critical analysis of Hegel's idealism in this section, see Chris Arthur, "Hegel's Master/Slave Dialectic and a Myth of Marxology," *New Left Review*, no. 142 (November–December 1983), 67–75.

satisfaction from the fact that the acting or suffering of the other, his positive or negative condition, offers itself to the dominator as the product of his will.... The practical function of this desire for domination ... is not so much the exploitation of the other as the mere consciousness of this possibility.... But still, even the desire for domination has some interest in the other person, who constitutes a value for it.... Even in the most oppressive and cruel cases of subordination, there is still a considerable measure of personal freedom.[30]

These formulations are characteristically idealist, treating power as an outgrowth of pure consciousness or will; but they insist on something ignored by empiricism—that power operates dialectically and not according to a Newtonian model of stimulus and response.

Giddens, in his discussion of this issue, emphasizes the dimension of free will in social life, the fact that, barring the confinements of a literal or figurative straitjacket, the ability to say no is always a live option. "This," he writes, "accounts for the intimate tie between agency and suicide. Self-destruction is a (virtually) always open-option, the ultimate refusal that finally and absolutely cancels the oppressive power of others; hence suicidal acts themselves can be understood as concerned with the exercise of power."[31] This is an important point insofar as it forces us to see all social outcomes as the contingent results of purposive human activity; and while it emphasizes the importance of choice (and, correlatively, of moral responsibility), it also recognizes the determinacy, as well as the possible oppressiveness, of circumstances and conditions not of our own choosing. But it also seems to be an incomplete account of the way the dialectic of power—the capability of the weak turning back resources against the strong—operates in social life outside of extreme situations like muggings and death camps.[32] Giddens

[30]Georg Simmel, *The Sociology of Georg Simmel*, ed. Kurt Wolff (New York: Free Press, 1950), pp. 181–82.

[31]Giddens, *Central Problems*, p. 149.

[32]Hannah Arendt, for instance, clarifying her views on the moral responsibility of those Jewish leaders who collaborated with Nazi policies, wrote: "I said that there was no possibility of resistance, but there existed the possibility of doing nothing." She was, however, very careful to distinguish the "limited freedom of decision and action" available in the ghetto with the "immediate pressure and impact of terror" within the concentration camp ("Letter to Gershom Scholem," reprinted in Hannah Arendt, *The Jew as Pariah*, ed. Ron H. Feldman [New York: Grove, 1978], pp. 248–49).

himself later observes: "Most circumstances of control, of course, are not nearly so all-embracing as those of captor and captive."[33]

In this sense Hegel's dialectic of master and slave is suggestive. The real dialectic of power in social life lies in the *real social powers* possessed by subordinate parties to enduring relationships, and in the reciprocity of social practice. The capacities possessed by the slave, which can be turned against the master, do not reside simply in the freedom of human agency as such; they reside in the definite social powers distributed by the master/slave relationship—plowing the fields, picking the cotton, and the like. The master-slave relationship, like all social relationships, is chronically negotiated and renegotiated on the basis of this reciprocal possession of powers. The "normal" practices of slavery distribute certain supervisory, disciplinary, and appropriative powers to masters and laboring powers to slaves. In the "normal" working out of this relationship masters tend to perform directive activities, and slaves laboring activities. But though this distribution of powers is a necessary feature of the structure of slavery, the successful exercise of them is a contingent outcome of the interaction between concrete masters and slaves. These outcomes depend on the respective abilities of the parties to mobilize the resources at their disposal and to use them effectively. The fact that social power characteristically involves relations of mutual dependence allows for a variety of modes of leverage, maneuvering, and strategic bargaining between agents.

Of course the forms the negotiation takes will vary according to the structure of the relationship. Industrial workers in advanced capitalist societies, for instance, have recourse to legal rights and a judicial machinery in negotiating their power with capitalists. Antebellum American slaves had no such recourse, and thus for them resistance and negotiation characteristically took more covert forms.[34] Giddens points out that Erving Goffman's distinction between "front" and "back regions" illuminates one frequent mode

[33]Giddens, *Contemporary Critique*, p. 63.
[34]See John W. Blasingame, *The Slave Community: Plantation Life in the Ante-Bellum South* (Oxford: Oxford University Press, 1972); Kenneth Stampp, *The Peculiar Institution* (New York: Vintage, 1956), esp. pp. 322–82; and Herbert W. Gutman, *The Black Family in Slavery and Freedom, 1750–1925* (New York: Pantheon, 1976).

by which subordinates negotiate power: "Performances in front regions typically involve efforts to create and sustain the appearance of conformity to normative standards to which the actors in question may be indifferent, or even positively hostile, when meeting in the back."[35] Goffman's writings emphasize the various games whereby everyday life—even in "total institutions" like asylums and prisons, where domination takes an extreme form—is negotiated by its participants.[36] John Blasingame's *The Slave Community: Plantation Life in the Antebellum South* similarly examines the different responses and forms of resistance to slavery evidenced by slaves. He concludes: "Rather than identifying with and submitting totally to his master, the slave held onto many remnants of his African culture, gained a sense of worth in the quarters, spent most of his time free from surveillance by whites, controlled important aspects of his life, and did some personally meaningful things on his own volition. This relative freedom of thought and action helped the slave to preserve his personal autonomy and to create a culture which has contributed much to American life and thought."[37] Much of the "new social history" is concerned with the subcultures and modes of self-organization of subordinate groups—peasants, workers, women, blacks and other racial groups—and the way in which these embody and facilitate resistance to forms of domination.[38]

What bears emphasis is that these forms of negotiation are not, as behavioralist formulations might suggest, situations from which power springs, as it were, ex nihilo. They are situations in which the exercise of structurally pregiven powers is negotiated and contested. It is at this level that the question of compliance—getting people to do things—can be broached. On the view I have developed power relations are not compliance relations. They are enduring relations of reproduced, reciprocal practices. The exercise

---

[35]Giddens, *Central Problems*, p. 208.

[36]See Erving Goffman, *The Presentation of Self in Everyday Life* (New York: Doubleday, 1959); *Asylums* (New York: Doubleday/Anchor, 1961); and *Relations in Public* (New York: Harper Torchbooks, 1971).

[37]Blasingame, p. viii.

[38]See Barry Goldberg, "A New Look at Labor History," *Social Policy* (Winter 1982), 54–63; and Gregor McLennan, *Marxism and the Methodologies of History* (London: Verso, 1981), pp. 112–28.

of power does sometimes involve problems of compliance, though often in social life powers are exercised rather matter-of-factly and unproblematically. Capitalists make investment decisions, workers work. Teachers give out assignments, students do them. Drill sergeants bark out orders, soldiers obey them. As William James once remarked, "habit is the enormous flywheel of society," and power is often (though, as we have emphasized, not always) exercised, and reproduced, rather routinely.

Although power relations are not best conceived as compliance relations, problems of compliance are chronic features of social life. The reproduction of practices, and of powers, is *always* problematic. In this sense, the specific individuals and groups who draw upon structural powers and exercise them in accordance with their own concrete purposes—meeting this production deadline, getting my students to do that assignment—are always faced with the problem of *achieving* these purposes. The mobilization of resources, the exchange of threats and counterthreats, the offering of positive and negative sanctions, the calculation of costs and benefits—all these figure importantly at this level of strategic interaction. Exchange theories of power shed light on the inherently problematic and negotiated exercise of power, though the assumptions about rationality and the transparency of interests entertained by most exchange theorists are unwarranted and highly suspect (see the following section).[39]

It is this indeterminacy in the exercise of power that accounts for the openness of history we discussed in Chapter 2. While power is a pregiven property of structurally located agents, these structures are only *relatively enduring*, and the activities of subordinate groups can play a crucial role in altering them. Students, for instance, can strategically withdraw their learning powers, forcing school administrators to allow them a greater role in school governance; and workers can collectively dispose of their labor power by organizing a trade union. These are examples of ways in which social struggle can renegotiate the terms of social power. And they

[39]See Brian Barry, ed., *Power and Political Theory: Some European Perspectives* (London: Wiley, 1976), for some good discussions of exchange theory. For a more general criticism of rational choice theory, see Roy Bhaskar, *The Possibility of Naturalism: A Philosophical Critique of the Contemporary Human Sciences* (Atlantic Highlands, N.J.: Humanities Press, 1979), pp. 137–46.

are also examples of the role solidarity and organization can play in enhancing the ability of particular agents to negotiate their interests. At the limit, however, are those instances in which relations of power are more fundamentally challenged and transformed. It is the nature of capitalism, as we shall see in Part II, that workers possess labor power that is put at the disposal of capitalists; but this is not to say that the practice of work could not be organized in different ways. It is the vision of socialist theory that workers, defined under capitalism as a subordinate class, might transform the structure of class relations, claiming for themselves powers previously in the hands of capitalists. In insisting that social power is a structural capacity we must not ignore the persistence, passion, and ingenuity with which living and breathing human beings exercise it, cope with it, and struggle to transform it.

Once again, our intention is not to rigidly bifurcate social structure and the manifold forms of human agency, but to see how power is implicated in both, and in fact links them together. The analysis of power must examine those structural relationships that distribute the capacity to act. But it must also examine the concrete history whereby these relationships are maintained and changed, and the forms of organization of those groups whose activity makes these things happen. A structural approach to social power thus does not license an invidious essentialism, whereby particular struggles and forms of organization are seen as no more than epiphenomenal "expressions" of underlying relations.

Barry Hindess, in a 1982 article, insists upon the "conditionality of outcomes" and argues that any concept of power as capacity must fail because "outcomes are not 'predictable' and 'unvarying' in the way this conception requires."[40] The unpredictability of social outcomes is something about which we agree; there can be no "guarantees" that power will be successfully exercised on any particular occasion. And more generally, as Hindess points out, the negotiation of power involves "struggles, not the playing-out of some pre-ordained script."[41] But Hindess equivocates between suggesting that (1) the exercise of power is contingent (he writes that

---

[40]Barry Hindess, "Power, Interests, and the Outcomes of Struggles," *Sociology* 16 (November 1982), 501.
[41]Ibid., p. 506.

outcomes are "rarely the *simple* products of initial conditions" [italics mine]; also note the scare quotes when he talks about the "unpredictability" of power), and (2) initial (structural) conditions are entirely irrelevant, there being nothing more than the exercise of power. The first suggestion is sound, and Hindess does well to remind us of the importance of struggle. The second is groundless, not only unhinging struggle from its conditions of existence, but rendering unintelligible what parties to struggle are struggling *about*.

Michel Crozier, in *The Bureaucratic Phenomenon*, has some very interesting things to say about the uncertainties surrounding the exercise of power in highly rationalized organizations, which compel even the most powerful officials to "bargain and compromise with all the people whose cooperation is indispensable at each level."[42] Yet, Crozier insists, "One should not translate the logic of the struggle into an overly black-and-white picture.... Other forces are operating which insure the minimum of consensus and organizational commitment that prevent people from extracting too much from, or being too much exploited in, their reciprocal deals."[43] Crozier's comments here caution us about being so sensitive to the role of struggle that we forget those structural conditions under which struggle takes place. They also raise another important question, to which we now turn—the question of interests, their constitution, and the problem of consensus.

Power, Interests, and Ideology

Lukes, we may recall, introduced the concept of interest into the three faces of power controversy. For Lukes, the concept of interest is necessary to the discussion of power insofar as it answers the question of the counterfactual—what would B do were it not for A's behavior? We have seen that this way of thinking about power is mistaken; and Lukes's counterfactual question does not figure in my realist account of power insofar as I reject the Newtonian

---

[42]Michel Crozier, *The Bureaucratic Phenomenon* (Chicago: University of Chicago Press, 1964), p. 163.
[43]Ibid., p. 167.

premise on which it rests. Rather than A getting B to do something B would not otherwise do, social relations of power typically involve both A and B doing what they *ordinarily* do. The structure of education, not teachers, causes students to act like students and teachers to act like teachers. Teachers and students, as the social identities that they are, would not "otherwise do" anything but what teachers and students tend to do. And neither a conflict of revealed preferences, nor of objective interests, must be discovered in order to attribute power to these roles.

As Lukes recognizes, a relation of power can exist even in the absence of a conflict of revealed preferences. Contrary to Lukes, however, a relation of power can also exist in the absence of a conflict of "objective interests." It might very well be the case that my power over my students is in their best interest; but the relationship is not for that reason any less one of domination and subordination. Lukes's own formulation would seem to deny this, defining away any form of power that seems or is claimed to be in the mutual interest of the parties involved, and thus opening him up to the charge of "vanguardism."[44] But to claim that the concept of power does not require recourse to the concept of interest in the way that Lukes argues is not to deny that the concept of interest plays a necessary role in the analysis of power. In acknowledging its centrality, however, we must also clarify the precise meaning of the concept.

I would suggest that there are at least three different meanings of the concept of interest that must be clearly distinguished. The first meaning of "interest" refers to the *subjective interests*, or revealed preferences, that are actually held by particular agents. We have suggested that in this sense the concept is not epistemically necessary to theoretical claims about social power. Different individuals have different preferences. Some may like their social role. Some may not. Some may not and yet prefer to do nothing about it, possibly because it is to them a means to other more preferential

[44]See Peter Abell, "The Many Faces of Power: Revealed Preference, Autonomy, and Teleological Explanation," *Sociology* 11 (January 1977), 3–23; K. Thomas, "Power and Autonomy: Further Comments on the Many Faces of Power," *Sociology* 12 (May 1978), 332–35; and G. W. Smith, "Must Radicals Be Marxists? Lukes on Power, Contestability, and Alienation," *British Journal of Political Science* 11 (1981), 405–25.

ends, like making money or graduating school. We can talk theoretically about the structure of power in the classroom without reference to the preferences of the students, who are subordinate even if they prefer to remain so. But while social relationships are not simply effects of subjective interests, being themselves important determinants of preference formation, subjective interests are crucially relevant to the exercise and the reproduction of social power. As we have insisted, the exercise of power is contingent, and the outcomes of its exercise are determined both by the structural distribution of power *and* the subjective understandings, preferences, and "will" of concrete social agents. Theoretical claims about the structural location of power may not require, as evidence, reference to the subjective interests of particular agents. But the analysis of the working out of relations of power, of their concrete reproduction and transformation, necessarily involves attention to the preferences and strategic objectives of socially situated individuals, groups, and organizations. A realist view of power does not reify social agents and their specific preferences. But neither does it take them as a given. Rather, it suggests that they be explained with reference, though not reduced, to the relatively enduring relationships in which agents participate.

The second meaning of "interest" is that suggested by Lukes—*objective interest*, or what is really in the interest, or good, of an agent, whether he or she thinks so or not.[45] I argued in Chapter 1 that we need not have recourse to this concept in order to justifiably identify a relation of power, and thus the peasant with a gun to her head is subordinate to the commissar of agriculture even if collectivization is in her interest. While it is thus possible to talk about power independently of the issue of objective interests, it does not follow that the concept is unintelligible or irrelevant, as many of Lukes's critics have claimed. We will return to this issue shortly.

These two usages of "interest"—subjective and objective—have preoccupied theorists in the debate on the concept of power. I will introduce a third meaning of interest—constitutive, or *real interest*.

[45]See William E. Connolly, "On 'Interests' in Politics," *Politics and Society* 2 (Summer 1972), 459–77; and also Isaac Balbus, "The Concept of Interest in Pluralist and Marxist Analysis," *Politics and Society* 1 (1971), 151–78.

This concept refers to those norms, values, and rationalities implicit in the practices of social life and associated with social roles as their principles of action. I label them "real" because they are causally effective in practice in the sense in which objective interests are clearly not. While objective interests may very well be ends that agents *should* subscribe to, real interests are those ends instantiated in their practice. To call them "real" is not to suggest that subjective interests, which are also causally effective in practice, are somehow epiphenomenal or less real. It is to suggest that certain interests are real, and causal, even if they are not avowed by social agents, and that these interests shape and limit (though they do not unequivocally determine) the development of subjective interests.

To revert to the teacher-student example: Ms. X, as an individual teacher, may have a preference for extreme discipline in her class; and as a pedagogue she may have an objective interest in teaching a seminar; but as a college English teacher she has a real interest in teaching a particular body of work within the guidelines of the university (grades, exams, schedules, room assignments). This is the interest that is shared by college English teachers in the university system as such. Similarly, her students may prefer to read *Rolling Stone* magazine; and they may have an objective interest in reading Shakespeare; but as students in the university system they have a real interest in going to class, somehow fulfilling the course requirements, and getting college credit. (This example is intended only as an illustration, not a theoretical claim, though if there is any truth to it, then we can see how far our system of higher education is from being organized around the pursuit of learning.)

What we have called real interests obviously play a central role in the constitution of social power. They are the practical norms, referred to in the "Power and Agency" section of this chapter, which justify and legitimate power relations. The rationality that characterizes the role of the university student, in the above example, sustains the subordination of students in the university system. Similarly, while the proletarian may prefer to make more money in order to buy a Sony television set, and may have an objective interest in the transformation of capitalism into socialism, as a proletarian in a capitalist society she has a real interest in finding and keeping a job. The satisfaction of her preferences must be tailored to this; and as her objective interest potentially threatens this (by engendering economic dislocations in the process of change), she is unlikely to challenge the system. Once again, the rationality that characterizes the role of worker in a capitalist society sustains the structure of power.[46]

By rationality here we mean something more than egoistic calculation, but less than Parsonian value consensus. As interpretative sociology has insisted, social conduct is rule-governed; and individuals, in becoming "socialized" into various practices, learn the rules, and expectations, that govern their conduct while performing these activities. Althusser has called this *interpellation*—the process of social identity formation, whereby human subjects are inserted into pregiven social practices, and learn how to "properly" participate in them.[47] Real interests are those purposes implicit in the performance of social practices, and therefore implicitly, and practically, held by participants in these practices. To be a student is simply to learn how to perform certain activities properly, and to assume this conduct as your interest. As we have seen, this role characteristically involves the possession of certain concepts— school, teacher, student, grade, homework—and certain norms regarding the value of education, the necessity of obedience, and the importance of merit and performance. But the learning of these concepts and norms, and the assumption of a real interest, as a student, in respecting them—and the teacher—is not necessarily the same as believing in and propositionally avowing the rightness of the teacher-student relationship. The concept of real interest directs our attention to the routinized character of social life and the practical character of norms. Giddens writes: " ... as large areas of social life are not directly motivated, they form a 'grey area' between knowledgeability and commitment. Social life, in all societies, contains many types of social practice or aspects of practice which are sustained in and through the knowledgeability of social

---

[46]See Joel Rogers and Joshua Cohen, *On Democracy* (London: Penguin, 1984).

[47]See Louis Althusser, "Ideology and Ideological State Apparatuses," in his *Lenin and Philosophy and Other Essays* (New York: Monthly Review Press, 1971), pp. 170–77. For a critique of Althusser's view of the role of the human subject in this process, see Michael H. Best and William E. Connolly, "Politics and Subjects: The Limits of Structural Marxism," *Socialist Review* (November–December 1979), 75–100.

actors but which they do not reproduce as a matter of normative commitment."[48]

Real interests are usually implicit, rather than explicitly avowed, in practice; and they are pragmatically sustained as much through habit as they are through "value consensus." John Dewey writes, commenting on James's remark that "habit is the enormous fly-wheel of society, its most precious conservative influence":

> The influence of habit is decisive because all distinctively human action has to be learned, and the very heart, blood, and sinews of learning is creation of habitudes. Habits bind us to orderly and established ways of action because they generate ease, skill, and *interest* in things to which we have grown used and because they instigate fear to walk in different ways, and because they leave us incapacitated for the trial of them. Habit does not preclude the use of thought, but it determines the channels within which it operates. Thinking is secreted in the interstices of habit [italics mine].[49]

Real interests are thus a constitutive dimension of social power. Just as powers are distributed by pregiven social relationships, so are interests, as those practical norms that govern the exercise of power. The analysis of power thus requires an analysis of the real interests, and the more inclusive ideologies, that sustain it. Göran Therborn defines ideology as "that aspect of the human condition under which human beings live their lives as conscious actors in a world that makes sense to them to varying degrees. Ideology is the medium through which this consciousness and meaningfulness operate ... [which] includes both everyday notions and 'experience' and elaborate intellectual doctrines, both the 'consciousness' of social actors and the institutionalized thought-systems and discourses of a given society."[50] It is ideologies in this sense that structure real interests, providing meanings and understandings of both the interests of social agents and their relationships to others,

---

[48]Giddens, *Contemporary Critique*, p. 65.

[49]John Dewey, *The Public and Its Problems* (Chicago: Swallow Press, 1927), pp. 159–60.

[50]Göran Therborn, *The Ideology of Power and the Power of Ideology* (London: Verso, 1980), p. 2.

situating them in a social context broader—spatially and temporally—than themselves.[51]

The analysis of ideology and its connection to power play a central role in what Mills calls "classical social theory," and yet the concept of ideology has received little attention in debates among political scientists about the concept of power. Lukes quite properly interjects the problem of ideology into the three faces of power debate, insisting, as we have seen, that it is "the supreme exercise of power to avert conflict and grievance by influencing, shaping, and determining the perceptions and preferences of others." For him ideology, instead of being a normative precondition of any social practice, is simply an instrument of one powerful agent in a contingent relation with another. As we have seen, Lukes is unable to articulate the structural nature of power. He is also unable to recognize that all social exercise of power is governed by pregiven norms, or real interests, and by more general ideologies that structure these interests.

Lukes is quite right, however, to see the securing of ideology as a central problem of the reproduction of power, and the "engineering of consent" as a primary subjective interest of dominant elements of power relations. As we have suggested in the previous section, the successful exercise of power is always a contingent and negotiated outcome of interaction. The interpretation of social norms, and the struggle over their meaning, is a crucial ambit of this negotiation. Promptness, for example, is a practical norm of capitalist relations of production as defined by bourgeois ideology; and prompt work is a real interest of the industrial worker. But what this means in practice, in particular instances, is always problematic and is chronically negotiated between managers and workers in the course of the work process. While interests are pregiven, what Dewey called their "conservative influence" is never guaranteed.

---

[51]Ibid., pp. 22–27. See also Anthony Giddens, "Ideology and Consciousness," in his *Central Problems*, pp. 165–97. Giddens also develops the notion of the "time-space constitution of social systems" in his *Contemporary Critique*, pp. 26–48. The importance of ideology in social life is debated in Nicholas Abercrombie, Stephen Hill, and Bryan S. Turner, "Determinacy and Indeterminacy in the Theory of Ideology," *New Left Review*, no. 142 (November–December 1983), 55–66, and Göran Therborn, "The New Questions of Subjectivity," *New Left Review*, no. 143 (January–February 1984), 97–107.

Once again, Hindess forces us to make a necessary qualification, insisting that " 'interests,' in the sense of recognized objectives and concerns, can hardly be regarded as attaching to particular agents as a given to power analysis." Hindess argues that interests are always "the product of some more or less complex discursive process," that they are *constructed* in the course of interaction, and are therefore always subject to variation. He writes: "To say this is to say not only that objectives are not always given independently of particular conditions of struggle, but also that they may be changed or developed in the course of struggle."[52] Hindess wishes to caution against the reification of the concept of interest, and its employment as a general explanation of specific outcomes and struggles. The specific manner in which, say, a group of factory workers at plant B in Chicago construe their situation, and define what we would call their subjective interest, cannot be taken as given by their structural position and their real economic interest in employment or income, as some simple-minded structural accounts might suggest. Neither can it be explained by their simple free choice to be so disposed (for to do so would be circular, their preferences being explained by their preferences). Rather, their subjective interest is the product of a complex discursive process that includes casual conversations, debates, the influence of mass media—a process of ideological persuasion and struggle. Whether they are inclined toward quiescence, reformism, or radicalism, whether they are divided by racism or sexism, cannot be simply "read off" of their structural position. These interests are constructed, and can be reconstructed, through struggle.

Ernesto Laclau and Chantal Mouffe, in their recent *Hegemony and Socialist Strategy*, similarly insist on the problematic, and discursive, construction of interests. In criticizing those perspectives (in their view Marxism in particular) which see social identities and interests as fixed by a totalizing structure, they develop the concept of "articulation," which they define as "any practice establishing a relation among elements such that their identity is modified as a result of the articulatory practice."[53] This rather

[52]Hindess, "Power," p. 507.
[53]Ernesto Laclau and Chantal Mouffe, *Hegemony and Socialist Strategy: Towards a Radical Democratic Politics* (London: Verso, 1985), p. 105.

circular definition points toward the characteristic openness of social life and the fact that social identities are never fully fixed. Articulation is, in their view, the always incomplete and precarious practice of defining circumstances and constructing interests; and *hegemony* is the practice of articulating various social interests to one another, and of constructing common interests and networks of alliances. Not only are the subjective interests of the factory workers in plant B constructed through a practice of articulation; but the relation of these interests to the interests of other workers, and to various nonworkers—feminist groups, student organizations, and the like—is established by a hegemonic practice that has no necessary outcome.

In insisting on the openness of social life and the nonfixity of interests, however, it is important not to go too far. Hindess, and Laclau and Mouffe, in objecting to deterministic understandings of social interests, border on the contention that there are no determinants of social identities at all, that the discursive process of interest construction takes place in a perfectly fluid field of interaction. The distinction between subjective interests and real interests is intended to mark the structural determinants of subjective identities. It is true that the subjective interests of the workers of plant B are not fixed, that they may identify under certain circumstances as white workers, or Catholic workers, or as simply whites or Catholics; and the fact that they are workers does not fix this. As we saw in the previous chapter, however, concrete social life is determined by a complex of structural relations (e.g., class, race, gender, ethnicity, citizenship), none of which exclusively determines social conduct, and any of which can be more important on a particular occasion, *but all of which are causally effective*. Furthermore, while on any particular occasion the fact that worker B is a worker may not determine his subjective interests, it is likely that most often it will be a crucial determinant. (Are the real interests of white workers—in employment, income, economic security—not implicated in their racist inclinations?) And finally, as I have insisted throughout this chapter, whatever the subjective interests of the workers in plant B, the fact remains that they are still workers, which means that they are still subordinated to their capitalist employers, with all that this entails regarding their economic status. Social identities may not be fully fixed, but social structures persist, partly through habit, partly through normative commitment, and partly through the mechanisms of compliance and coercion. Social struggle is an important determinant of social life; but it always takes place within the limits and constraints of social power and ideology.

The analysis of power, then, requires attention to the concrete discursive processes whereby subjective interests are constructed; but it also requires attention to the real interests, and ideologies, implicated in ongoing relations of power. I would also argue, through, that the analysis of power requires, in a different sense, an analysis of *objective interests*. This hinges, of course, on the question of the relationship between "facts" and "values," and of description versus evaluation, in social science. Many of Lukes's critics, particularly Polsby, have ridiculed any attempt to move from an analysis of social reality to a critique of it.[54] Many contemporary philosophers, however, have argued that it is both possible and necessary to do so.[55] There are two ways in which writers dealing with the concept of power have dealt with this, and while I would suggest that they are both problematic, this is not to reject their project of an analysis of power with practical, emancipatory intent.

The first strategy is that of Lukes and, more generally, of Habermas. We might call this the neo-Kantian approach. In this view the theorist of power must judge empirical reality against a postulated ideal condition of autonomous agency. Habermas's ideal speech situation, in which individuals could hypothetically engage in "undistorted communication" about their practical interests, is paradigmatic. As Habermas writes in *Knowledge and Human In-*

---

[54]See Nelson Polsby, *Community Power and Political Theory*, 2d ed. (New Haven: Yale University Press, 1980), p. 224: "Where, then, is the relevant knowledge to be found that permits people not merely to choose but to choose in accordance with their interests? If such knowledge exists at all, we must conclude it is in the possession of self-proclaimed 'radicals' or third-dimensionalists (or even reactionaries) who know enough to be able to tell when it is appropriate to reject the choices of ordinary citizens as insufficiently enlightened to reflect their real interests. A definition relying upon 'enlightenment' of some form of other amounts to an argument that actors would choose differently if they knew what analysts knew; in short, it consists of a substitution of analysts choices for actors' choices."

[55]See Bhaskar, *Possibility*, pp. 69–83, and his "Scientific Explanation and Human Emancipation," *Radical Philosophy* (Autumn 1980), 16–28.

terests: "The goal is 'providing a rational basis for the precepts of civilization': in other words, an organization of social relations according to the principle that the validity of every norm of political consequence be made dependent on a consensus arrived at in communication free from domination."[56] The problem with this approach is not that it proposes that the theorist make normative judgments about the actions of others (claiming, for instance, that contemporary liberal democratic states are not in the objective interests of their citizens). All normative theory, from Plato to Rawls to Dahl's *A Preface to Democratic Theory*, does this. The problem is that it detaches the analysis of objective interest from the analysis of actual power relations. I label it neo-Kantian because, as in Kant, this view seems to rest on a sharp dualism between the real world of causal relations (understood, as Kant did, in Humean terms) and an ideal world of autonomy.[57] How those subject to relations of power might identify with this ideal condition, and be inclined to bring it about, is left unexplained.[58]

[56]Jürgen Habermas, *Knowledge*, p. 284; see also his "On Systematically Distorted Communication," *Inquiry* 13 (1970), 205–18.

[57]As Habermas writes of social science, it has the goal "of producing nomological knowledge. A critical social science, however, will not remain satisfied with this. It is concerned with going beyond this goal to determine when theoretical statements grasp *invariant regularities of social action as such* and when they express ideologically frozen relations that can in principle be transformed" (italics mine). We can see here the dualism between empiricist causal relations of heteronomy, and the ideal of autonomy. On this dualism see Quentin Skinner's "Habermas's Reformation," *New York Review of Books*, October 1, 1982, pp. 35–39.

[58]Ironically, Lukes has pointed this out in his "Of Gods and Demons: Habermas and Practical Reason," in John B. Thompson and David Held, eds., *Habermas: Critical Debates* (Cambridge, Mass.: MIT Press, 1982). As Lukes insists, there is no reason for supposing that actual agents subject to relations of power could ever reach a rational decision on the basis of undistorted communication, as these actual agents (as opposed to the ideal agents of Habermas's theory) would "continue to exhibit all kinds of traits conducive to 'distorted communication'—prejudices, limitations of vision and imagination, deference to authority, fears, vanities, self-doubts, and so-on" (pp. 138–40). Benton, 1981 "Objective Interests," calls this the "paradox of emancipation"—the transformation of relations of domination requires that agents come to see these as contrary to their objective interests; and yet, in the Habermassian view, it is only possible for agents to see this under transformed, genuinely free circumstances. Of course, this paradox is mitigated once we cease thinking of relations of domination as relations of heteronomy, and once we cease thinking of objective interests as transcendental to this heteronomous reality.

The second strategy is that most often associated with the Lukácsian tradition of Marxism. If the first strategy fails to bridge the gap between the real and the ideal, the second obliterates it. It does this by positing a teleology, whereby those in a subordinate position are either actually or immanently in opposition to the existing system of power. Lukács, for instance, notes the irresolvable antinomy of Kantian practical reason: "For, just as objective necessity, despite the rationality and regularity of its manifestations, yet persists in a state of immutable contingency because its material substratum remains transcendental, so too the freedom of the subject which this device is designed to rescue, is unable, being an empty freedom, to evade the abyss of fatalism."[59] On the other hand, Lukács argues, Marxism represents the "consciousness of the proletariat [which has] elevate[d] itself to the self-consciousness of society in its historical development," aware of the "immanent meanings" of its own struggles and their necessary end—socialist liberation.[60] One consequence of this teleological treatment of the problem of interests is that discrete acts of resistance, and more ordinary forms of negotiation and conflict, are inaccurately interpreted as signs of a movement toward social transformation. This mistake leads toward the moralizing of theoretical analysis, and a failure to acknowledge the coherence and stability of social forms. A second consequence of this is an inattention to real normative questions. Insofar as change is seen as immanent, it becomes less

[59]Georg Lukács, "Reification and the Consciousness of the Proletariat," in *History and Class Consciousness* (Cambridge, Mass.: MIT Press, 1971), p. 133. He writes elsewhere in language presaging Lukes's Critique of Habermas: "... in the philosophy of Kant the category of 'ought' presupposes an existing reality to which the category of 'ought' remains *inapplicable* in principle. Whenever the refusal of the subject simply to accept this empirically given existence takes the form of an 'ought,' this means that the immediately given empirical reality receives affirmation and consecration at the hands of philosophy: it is philosophically immortalised. 'Nothing in the world of phenomena can be explained by the concept of freedom,' Kant states, 'the guiding threat in that sphere must always be the mechanics of nature' " (p. 160).

[60]Lukács, pp. 180, 197. Ironically, the same problem can be found in Ralf Dahrendorf's *Class and Class Conflict in Industrial Society* (Stanford: Stanford University Press, 1959), pp. 175–79. I have also criticized this in my "On Benton's 'Objective Interests and the Sociology of Power': A Critique," *Sociology* 16 (August 1982), 440–44.

imperative to figure out why change is justified and how the future should be better organized.[61]

Somewhere between the idealism of the first strategy and the historicist reductionism of the second lies the terrain on which the analysis of power can properly broach the question of objective interest. Normative theory, as an analysis of what forms of social life are just and morally legitimate, must always address questions of actual social practice, of real social interests, and of historical possibility. Yet it can never be reduced to a mere corollary of descriptive analysis. And it is only at the limit case, as a product of a protracted process of ideological struggle and political persuasion, that the conclusions of normative theory can become causally effective as the subjective interests of a real social group. Such a process, to be sure, takes us outside the realm of pure theory and into the realm of political practice. And while success in such endeavors is surely no mark of the epistemic validity of our theories, it is arguably the great promise of such an emancipatory theory which provides us with the most compelling reason to undertake the analysis of social power.

[61]On this problem within classical Marxism, see Svetozar Stojanovic, *In Search of Democracy in Socialism: History and Party Consciousness* (New York: Prometheus, 1981). See also Norman Geras, "The Controversy about Marx and Justice," *New Left Review*, no. 150 (March–April 1985), 47–88.

MARXISM
AND POWER

In Part I I criticized the empiricist consensus surrounding the three faces of power controversy and outlined an alternative, realist concept of power. In Part II I turn to more substantive matters, arguing that contemporary Marxian social theory represents a realist approach to the analysis of social power. As such it deserves to be taken seriously as a genuine scientific theory. It may not provide a wholly adequate or correct analysis of social power. It may require the supplementation of other theories—feminist theory, for instance—in order for us to better understand the diverse relations of power existing in contemporary societies. And it may even be incorrect with regard to the analysis of its primary object of explanation—class relations under capitalism. I will make no attempt to corroborate or defend the substantive validity of Marxism as a theory of power, only to insist upon its realist, and scientific, character. It might be helpful to briefly set out the sense in which the Marxian analysis of power is realist.

First, Marxian theory does not conform to the deductive-nomological ideal. It is not interested in behavioral regularities; rather, it is a theory of the class relations of capitalism and the enduring powers distributed by these relations. In the Marxian view classes are collectivities engaged in structural relations and possessing those capacities to act that are characteristic of these relations. Because these powers are asymmetrically distributed, the class relations of capitalism are relations of domination and subordination as I defined them in Chapter 3.

Second, Marxian theory acknowledges both the reciprocity characteristic of social relations of power and the continuous negotiation endemic to them. The concept of "class struggle," one of the central concepts of Marxian analysis, denotes this process of continuous negotiation of power, and the specific basis of this negotiation in structural relations of domination. In analyzing class struggle, many recent Marxian theorists have made use of a concept of "class capacities," which refers to the specific structural and organizational relations within classes, examining how these relations determine the specific means by which classes engage in struggle and the specific abilities they develop through struggle.

Third, contemporary Marxian theorists have not only been concerned with class powers and their reproduction and transformation through struggle. They have also concerned themselves with the state and with the theoretical analysis of state power and its connections with class power.

In short, Marxian theory employs a core set of concepts—class, class domination, class struggle, capitalist state—which are realist, which denote enduring features of social life, and which are designed to explain the constitution and reproduction of the economic and political practices of capitalist societies. Ellen Wood writes:

> The fundamental secret of capitalist production disclosed by Marx— the secret that political economy systematically concealed, making it finally incapable of accounting for capitalist accumulation—concerns the social relation and the disposition of power that obtains between the worker and the capitalist to whom he sells his labour-power. This secret has a corollary: that the disposition of power between the individual capitalist and worker has as its condition the political configuration of society as a whole—the balance of class forces and the powers of the state which permit the expropriation of the direct producer, the maintenance of absolute private property for the capitalist, and his control over production and appropriation.[1]

[1] Ellen Meiksins Wood, "The Separation of the Economic and the Political in Capitalism," *New Left Review*, no. 127 (May–June 1981), 68.

Once we acknowledge the manifest weaknesses of empiricism as a way of thinking about power, we can also begin to appreciate the radically different meta-theoretical groundings of Marxian theory.

It is, of course, true that there is currently no consensus among Marxists or their critics on the methodological underpinnings of Marxian theory.[2] But many recent commentators have emphasized the realist presuppositions of Marxian theory, tracing this realism back to Marx himself.[3] James Farr is representative when he proposes that "we best understand Marx's methodology as developing within and contributing to the tradition of scientific realism. From 1843 on, realism was the working language of his science, the language of 'essences,' 'inner mechanisms,' 'real relations,' and 'natural necessity.' "[4] Empiricist critics like Popper, in distinguishing between the "essentialism" characteristic of Marxian theory and "real" scientific method, have similarly underlined the nonempiricist premises of Marxist theory.

First, Marxian theory embodies a *relational* social ontology.[5] For Marx, "the individual is the social being," a being "which can

[2]Jon Elster, for instance, has even attempted to reconstruct Marxian theory on the basis of methodological individualism. See his "Marxism, Functionalism, and Game Theory: The Case for Methodological Individualism," *Theory and Society* 11 (1982), 453–82. On this dissensus within Marxism, see Terence Ball and James Farr, eds., *After Marx* (Cambridge: Cambridge University Press, 1984).

[3]See the following: Russell Keat and John Urry, *Social Theory as Science* (London: Routledge & Kegan Paul, 1975); Ted Benton, *Philosophical Foundations of the Three Sociologies* (London: Routledge & Kegan Paul, 1977); John Mepham and David Hillel-Ruben, eds., *Issues in Marxist Philosophy*, 3 vols. (Brighton, Sussex: Harvester Press, 1979); Roy Bhaskar, *The Possibility of Naturalism: A Philosophical Critique of the Contemporary Human Sciences* (Atlantic Highlands, N.J.: Humanities Press, 1979); David Hillel-Ruben, *Marxism and Materialism: A Study in Marxist Theory of Knowledge* (Atlantic Highlands, N.J.: Humanities Press, 1979); Derek Sayer, *Marx's Method: Ideology, Science, and Critique in 'Capital'* (Atlantic Highlands, N.J.: Humanities Press, 1979); Alan Gilbert, *Marx's Politics: Communists and Citizens* (New Brunswick, N.J.: Rutgers University Press, 1981); John Urry, "Science, Realism, and the Social," *Philosophy of the Social Sciences* 12 (1982), 311–18; James Farr, "Marx and Positivism," Terence Ball, "Marxian Science and Positivist Politics," and Alan Gilbert, "Marx's Moral Realism: Eudaimonism and Moral Progress," in Ball and Farr, *After Marx*; and Peter T. Manicas, *A History and Philosophy of the Social Sciences* (Oxford: Blackwell, 1987).

[4]James Farr, "Marx's Laws," *Political Studies*, 34 (Spring 1986), 202–22.

[5]See Bertell Ollman, *Alienation: Marx's Conception of Man in Capitalist Society* (Cambridge: Cambridge University Press, 1971); Carol Gould, *Marx's Social Ontology* (Cambridge, Mass.: MIT Press, 1980); and Shlomo Avineri, *Karl Marx's Social and Political Thought* (Cambridge: Cambridge University Press, 1968).

individuate itself only in the midst of society."[6] Marx consistently rejected the individualist premises of classical political economy; and while he ascribed certain fundamental properties and powers—creative, intellectual, and material—to human beings as such, he also rejected the explanatory reliance on any notion of a transhistorical abstract human essence. "Society does not consist of individuals," he wrote, "but expresses the sum of interrelations, the relations within which these individuals stand. As if someone were to say: Seen from the perspective of society there are no slaves and no citizens: both are human beings. Rather, they are that outside of society. To be a slave, to be a citizen, are social characteristics, relations between human beings A and B. Human being A, as such, is not a slave. He is a slave in and through society."[7] In other words, to understand society in terms of the (equal, species) properties of generic individuals is to "abstract from just the specific difference on which everything depends."[8] For Marx it is the historically evolved and relatively enduring relations between agents that constitute society—"wipe out these relations and you annihilate all society."[9]

Second, Marx's social ontology is *transformational.* "Just as society produces man as man," he wrote, "so is society produced by him."[10] Human agency, in all its complexity, is thus at the center of Marx's ontology. But for Marx human agency must be seen as socially conditioned. This conception is consistent with Giddens's notion of the "duality of structure," and on it the historical process is seen as a process of ongoing human transformation: "History is nothing but the succession of the separate generations, each of which exploits the materials...handed down to all by preceding generations, and thus, on the one hand, continues the traditional activity in completely changed circumstances and, on the other, modifies the old circumstances with a completely changed activ-

---

[6]Karl Marx, "Economic and Philosophical Manuscripts," in Robert C. Tucker, ed., *The Marx-Engels Reader,* 1st ed. (New York: Norton, 1972), p. 72; Karl Marx, *Grundrisse,* trans. Martin Nicolaus (New York: Vintage, 1973), p. 84.

[7]Marx, *Grundrisse,* p. 265.

[8]Ibid.

[9]Karl Marx, *The Poverty of Philosophy,* in Karl Marx and Frederick Engels, *Collected Works,* vol. 6 (New York: International Publishers, 1977), p. 159.

[10]Marx, "Economic," p. 71.

ity."[11] As this text suggests, for Marx social structures are the material causes of social life, but human activity is the efficient cause; or as he put it elsewhere: "Men make their own history, but they do not make it just as they please, they do not make it under circumstances chosen by themselves, but under circumstances directly found, given, and transmitted from the past."[12]

Third, Marx operated on the basis of characteristically realist distinctions between appearance and reality and experience and knowledge. "All science," he wrote, "would be superfluous if the outward appearance and the essence of things directly coincided."[13] For Marx science explains the underlying causal mechanisms that generate the phenomena of experience. In order to do this, the theorist must isolate the relevant causal processes. In this regard social science is no different from natural science. As Marx points out, discussing his method in the preface to the first German edition of *Capital*: "The physicist either observes physical phenomena where they occur in their most typical form and most free from disturbing influence, or whenever possible, he makes experiments under conditions that insure the occurrence of the phenomenon in its normality."[14] However, Marx recognized, in social science, unlike natural science, experimental closure is impossible. Thus, "in the analysis of economic forms . . . neither microscopes nor chemical reagents are of use. *The force of abstraction must replace both*" (italics mine).[15]

As Marx acknowledges in *Capital*, the "classic ground" of capitalist development is England. But he is quite clear that England serves for him only as a model of the essential characteristics of capitalism, as "the chief illustration in the development of my theoretical ideas."[16] Marx recognizes that all capitalist societies do not share the empirical characteristics of England; he insists, however, that his theory is not a concrete analysis of England but an abstract analysis of capitalism in general. He writes, in deliberately

[11]Quoted in Bhaskar, *Possibility*, p. 93.

[12]Karl Marx, *The Eighteenth Brumaire of Louis Napoleon*, in Marx and Engels, vol. 11, 1977, p. 103.

[13]Karl Marx, *Capital*, vol. 3 (New York: International Publishers, 1967), p. 817.

[14]Ibid., vol. 1, p. 8.

[15]Ibid.

[16]Ibid.

polemical and naturalist language: "Intrinsically, it is not a question of the higher or lower degree of development of the social antagonisms that result from the *natural laws of capitalist production.* It is a question of these laws themselves [italics mine]."[17] The phenomena of the production and exchange of commodities, a class of wage laborers, the factory system, and class conflict are thus explained by subsuming them under a general theory of underlying relations. Russell Keat and John Urry write:

> Marx's theoretical purpose is to produce descriptions of the structures of different modes of production. However, no such mode is ever found in pure form. Different modes are always co-present within any actual society, although if the capitalist mode is dominant we will characterize that society as capitalist; for example, nineteenth century Britain. It thus follows that social analysis consists of at least two stages: first, the elucidation of the internal structure of each mode of production, a theoretical activity involving the positing of models of the relevant causal mechanisms; second, the analysis of the ways in which different modes of production are co-present within a given society and the social and political consequences that follow.[18]

As pointed out in Chapter 2, social scientific investigation typically involves operating at many different levels of abstraction. Marx's general theory of capitalist economic relations, as set forth in *Capital*, must thus be distinguished from the analysis of specific capitalist societies, in specific times and places. The Althusserian distinction between a capitalist mode of production (the properties of capitalism in its "pure" state, its "normality") and a capitalist social formation (a concrete society in which capitalist relations coexist with others in a particular way) highlights this point. As Althusser insists, however, the theoretical conceptualization of capitalism as a pure mode of production is not simply a heuristic or an ideal type; rather, it is "the *concept* of the real."[19]

---

[17]Ibid. On Marx's "natural laws," see Farr, "Marx's Laws."

[18]Keat and Urry, p. 97.

[19]Louis Althusser and Etienne Balibar, *Reading Capital* (London: New Left Books, 1970), p. 196. For a realist interpretation of Althusser, see Ted Benton, *The Rise and Fall of Structural Marxism: Althusser and His Influence* (New York: St. Martin's, 1984).

In Part II I outline in detail the realist features of the Marxian analysis of power. My discussion of Marxism should help concretize, and clarify, some of the meta-theoretical arguments presented in Part I. But, one hopes, bringing realism to bear explicitly upon Marxian analysis will also help to clarify some of the basic themes of contemporary Marxian theory. This is particularly germane given what appears to be something of a scholarly consensus that Marxian theory lacks any account of power and domination. Regis Debray writes, for instance, that "owing to Marx and his descendants something is known about the exploitation of man by man. Very little is known about the domination of man over man, regarding which Marxism falls short."[20] And Isaac Balbus contends that "the roots of domination are not visible from a Marxian standpoint."[21] These criticisms smack of historicism, suggesting that Marxism fails because it provides no transhistorical theory of social power and domination—a point to which we shall return. But the burden of the following chapters is to demonstrate that, whatever deficiencies might be laid at the feet of historical materialism—the Marxist theory of history set out schematically in Marx's preface to a *Contribution to a Critique of Political Economy*, and systematically defended by G. A. Cohen in *Karl Marx's Theory of History: A Defense*—the Marxian analysis of capitalism is, as Wood insists, an account of the distribution of *power* in capitalist societies.[22] This itself is an important point, given the scholarly mobilization of bias against Marxism, and given recent converts to the chorus of voices attacking its reductionism. Necessary though this defense of Marxism is, however, it is not sufficient. And so I will conclude, in Chapter 6, with a critical analysis of the substantive virtues and vices of Marxism as a theory and practice of power.

[20]Quoted in Alex Callinicos, *Is There a Future for Marxism?* (Atlantic Highlands, N.J.: Humanities Press, 1982), p. 10.

[21]Isaac Balbus, *Marxism and Domination* (Princeton, N.J.: Princeton University Press, 1982), p. xi.

[22]For two recent attempts to critically reconstruct historical materialism, see G. A. Cohen, *Karl Marx's Theory of History: A Defense* (Princeton, N.J.: Princeton University Press, 1978); and Richard W. Miller, *Analyzing Marx: Morality, Power, and History* (Princeton, N.J.: Princeton University Press, 1984).

CHAPTER 4

Marxism, Class, and Power

In this chapter I examine some of the basic concepts of contemporary Marxian class analysis and propose a realist interpretation of these concepts. First, I discuss the structural focus of recent writing on class, particularly that produced out of the Althusserian tradition of Marxism. Second, I argue that the concept of power not only figures in, but lies at the heart of, the Marxian analysis of capitalism. Having established this, I then discuss how the concept of power figures not simply in the analysis of the basic structure of capitalist class relations, but also in the analysis of the forms of economic and political organization of classes and their struggles. In short, the Marxian analysis of class power is not essentialist and does not reduce all power to the level of production relations. Finally, I return to some of the recent critics of Marxism, arguing that while they quite properly reject the essentialism entailed by certain variants of Marxist historicism, they do no better, simply substituting in its place a non-Marxist historicism. As I will conclude, "power" does not figure in Marxian theory as an "ultimate explanation" of anything, a virtue of Marxism that should be emulated by any adequate social theory.

Class and the Structure of Capitalism in Recent Writings

Although there are important disagreements among Marxian theorists about the precise meaning and implications of the concept of class, there is a general agreement that classes are "social ag-

116

gregates that occupy common positions within the social relations of production."[1] This understanding of class is a *structural* one, which focuses on the basic economic positions, and the enduring relations between positions, which constitute capitalist society as such. Poulantzas writes that class "designates certain objective places occupied by the social agents in the division of labor: places which are independent of the will of these agents."[2] This is not to suggest, as Poulantzas's remark might, that class relations are independent of the practical activities of members of classes. But it does highlight an important, if sometimes overlooked, consensus within Marxian theory that it is only with reference to structural relationships that the activities of members of classes become fully intelligible. Even E. P. Thompson, who has insistently criticized structural Marxist accounts of class for their reification of the concept and their neglect of the texture of class experience, contends that class is an enduring historical relationship (see the section "Class Formation" later in this chapter).

On the Marxian view class is not simply a structural relation; it is a structural relation of production. In the most general and commonly understood terms, class relations are relations between those who own and control the means of production (capitalists) and those direct producers dependent on the owners for employment (workers). Originating with Marx, Marxian theorists have contended that this division into two mutually dependent, and mutually antagonistic, classes is the *differentia specifica* of capitalism, and that the theoretical analysis of these basic relations holds the key to the analysis of capitalist societies. This is not to say that Marxian theory posits that these two classes, in their theoretically postulated purity, exhaust the relations that obtain in any particular capitalist society. Poulantzas, clarifying a view that has always been at the center of Marxian analysis, writes: "A concrete society [a social formation] involves more than two classes, in so far as it is composed of various modes and forms of production. No social formation involves only two classes, but the two fundamental classes of any social formation are those of the

---

[1]Alan Hunt, "The Identification of the Working Class," in Alan Hunt, ed., *Classes and Class Structure* (London: Lawrence and Wishart, 1977), p. 98.

[2]Nicos Poulantzas, *Classes and Contemporary Capitalism* (London: New Left Books, 1975), p. 14.

dominant mode of production in that formation."[3] In other words, while contemporary capitalist societies are not characterized simply by capitalists and workers in stark polarity, these are the two most important classes in these societies. The Marxist analysis of these basic classes and their properties is based upon what we have called earlier, following Giddens, a methodological epoché—a theoretical abstraction that isolates certain general, underlying structures in their "pure" form.[4] Although only capitalists and workers figure at the level of discussing the basic features of capitalism in general, as we descend the ladder of abstraction to analyze concrete societies and specific conjunctural moments, Marxian analysis introduces other classes, relations, and causal agents into the picture, viewing actual social outcomes as a "rich totality of many determinations and relations."[5]

A number of contemporary Marxian theorists, drawing upon Marx's observations in the *Grundrisse* and *Capital*, have elucidated some of the major features of the class relations of capitalism by contrasting them with those of the feudal mode of production. Etienne Balibar points out that feudal class relations were hierarchical relations between lords and peasants, typically sustained by oaths of personal allegiance.[6] Peasants were characteristically bound to the land by tradition, backed up by the military force unilaterally wielded by their lords. The relation between lord and peasant was indissolubly economic and political. It not only involved the appropriation on the part of the lord of a part of the product, a "surplus product," of the peasant's labor; it involved the direct, "naked" appropriation of the surplus through the po-

[3]Ibid., p. 22.

[4]Poulantzas is good on this point: "The mode of production constitutes an abstract-formal object *which does not exist in the strong sense*" (italics mine). In other words, the concept of the mode of production is an abstraction denoting a complex social structure that is real, but that exists insofar as it is instantiated in the concrete practices of specific societies. Thus, only social formations exist "in the strong sense," although these formations are structured by modes of production. See Nicos Poulantzas, *Political Power and Social Classes* (London: New Left Books, 1973), pp. 15–17.

[5]Karl Marx, *Grundrisse*, trans. Martin Nicolaus (New York: Vintage, 1973), p. 100.

[6]Etienne Balibar, "On the Basic Concepts of Historical Materialism," in Louis Althusser and Etienne Balibar, *Reading Capital* (London: New Left Books, 1970), pp. 209–53.

litical domination of the peasant by the lord. Feudalism, as Perry Anderson argues, was a structure of "parcellized sovereignty," based on the lord's control of territory and of the means of violence.[7] All existence for the peasant took place within the literal "domain" of the lord. Poulantzas, however, following Balibar, distinguishes between economic ownership—"real economic control of the means of production, i.e., the power to assign the means of production to given uses and so to dispose of the products obtained"—and possession, "the capacity to put the means of production into operation."[8] While the lords were a class of appropriators, who both economically and politically dominated the peasants, the peasants as a class maintained effective control over the means of production sufficient to guarantee their own means of subsistence. Surplus was thus extracted visibly, in "palpable form," as surplus labor—peasants were required to work a certain number of days every month on a separate plot of land for the lord. The surplus labor of the peasant was thus separated, in both space and time, from the labor necessary for subsistence; and the performance of surplus labor was regulated by traditional obligations and customs, and enforced by the direct and localized political power of the lord.[9]

Contemporary Marxist theorists have written a great deal on the transition from feudalism to capitalism, emphasizing two basic developments. The first was the development of the modern state, which centralized political power and territorial control, undermining much of the power of the feudal lords and establishing juridical equality among homogenous subject populations. The second was the development of a class of wage laborers dispossessed of the means of production and possessing nothing but their ability

---

[7]Perry Anderson, *Lineages of the Absolutist State* (London: New Left Books, 1974), p. 19. See also Marc Bloch, *Feudal Society*, vol. 1 (Chicago: University of Chicago Press, 1974), pp. 241–54, for a discussion of the feudal manor as a self-contained political-economic entity.

[8]Poulantzas, *Political Power*, pp. 26–27, and *Classes*, p. 18.

[9]This analysis draws from Marx's observation that "it is evident that in all forms in which the direct labourer remains the 'possessor' of the means of production and labour conditions necessary for the production of his own means of subsistence, the property relationship must simultaneously appear as a direct relationship of lordship and bondage, so that the direct producer is not free" (*Capital*, vol. 3 [New York: International Publishers, 1967], p. 790).

to work.[10] Marx writes: "For the conversion of his money into capital, therefore, the owner of money must meet in the market with the free labourer, free in the double sense, that as a free man he can dispose of his labour-power as his own commodity, and that on the other hand he has no other commodity for sale, is short of everything necessary for the realization of his labour power."[11]

Labor markets are thus a necessary feature of capitalism—workers are legally free to dispose of their ability to work as they choose, and there is no authoritative allocation of labor. On the Marxian view, however, the existence of labor markets takes its importance from its connection to production. The commodity sold on the labor market is not labor, but labor *power*. What is sold to the capitalist is neither a completed task or product (which embodies labor) nor a definite amount of labor specified in advance. It is an abstract capacity to labor on the part of human agents, a capacity that is only concretized, and rendered useful to the capitalist, when it is exercised in the labor process. It is not in the sphere of exchange but in the sphere of production that labor power assumes its significance as a capacity to act whose usefulness to the capitalist is contingent upon its proper exercise.

Capitalism as a mode of production is based, then, upon the purchase of labor power by the capitalist and its translation into actual labor in the labor process, for the purpose of producing commodities. The worker typically engages in this process in order to "make a living"; the real interest of workers is to earn their means of subsistence in the form of a wage. The capitalist typically engages in this process for quite a different reason—in order to earn a profit, to earn more than has been laid out in investment. This mode of production differs from feudalism in some important respects that are pertinent to the question of power.[12]

[10]See Rodney Hilton, ed., *The Transition from Feudalism to Capitalism* (London: New Left Books, 1976); Maurice Dobb, *Studies in the Development of Capitalism* (New York: International Publishers, 1976); and Immanuel Wallerstein, *The Modern World System* (New York: Academic Press, 1976). On the state, see Anderson, *Lineages*, and Peter Gourevitch, "The International System and Regime Formation: A Critical Review of Anderson and Wallerstein," *Comparative Politics* 10 (April 1978), 419–38. On labor markets, see Robert Brenner, "The Origins of Capitalist Development: A Critique of Neo-Smithian Marxism," *New Left Review*, no. 104 (1977), 25–92.

[11]*Capital*, vol. 1, p. 169.

[12]See Balibar, "Historical Materialism."

First, the class relation between capital and labor is a purely "economic" relation in that it is based on formally free contracts and economic necessity; the capitalist, unlike the feudal lord, does not possess powers of physical coercion and control over territory, and thus cannot directly employ political means to enforce compliance. Moreover, there are no traditional bonds and obligations between class actors. All is reduced to the "cash nexus." (There are, of course, important political and ideological determinants of class relations, but they are not directly present within these relations, which are relatively autonomous and work according to the modus operandi of market exchange and economic necessity.)[13]

Second, the securing of the subsistence of the worker and the surplus (profit) of the capitalist, respectively, is achieved through the market. Laborers do not produce their own subsistence directly in the form of their own useful concrete products, in accordance with traditional rights and customs; and capitalists do not appropriate surplus directly in the form of surplus labor or product, in accordance with traditional obligations enforced upon laborers. Rather, workers secure their subsistence through exchanging their wages for products on the market, and capitalists secure their profit through their efficient employment of labor power, and through the sale of the products in the market and the realization of a price greater than the costs of production.

Third, unlike feudalism, necessary and surplus labor are not separated in time and space; both are performed simultaneously and conjointly. This is related to the previous point—the surplus appropriated by capitalists in the form of profit is not directly appropriated as surplus labor, but only gotten indirectly through the sale of commodities. The crucial implication of this is that, unlike feudal lords, capitalists do not know in advance of the circulation of commodities whether they have appropriated surplus (moreover, their very survival depends, directly and in the short run, on whether or not they have done so). They are thus forced to maximize the efficiency of the labor process and to translate the

---

[13]As Marx writes: "The contrast between the power, based on the personal relations of dominion and servitude, that is conferred by landed property, and the impersonal power that is given by money, is well expressed by the two French proverbs: 'Nulle terre sans seigneur,' and 'L'argent n'a pas de maître'" (*Capital*, vol. 1, p. 46).

labor power they have purchased into as much actual labor as possible. This means that capitalists directly control the entire labor process in the interests of profit maximization. Unlike the requirements of feudal surplus labor, which were set in advance outside of the labor process in accordance with custom and manorial procedures, the labor process under capitalism is purely "despotic"— capitalists try to get as much labor as they can, by whatever means possible, from laborers (even the law is often a negligible constraint on capitalists, given their actual control of the spatial confines of the factory or office).[14] If under feudalism, then, the powers of economic appropriation and possession are separated, the latter being possessed by the peasant class, under capitalism the working class is dispossessed of both powers, which are united in the hands of the capitalist.

Marxism and Class Powers

Contemporary Marxian theorists of capitalism have explicitly acknowledged the centrality of power to their analyses. Ellen Wood insists that the "disposition of power" is at the center of Marxian political economy, a virtue that distinguishes it from marginalism's

[14]Cf. Marx: "Division of labour within the workshop implies the undisputed authority of the capitalist over men, that are but parts of a mechanism that belongs to him" (*Capital*, vol. 1, p. 356). Marx, however, while emphasizing the "despotic" power of capital, also treats this power as an "embodiment" of structural relations and insists that the color of this power is shaped by dynamics of capital accumulation. It is worth quoting him at length: "The authority assumed by the capitalist as the personification of capital in the direct process of production, the social function performed by him in his capacity as manager and ruler of production, is essentially different from the authority exercised on the basis of production by means of slaves, serfs, etc.

"Whereas, on the basis of capitalist production, the mass of direct producers is confronted by the social character of their production in the form of strictly regulating authority and a social mechanism of the labour-process organised as a complete hierarchy—this authority reaching its bearers, however, only as the personification of the conditions of labour in contrast to labour, and not as political or theocratic rulers as under earlier modes of production—among the bearers of this authority, the capitalists themselves, who confront one another only as commodity-owners, there reigns complete anarchy within which the social interrelations of production assert themselves only as an overwhelming natural law in relation to individual free will" (*Capital*, vol. 3, p. 881). The market, then, both shapes and places constraints on the exercise of capitalist power.

exclusive concern with commodities.[15] And Poulantzas, to whose analysis of power we shall return, contends that "class relations are relations of power."[16] The concept of power is ubiquitous in Marxian analysis; and yet while certain theorists have offered arguments regarding the meaning of the concept (see the section "Objections Overturned" later in this chapter), there has been little attention to meta-theoretical issues in the analysis of power. More specifically, while the Marxian analysis of power is implicitly realist, this point and certain corollary points regarding what we have called the "dialectic of power" have not been made sufficiently explicit.

This is peculiar given the great emphasis Marx placed on labor power as the key to capitalist production. Marx writes that labor is the "motive power of capital." He contends that "the laborer therefore constantly produces material, objective wealth, but in the form of an *alien power* that dominates and exploits him" (italics mine).[17] This text refers to the fact that the surplus value produced by the working class functions as additional capital to be reinvested in the cycle of production and exploitation, "chaining" the laborers to constant capital and to the capitalist, and further reducing their status. It highlights the centrality to Marx's analysis of the capacities of the working class, which reproduces its own domination through its participation in the practices of production.[18] Domination is not simply imposed on workers, and the subordination of workers is not constituted by their heteronomous responses to the behaviors of capitalists. Rather, domination is an enduring feature of class relations, which are also characterized by the powers of the subordinate element, the working class.

---

[15]Ellen Meiksins Wood, "The Separation of the Economic and the Political in Capitalism," *New Left Review*, no. 127 (May–June 1981), 66–95.

[16]Poulantzas, *Political Power*, p. 99. He writes in a realist vein: "The relations of production and the relationships which comprise them (economic ownership/possession) are expressed in the form of powers which derive from them, in other words class powers" (*Classes*, p. 21).

[17]*Capital*, vol. 1, p. 57.

[18]Cf. Marx: "If the capitalist mode of production presupposes this definite social form of the conditions of production, so does it reproduce it continually. It produces not merely the material products, but reproduces continually the production relations in which the former are produced, and thereby also the corresponding distribution relations" (*Capital*, vol. 3, p. 879).

The basic power workers possess as such is labor power. The concept of labor power lies at the heart of Marx's analysis of capitalism. Marx defines labor power as "the aggregate of those mental and physical abilities existing in a human being, which he exercises whenever he produces a use-value [product] of any description."[19] As he makes clear, the general concept of labor power implicates a social ontology and refers to certain basic properties of human individuals, or *human powers*.[20] Marx writes in a classic passage:

> We pre-suppose labour in a form that stamps it as exclusively human. A spider conducts operations that resemble those of a weaver, and a bee puts to shame many an architect in the construction of her cells. But what distinguishes the worst architect from the best of bees is this, that the architect raises his structure in imagination before he erects it in reality. At the end of every human labour-process, we get a result that already existed in the imagination of the labourer at its commencement. He not only effects a change of form in the material on which he works, but he also realises a purpose of his own that gives the law to his modus operandi, and to which he must subordinate his will.[21]

As Marx makes clear, however, though the concept of labor power denotes certain species characteristics of humans, it figures as an explanatory concept only in the analysis of capitalism. He writes in the *Grundrisse*: "This example of labour shows strikingly how even the most abstract categories, despite their validity—precisely because of their abstractness—for all epochs, are nevertheless, in the specific character of this abstraction, themselves likewise a product of historic relations, and possess their full validity only for and within these relations."[22]

In all modes of production laborers possess and exercise socially

---

[19]*Capital*, vol. 1, p. 167.

[20]On human powers, see chap. 3, "Agency," of Roy Bhaskar, *The Possibility of Naturalism: A Philosophical Critique of the Contemporary Human Sciences* (Atlantic Highlands, N.J.: Humanities Press, 1979).

[21]*Capital*, vol. 1, p. 178.

[22]*Grundrisse*, p. 105. On this point, see Derek Sayer, *Marx's Method: Ideology, Science, and Critique in 'Capital'* (Atlantic Highlands, N.J.: Humanities Press, 1979).

defined capacities to labor. But only in the capitalist mode of production does productive activity exist qua productive activity, disembedded, to use Polanyi's phrase, from other social practices.[23] As Marx notes, only under capitalism does laboring, the paradigmatic human transformative activity, become not a mode of social being but a *means* of social existence and of human subsistence.[24] Under capitalism labor power becomes a commodity, the only commodity possessed by the worker; and the central dynamic of capitalism is the purchase of this commodity by the capitalist, and its translation into actual labor productive of profitable commodities.

Marx writes in *Capital* that as a commodity the capacity to labor becomes abstract, labor power pure and simple—the ability to labor irrespective of any other social meanings. It is, from the point of view of the production of commodities, devoid of all particular characteristics as concrete types of labor, and reduced to a common denominator whose function is simply to be employed to produce commodities profitably. Marx describes the ways in which craft production and craft skills are broken down, and how they give way to the production of commodities as cheaply and as profitably as possible. The specific skills embodied in labor power are, from the point of view of the capitalist, at best "factors of production" to be employed in the pursuit of profit, at worst impediments to cost-efficient production. Cornelius Castoriadis, highlighting this reduction of specific skills and powers to abstract labor power, writes: "in real life, capitalism is obliged to base itself on people's capacity for self-organization, on the individual and collective creativity without which it would not survive for a day, while the whole 'official organization' of modern society both ignores and seeks to suppress these abilities to the utmost."[25]

[23] See Karl Polanyi, *Primitive, Archaic, and Modern Economics* (Boston: Beacon Press, 1968).

[24] As the early Marx writes on estranged labor, reflecting upon power and spatial relations: "[Man] is at home when he is not working, and when he is working he is not at home.... What is animal becomes human and what is human becomes animal" ("Economic and Philosophical Manuscripts," in Robert C. Tucker, ed., *The Marx-Engels Reader* [New York: Norton, 1972], p. 60).

[25] Cornelius Castoriadis, *Workers' Councils and the Economics of Self-Management*, quoted in Michael Albert and Robin Hahnel, "A Ticket to Ride: More Locations on a Class Map," in Pat Walker, ed., *Between Labor and Capital* (Boston: South End Press, 1979), p. 259.

It is in the labor process that this contradiction—"the simultaneous exclusion and participation of people in relation to their activities"— is worked out. It is here that labor power, as a commodity purchased by the capitalist, is employed; and it is here that the *powers* possessed by the working class are exercised under the rubric of the capitalist. Marx writes: "The labour process, turned into the process by which the capitalist consumes labour-power, exhibits two characteristic phenomena. First, the labourer works under the control of the capitalist. Secondly, the product is the property of the capitalist and not that of the labourer, the immediate producer."[26] The capitalist class thus possesses two basic powers: the power of control over investment, or appropriation; and the power to direct and supervise the labor process itself, or what Balibar calls economic possession. The capitalist class has power over the working class insofar as it possesses the power to determine the conditions of labor. The capitalist purchases labor power in a legally free contractual agreement; for a specified wage the workers agree to work for a specified number of hours. For that time the labor power of the workers legally belongs to the capitalist, who (metaphorically) consumes it in the form of actual labor, appropriating the products of that labor and the revenues realized through the sale of those products. The capital-labor relation is thus a relation of domination and subordination as I have defined it; it is a relation based on the *asymmetrical distribution of powers*. It is also a relation characterized by the reciprocity of practice discussed in Chapter 3. It is easy to see how this is so.

Workers, as owners of no property but their labor power, are dependent on the capitalist class in order to employ their skills and to earn a living. Capitalists, as owners of capital (which includes not only raw materials and instruments of production, but a wage fund, or "variable capital"), are dependent on the working class in order to set the production process in motion and to produce commodities that can be sold for a profit on the market. The relation between these two collectivities is thus one of mutual dependence and reciprocity. The structure of this relation, the various forms it has taken over the course of capitalist development, and

---

[26]*Capital*, vol. 1, p. 185.

the chronic negotiation of the exercise of power have been a primary focus of Marxian theory.

Marx, in *Capital*, discusses the transformations in the power of capital in the course of capitalist development, distinguishing three stages in the development of the domination of capital. The first stage he calls *simple cooperation*, whereby many workers are organized under the control of a single capitalist. Here workers, under the general supervision of capital, employ their craft skills in order to produce commodities for the capitalist. The second stage he calls *manufacture*, which involves cooperation based on the division of labor within the factory. This stage involves a more extensive supervision of labor and also involves the development of the "detail laborer."[27] The laborer here no longer produces an entire product, but specializes through repetition in producing a part of a product. Marx calls the third stage *machinofacture*, which is manufacture based on the introduction of machinery into production. Here the speed and rhythm of work is subordinated to that of the machine, which is of course owned and controlled by the capitalist in the pursuit of profit. Marx describes the effects of this as follows:

> At the same time that factory work exhausts the nervous system to the uttermost, it does away with the many-sided play of the muscles and confiscates every atom of freedom, both in bodily and intellectual activity ... it is not the workman that employs the instrument of labour, but the instruments of labour that employ the workman. But it is only in the factory system that this inversion acquires technical and palpable reality. By means of its conversion into an automaton, the instrument of labour confronts the labourer, during the labour process, in the shape of capital, dry, dead labour, that dominates, and pumps dry, living labour-power. ... The technical subordination of the workman to the uniform motion of the machine instruments of labour ... gives rise to a barrack discipline, which is elaborated into a complete system in the factory, and which fully develops the before-mentioned labour of over-looking, thereby dividing the work-people into operatives and overlookers, into private soldiers and sergeants of an industrial army.[28]

[27]See *Capital*, vol. 1, pp. 349–68. The phenomenon of the detail laborer was, of course, recognized by Adam Smith in his famous discussion of the pin factory in chap. 1, "The Division of Labor," *The Wealth of Nations* (New York: Modern Library, 1965).

[28]*Capital*, vol. 1, pp. 423–24.

This process of structuration, of the transformation of the formal (legal) subordination of the worker through the labor contract into what Marx calls the "real subordination" of the factory system, is an outcome of the capital accumulation process and is generated by two constraints: (1) the capitalist's need to minimize costs in the interests of profitability,[29] and (2) the capitalist's need to minimize worker autonomy, skill, and craft knowledge. In order to produce profitably, it is not only imperative to introduce cost-effective technologies and production processes; it is also necessary to control labor time and to eliminate traditional craft and labor practices in order to maximize the amount of labor gotten out of labor power.[30] Giddens argues that the Marxian analysis of this process highlights a crucial feature of capitalist society—the radical transformation of the social control of space and time.[31] Under capitalism production becomes spatially concentrated and methodically organized in factories, and the labor process becomes governed by the strict control and accounting of time. Erik Olin Wright argues that the emphasis on this constitutes the chief virtue of Marx's labor theory of value and exploitation.[32]

Marx saw, as any reader of *Capital* may recall, that struggles over the disposition of time, more specifically over the amount of time that workers would be working for capitalists to increase surplus value–profit, were central to the development of capitalism.

[29]Max Weber refers to the "conditions affecting the optimization of calculable performance of labor engaged in carrying out specifications" (*Economy and Society*, ed. Guenther Roth and Claus Wittich [Berkeley: University of California Press, 1978], p. 150).

[30]See Stephen Marglin, "What Do Bosses Do?" *Review of Radical Political Economics* 6 (1974), 33–60, on the early establishment of control over labor time. See also Herbert Gintis, "The Nature of Labor Exchange and the Theory of Capitalist Production," *Review of Radical Political Economics* 8 (Summer 1976), 36–54, for a critique of the failure of marginalist economic theory to account for this.

[31]Anthony Giddens, *A Contemporary Critique of Historical Materialism* (Berkeley: University of California Press, 1981), pp. 117–21. For an interesting, non-Marxist account of the modern transformation of time, see David S. Landes, *Revolution in Time: Clocks and the Making of the Modern World* (Cambridge, Mass.: Harvard University Press, 1983).

[32]See Erik Olin Wright, "The Value Controversy and Social Research," *New Left Review*, no. 116 (July–August 1979), 52–82, and E. P. Thompson, "Time, Work Discipline, and Industrial Capitalism," *Past and Present*, no. 38 (1967), 56–97. For a more general discussion of the labor theory of value and exploitation, see Ian Steedman et al., *The Value Controversy* (London: Verso, 1981).

According to Marx, these struggles over "the working day" (the title of chapter 10 of *Capital*, volume 1) could be divided into two kinds: struggles over the length of the working day (or what Marx called struggles about absolute surplus value) and struggles over the labor process and the intensity of work (by minimizing the time necessary to produce commodities in order to produce more efficiently, reduce prices, and remain profitable, capitalists were also reducing the costs of reproducing the labor force, reducing necessary labor time, and increasing what Marx calls relative surplus value).

Contemporary Marxian theorists have pursued and extended this analysis of the mechanisms of class power. Particularly influential has been Harry Braverman's *Labor and Monopoly Capital: The Degradation of Work in the Twentieth Century*.[33] Braverman describes in great detail the reduction of the craft skills of workers and the institutional separation of the conception and execution of production in the course of capitalist development, a process he calls "deskilling." Braverman devotes a great deal of attention in particular to the various capitalist strategies of securing control over the labor process, particularly the time-and-motion studies initiated by Frederick Taylor and the Scientific Management Movement in the United States.

The controversies within Marxian theory over Braverman's thesis highlight the centrality of an implicitly realist understanding of power in Marxian analysis. The most general objection against Braverman has been summarized by Andrew Zimbalist: "The most common Marxist criticism has been that Braverman ignored or minimized the role of class struggle in forming the labor process ... that as a result capital is portrayed as having uncontested, unilateral control over the labor process; Taylorism and technology are juggernauts introduced at will to subjugate the workforce."[34] Braverman is seen as having presented Taylorism as the triumphant

---

[33]Harry Braverman, *Labor and Monopoly Capital: The Degradation of Work in the Twentieth Century* (New York: Monthly Review Press, 1974). See also Andrew Zimbalist, ed., *Case Studies in the Labor Process* (New York: Monthly Review Press, 1979), and Dan Clawson, *Bureaucracy and the Labor Process* (New York: Monthly Review Press, 1980), for empirical analyses following Braverman's model.

[34]Zimbalist, p. xii.

solution to the problem of capitalist control of the labor process, committing what Craig Littler and Graeme Salaman have called the "Panacea Fallacy."[35] Rather, it is argued by the critics, emphasis should be placed on the variability of control, on its specific mechanisms, and on forms of worker resistance. In other words, Braverman's analysis is seen as having minimized what we have called the reciprocal and negotiated character of relations of power.

Two subsequent studies by Marxian theorists have addressed these problems. The title of the books, Richard Edwards's *Contested Terrain* and Michael Burawoy's *Manufacturing Consent,* indicate the centrality of working-class power and struggle in the labor process.[36] Edwards views the workplace as a "battleground" where social outcomes are the result of structural constraints and collective strategies. He traces the specific forms of control of the labor process over the course of American history, arguing that Taylorism was one of many forms, and never the dominant one, of capitalist control. Edwards insists that we distinguish between the preferences and strategies of capitalists and the real structure of power; and he further insists that transformations of the structure of power were the products of the activities of capitalists *and* workers. Edwards discerns three different forms of control of production, each the resultant of class conflict and managerial strategies: (1) *supervision* by the foreman, which characterized early capitalism before the advent of large corporations; (2) *technical control*, where the continuous flow of production and the pace of machinery (regulated by the capitalist) served as the primary mechanism of control of labor; and (3) *bureaucratic control*, characterized by the bureaucratic "institutionalization of organized power" within the production unit through finely graded divisions and the stratification of workers through job titles, pay and promotion schemes, and the proliferation of supervisory positions. This form of control of labor is, according to Edwards, the dominant form in contemporary capitalist societies. And, he insists, it

[35]See Craig Littler and Graeme Salaman, "Bravermania and Beyond: Recent Theories of the Labour Process," *Sociology* 16 (May 1982), 251–69.

[36]Richard Edwards, *Contested Terrain: The Transformation of the Workplace in the Twentieth Century* (New York: Basic Books, 1979), and Michael Burawoy, *Manufacturing Consent: Changes in the Labor Process under Monopoly Capitalism* (Chicago: University of Chicago Press, 1979).

must be seen as the outcome of class struggles in which workers and their collective organization through unions played a crucial role. Edwards thus analyzes both the basic powers of capitalists and workers in production and the *organizational power* of workers through their unions; although he suggests that unions in fact reinforce the bureaucratic procedures of capitalist labor control in exchange for higher wages in the large corporate sector of the economy.[37]

Burawoy also focuses on bureaucratic mechanisms of power, referring to the large corporation as an "internal state" with its own "internal labor market." But he also emphasizes what he calls the "organization of consent." He insists that contemporary theorists confront new realities of labor control and thus must supplement Marx's analysis: "Marx has no place in his theory of the labor process for the organization of consent, for the necessity to elicit a willingness to cooperate in the translation of labor power into labor... the labor process, therefore, must be understood in terms of the specific combinations of force and consent that elicit cooperation in the pursuit of profit."[38] Burawoy argues that the control of the labor process by capital involves the cooperation of workers in the exercise of their labor power, and that mechanisms of consent, not simply supervision and degradation, are important elements of this control. He proposes that the labor process be viewed as a "game" in which consent is generated and sustained, and he labels this game "making out"—the seductive practice of fulfilling quotas and getting assigned work done with the least amount of effort. This game has a logic of its own, which lures even the most antagonistic workers (Burawoy is a Marxist sociologist who spent nine months of participant observation at a major U.S. corporate machine shop) into participating in the interest of achievement, piece-rates, and promotion. In the terms developed in Chapter 3, "making out" induces workers to pursue their *real interest* in secure employment and income. Burawoy argues that this form of pragmatic acceptance of capitalist domination on the part of workers disperses conflict laterally (between workers) in-

[37]On this theme see also André Gorz, ed., *The Division of Labor: The Labor Process and Class Struggle in Modern Capitalism* (Atlantic Highlands, N.J.: Humanities Press, 1976).
[38]Burawoy, p. 30.

stead of vertically (between workers and capitalists), muting class antagonisms. He also insists, however, that this legitimacy of class relations is chronically contested and negotiated as class actors redefine their interests. "The game," he writes, "does not reflect an underlying harmony of interests; on the contrary, it is responsible for and generates that harmony. The sources of the game itself lie not in a preordained value consensus but in historically specific struggles to adapt to the deprivation inherent in work and in struggles with management to define the rules."[39]

The analyses of Edwards and Burawoy highlight a crucial feature of power discussed in Chapter 3—that its exercise is contingent and is continually negotiated by the parties to power relations. Marxian theory has produced an extensive literature describing the mechanisms through which capitalists have been able to secure, maintain, and further their power over workers and their control over the labor process. This effort on the part of capital involves various strategies, some aimed intentionally at gaining control over labor, others concerned primarily with the accumulation of capital and only consequentially concerned with the subordination of labor.[40] But in most of the Marxian analyses of this process the working class is not viewed as a passive object of the strategies of capital. Rather, the strategies and responses of workers—running the gamut from shop-floor resistance to collective economic and political organization—are acknowledged as playing a crucial role in the exercise and reproduction of class power.[41]

Class Formation: Agency, Struggle, and Collective Organization

As we have seen, the Marxian analysis of the relations of production in capitalist society provides an account of the distribution of class powers and the contestation and transformation of these

[39]Ibid., p. 82.

[40]See Katherine Stone, "The Origins of Job Structures in the Steel Industry," *Review of Radical Political Economics* 6 (Summer 1974), 61–97, and Gabriel Kolko, *Main Currents in American History* (New York: Harper & Row, 1976).

[41]See David Montgomery, *Worker's Control in America* (Cambridge: Cambridge University Press, 1979), and Nina Shapiro-Perl, "The Piece Rate: Class Struggle on the Shop Floor," in Zimbalist, for discussions of forms of working class resistance.

powers. It would be a mistake to imply, however, that the Marxian analysis of class power is exhausted at this level. For Marxian theorists have not only provided analyses of the basic economic structure of capitalism and the transformations of the relations of production and the labor process; they have also focused on the more specific forms of class agency and class organization.

E. P. Thompson, from within the Marxian tradition, has presented the most forceful critique of a view of class pitched exclusively at the level of the structure of the mode of production. Thompson argues for a thoroughly historical approach, viewing history as "unmastered human practice," and examining the finely textured realm of class experience. "No historical category," he writes, "has been more misunderstood, tormented, transfixed, and de-historicized than the category of social class; a self-defining historical formation, which men and women make out of their own experience of struggle, has been reduced to a static category, or an effect of an ulterior structure of which men are not the masters but the vectors."[42]

Thompson's criticism is directed against the deliberately exaggerated claim made by Althusser that for Marxism history is a process without a subject. But it is also an eloquent argument against the reduction of the varied forms of class activity and culture to their structural determinants.[43] Perry Anderson has remarked, however, that Thompson's dismissiveness toward structural theory is not only too sweeping; it also renders unintellible the significance of class agency that Thompson himself wishes to register.[44] G. A. Cohen writes of Thompson's *The Making of the English Working*

[42]E. P. Thompson, *The Poverty of Theory and Other Essays* (New York: Monthly Review Press, 1978), p. 46.

[43]On Althusser's structuralism, see Ted Benton, *The Rise and Fall of Structural Marxism: Althusser and His Influence* (New York: St. Martin's, 1984), and Steven B. Smith, *Reading Althusser: An Essay on Structural Marxism* (Ithaca, N.Y.: Cornell University Press, 1984).

[44]Anderson has suggested that, while Thompson's emphasis on historical agency is indispensable, his methodological assertions about history as "unmastered human practice" would, if taken to their logical conclusion, undermine class analysis altogether, rendering Thompson's own research into the formation of the English working class unintelligible. "The paradoxical result of Thompson's critique of Althusser," he writes, "is thus actually to reproduce the fundamental failure of the latter, by a polemical inversion" (*Arguments within English Marxism* [London: Verso, 1980], p. 21).

Class: "Thompson asks, in effect, 'Under what conditions may we identify the working class as an active historical subject?' He supplies a sensitive answer and a book which is a brilliant illustration of it. But there is a distinct question, namely 'In virtue of what do members of the working class count as members of that class?' The traditional answer is structural, and rightly so. Issues relevant to the first question have deformed Thompson's treatment of the second."[45] Giddens's notion of the "duality of structure" is helpful here; it emphasizes that class structure is *both* the medium and the effect of the practices of members of classes.[46]

In this light we should note that in Marxian theory the concept of class is paradigmatically ambiguous, denoting both a structural relation between economic positions and the collectivities that occupy these positions and reproduce them in the course of their activity. Class analysis has concerned itself with both class structure and *class formation*— the process whereby class collectivities develop group solidarities and act collectively to negotiate and transform class relations. This distinction between class structure and class formation parallels the classical Marxist distinction between class-in-itself and class-for-itself.

Adam Przeworski highlights the centrality of class self-organization, and its irreducibility to structural relationships: "Classes as historical actors are not given uniquely by any objective positions, not even those of workers and capitalists... the very relations between classes as historical actors (classes-in-struggle) and places within the relations of production must become problematic. *Classes are not given uniquely by any objective positions because they constitute effects of struggles, and these struggles are not determined uniquely by the relations of production.*"[47] Przeworski refers here to political determinants of class formation, which, as

---

[45]G. A. Cohen, *Karl Marx's Theory of History: A Defense* (Princeton, N.J.: Princeton University Press, 1978), p. 76.

[46]See my "Realism and Social Scientific Theory: A Comment on Porpora," *Journal for the Theory of Social Behaviour* 13 (October 1983), 301–308.

[47]Adam Przeworski, "Proletariat into a Class: The Process of Class Formation from Karl Kautsky's 'The Class Struggle' to Recent Controversies," *Politics and Society* 7 (1977), 367. For further discussion of class formation see Erik Olin Wright, "Varieties of Marxist Conceptions of Class Structure," *Politics and Society* 9 (1980), 323–70, and "Class and Occupation," *Theory and Society* 9 (January 1980), 177–214.

we shall see in Chapter 5, have been analyzed at length by contemporary Marxian theorists. He also insists on something we discussed in Chapter 3 with reference to Hindess's cautionary remark about "interests"—that the identities of parties to relations of power, and their corresponding subjective interests, are the contingent outcomes of struggle and are never given in advance. Class struggle, it follows, is an inherent feature of class relations. Poulantzas writes: "Social classes do not firstly exist as such, and only then enter into a class struggle. Social classes coincide with class practices, i.e., the class struggle, and are only defined in their mutual opposition."[48] Conflicts between the real interests of workers and capitalists—in secure employment and profit, respectively—structure antagonism into the very foundation of class relations. On the basis of these antagonisms particular class collectivities develop specific forms of solidarity and organization.

The phrase "on the basis of" is ambiguous, suggesting that the forms of organization are somehow less essential and less real than the structure of production relations. Contemporary Marxists have insisted that class organizations are rooted in class structure, meaning that class structure establishes certain parameters of struggle—social identity, interests, and most important, *power*. The direction of much recent research, however, attests to the seriousness accorded class formation and class organization as sui generis realities. Erik Olin Wright has introduced the term "class capacities" to cover these forms of collective organization. Wright defines class capacities as *"the social relations within a class* which to a greater or lesser extent unite the agents of that class into a class formation ... capacities constitute the potential basis for the realization of class interests within the class struggle."[49] He distinguishes between *structural capacities* and *organizational capacities*. The former are those properties of classes generated by the basic structure of capitalism itself. Most important would be what we have called class powers. The ability of the working class to dispose of its labor, and the ability of the capitalist class to dispose of its capital, are structural properties of these collectivities that are drawn upon in struggle. Wright also discusses the structural property of what

[48]Poulantzas, *Classes*, p. 14.
[49]Erik Olin Wright, *Class, Crisis, and the State* (London: Verso, 1979), p. 98.

Marx called "the collective laborer": the development of capitalism brings many workers together under the same factory roof, creating the possibility of an increased sense of commonality and solidarity. Organizational capacities, on the other hand, are "those links which are constituted by the conscious organization of members of that class"[50]—mutual aid societies, trade unions and union confederations, and political parties. These concepts highlight the importance for many Marxists of the power of economic and political organizations and of the many levels at which power is contested and brought to bear in capitalist society.

Claus Offe and Helmut Wiesenthal, building upon the work of Mancur Olson, argue that in capitalist society there are two "logics of collective action," which correspond to the class division between capitalists and workers. Their major thesis is that "differences in the position of a group in the class structure (we consider here only the classes of labor and capital), not only lead to differences in power that the organizations can acquire, but also lead to differences in the *associational practices*, or logics of collective action, by which organizations of capital and labor try to improve their respective position vis-à-vis each other."[51] While capitalists are a relatively small group, possessing financial resources and a monological, easily defined utilitarian interest in profitability, workers are a much larger, more heterogeneous group, to whom the costs of organization are much higher. Instrumental rationality will not lead workers to organize themselves; this will only occur if workers can develop a sense of collective identity and solidarity. The working class under capitalism thus faces significant obstacles to its organizational empowerment. Offe and Wiesenthal further suggest that working-class organizations, particularly unions, confront a dilemma similar to Robert Michels's iron law of oligarchy—in order for them to operate and bargain effectively they must possess a high degree of centralized power; but this source of power is also a source of weakness insofar as it necessarily constrains popular participation and mobilization. For the working class, or-

[50]Ibid., p. 99.

[51]Claus Offe and Helmut Wiesenthal, "Two Logics of Collective Action: Theoretical Notes on Social Class and Organizational Form," in Maurice Zeitlin, ed., *Political Power and Social Theory*, vol. 1 (Greenwich, Conn.: JAI Press, 1980), p. 76.

ganization is, to use Michels's phase, "the weapon of the weak"; but it is also a limit upon a more radical political practice.

Scott Lash and John Urry propose the extension of this line of inquiry into the different logics of class organization, suggesting that certain insights of game-theoretic Marxism must be integrated into accounts of the determinants of class conflict. The basic framework of their programmatic involves the following assumptions:

> (i) that class and other collective actors are possessed with resources; (ii) that "class capacity" (or conversely the capacities of other collective agents) be defined as the strength of the organizational resources which the grouping can mobilize, especially over time and across space; (iii) that social change in civil society and the state in capitalism can be well understood through the consideration not simply of the dominant class, but through the analysis of the capacities of the *subordinate* class (and other collective) agents; (iv) that instrumental reason and other forms of consciousness must not be understood as unconditioned but as constituted, in particular via the medium of language.[52]

These theoretical insights about collective organization and class capacities have been developed in a number of recent empirical inquiries. Therborn, for example, has argued that class capacities are shaped by the historical timing of class formation, and he has suggested that the hegemonic influence of the Swedish working class is due in no small part to its early and broad political unification in the 1880s.[53] Allin Cottrell has provided an analysis of the "formidable defensive conservatism of the organized working class" of Great Britain, and of the interaction between the British union movement, the Confederation of British Industries, and the Liberal, Conservative, and Labour parties which has led to the politics of Thatcherism.[54] Niels Christiansen has analyzed the crisis of the Danish welfare state, explaining the current impasse in terms of the balance of forces between class and political party organi-

[52]Scott Lash and John Urry, "The New Marxism of Collective Action: A Critical Analysis," *Sociology* 18 (February 1984), 46.

[53]Göran Therborn, "Why Some Classes Are More Successful than Others," *New Left Review*, no. 138 (March–April 1983), 37–56.

[54]Allin Cottrell, *Social Classes in Marxist Theory* (London: Routledge & Kegan Paul, 1984), pp. 194–265.

zations.[55] And a number of recent studies have analyzed the structure of the postwar American accords between the major trade unions and the corporate sector, emphasizing the real power and benefits institutionalized through these arrangements, their contradictory effects, and their demise under the Reagan administration.[56]

In all of these discussions the powers—the enduring capacities to act and intervene—of class organizations and political parties are treated as effective realities not reducible to the structure of production relations. But while Marxian theorists have avoided any such essentialism in their analyses of class power, they have also insisted that it is theoretically mistaken to detach the analysis of organizations from the analysis of the general structure of capitalism. David Coates, for instance, in discussing the power of unions in contemporary capitalism, insists that "if trade unions have power, it is on a very narrow range of issues: wages, working conditions, levels of manning, speed of work.... And even here that power is more negative than positive, a power to block unacceptable managerial initiatives rather than to dictate a wholly new set of working practices. It is shared power too, a capacity to negotiate and bargain, not (as with management's power elsewhere in industrial decision-making) to decide unilaterally."[57]

Leo Panitch, in his critique of mainstream theorists of neocor-

[55]Niels Christiansen, "Denmark: End of the Idyll," *New Left Review*, no. 144 (March–April 1984), 5–32.

[56]On class compromise, see Samuel P. Bowles, "The Post-Keynesian Capital-Labor Stalemate," *Socialist Review*, no. 65 (September–October 1982), 45–72, and Alan Wolfe, *America's Impasse: The Rise and Fall of Growth Politics* (New York: Pantheon, 1980). On the divisions within the American working class, see Ira Katznelson, *City Trenches: Politics and the Patterning of Class in the United States* (Chicago: University of Chicago Press, 1981), and David M. Gordon, Richard Edwards, and Michael Reich, *Segmented Work, Divided Workers* (Cambridge: Cambridge University Press, 1982). On the breakdown of the class compromise, see Mike Davis, "The Political Economy of Late Imperial America," *New Left Review*, no. 143 (January–February 1984), 6–38, and Rob Wrenn, "The Decline of American Labor," *Socialist Review*, nos. 82–83 (July–October 1985), 89–118. For a superb, non-Marxist treatment that complements these analyses, see Thomas Byrne Edsall, *The New Politics of Inequality* (New York: Norton, 1984).

[57]David Coates, "The Question of Trade Union Power," in David Coates and Gordon Johnston, eds., *Socialist Arguments* (Oxford: Martin Robertson, 1983), p. 67. See also Andrew Martin and George Ross, "European Trade Unions and the Economic Crisis: Perceptions and Strategies," *West European Politics* (June 1980), 32–66.

poratist representation of capital and labor within the state, also argues that one must account for the structural context and consequences of group bargaining:

> Trade union power is based on the effectiveness of its collective organization. But the power of capital is based on control of the means of production, and this control is not transferred to the interest associations of business by individual firms. This means that these associations' incorporation via state structures is less significant for capital than is the incorporation of trade unions for labor, precisely because these associations play a less critical role for their class as agencies of struggle, of representation, and of social control than do trade unions for their class.[58]

Panitch thus contends that the underlying structure of domination characteristic of capitalism provides capital with powers of appropriation unmatched by labor, and that corporatism, far from negating these powers, functions to compromise—at the price of material concessions—the independence and militancy of the labor movement.

Jonus Pontusson offers a similar argument in his critique of the thesis of the Swedish "transition to socialism" put forth by J. Stephens, V. Himmelstrand, and most notably by Walter Korpi. While acknowledging the organizational power of the major Swedish trade union organization—the LO—and the Swedish Social Democratic Party, Pontusson rejects the voluntarism of what he calls the "power resources model" of Korpi et al., which suggests that this organizational power translates into the counterbalancing, if not the overcoming, of the power of capital. He argues that such a view "ignores the structural constraints on the exercise of working-class power within capitalism," and that the contradictions of the capital accumulation process as well as the powers (of economic possession and appropriation) of the capitalist class place

[58]Leo Panitch, "Trade Unions and the Capitalist State," *New Left Review*, no. 125 (1981), 26. See also his earlier "The Development of Corporatism in Liberal Democracies," in Phillipe C. Schmitter and Gerhard Lehmbruch, eds., *Trends Toward Corporatist Intermediation* (Beverly Hills: Sage, 1979), and "Recent Theorizations of Corporatism: Reflections on a Growth Industry," *British Journal of Sociology* 21 (June 1980), 159–87.

necessary limits upon social democracy and introduce severe antagonisms into the fragile class compromise.[59]

Objections Overturned: or What a Theory of Power Cannot Do

Despite the centrality of the concept of power to Marxian theory, a number of recent critics of Marxism have faulted it precisely for its failure to seriously treat the issue of power. One should note that, while all of the critics direct their criticisms against a historically determinist Marxism largely out of fashion among contemporary theorists, at the same time they propose to replace this Marxism with an equally historicist theory in which the concept of power acquires substantive explanatory force. These critics misinterpret Marxism, failing to see that domination and the dialectic of power lie at the heart of its analysis. And they also mistakenly suppose that the concept of power can provide the substantive foundation of a theoretical explanation, a supposition no more absurd in the case of social science than the view that the concept of "cause" can furnish the natural sciences with proper explanatory theories.

Frank Parkin, in his polemic entitled *Marxism and Class Theory: A Bourgeois Critique*, rejects the Marxian emphasis on production relations, insisting that it results in a deterministic account of social life. He proposes to replace the Marxian concept of class with the concept of *closure*, which denotes the process whereby social groups seek to maximize their rewards and life chances by restricting access to resources and opportunities to a limited circle of eligibles. For Parkin the concept of closure designates two processes. Exclusionary closure is "the attempt by one group to secure for itself a privileged position at the expense of some other group through a process of subordination. That is to say, it is a form of collective social action which, intentionally or otherwise, gives rise to a social category of ineligibles or outsiders." Usurpatory closure, in contrast, is the countervailing action by negatively privileged

[59]Jonus Pontusson, "Behind and beyond Social Democracy in Sweden," *New Left Review*, no. 143 (January–February 1984), 69–96. For Korpi's analysis, see his *The Working Class in Welfare Capitalism: Work, Unions, and Politics in Sweden* (London: Routledge & Kegan Paul, 1978).

groups to "win a greater share of resources."[60] Parkin argues that these concepts allow us a more accurate understanding of the "principle lines of cleavage" in a society.

Parkin's book provides a valuable critique of certain reductionist tendencies within historical materialism, incisively rejecting the view of production relations as "the structural fault running through society to which the most serious disturbances on the political landscape are ultimately traceable."[61] He rightly argues that there are a multiplicity of relations and conflicts in society, and that these are not reducible to a single underlying antagonism. In pushing these points, however, he seems to ignore a large body of recent Marxian theory that is not liable to these objections. He also mistakenly, and without justification, implies that the concept of closure can substitute for the concept of production to disclose the "fundamental source of cleavage" in society, and that it has the virtue of placing *power* at the center of study.

This argument suffers from two basic difficulties. First, Parkin's own account is excessively voluntarist. "For Marxism," he writes, "classes are defined in terms of systemic properties, independently of the make-up of constituent groups. . . . The human raw material of class analysis that Weberian usage designates as 'actors,' thereby singling out the role of conscious agency and volition, is transformed by Marxist usage into the status of 'embodiments' or 'repositories' of systemic forces."[62] We have already encountered a similar criticism by E. P. Thompson, and a response by G. A. Cohen that indicates the centrality of *both* class structure and class agency to Marxian theory. Parkin, in objecting to structural determinism, proposes in its stead an equally hopeless indeterminism, failing to recognize the duality of structure and agency implicit in Marxian theory. And he simply ignores the body of theory by contemporary Marxists exploring the complex forms of class agency and organization, and their connection with noneconomic practices and struggles. Furthermore, his own account of closure fails to grasp the reciprocity that is constitutive of social practice and central to the Marxian analysis of capitalism. On the Marxian view the cap-

[60]Frank Parkin, *Marxism and Class Theory: A Bourgeois Critique* (New York: Columbia University Press, 1979), p. 44.
[61]Ibid., p. 3.
[62]Ibid., p. 4.

italist furnishes the means and instruments of production and controls the labor power supplied by the worker. Within the confines
of this relation a reciprocity obtains, no matter how dominated or
exploited the subordinate group is. Both groups possess and exercise power, and both require their opposites for capitalist production to take place. Capitalists do not want to exclude workers,
whose inclusion within the process of production is an absolutely
essential precondition of the "reward" that accrues to the capitalist.
(Capitalists may wish to reduce the costs of labor power, and even
lessen their reliance on human labor through automation, but they
still rely on the labor of the working class; furthermore, let us not
forget one of the basic contradictions of capital accumulation—
while each individual capitalist may wish to limit his or her wage
bill, capitalists as a class require a class of workers not only to
produce but to consume commodities.)[63]

The concept of usurpation is no more successful in capturing the
forms of working-class resistance to the power of capital. To be
sure, much of the distributional class struggle that takes place under
capitalism might be described as the attempt of working-class
groups to "usurp" the rewards accruing to capitalists; but this
usurpation in no way contests the right of capitalists to their capital
and their powers of appropriation and possession, features of the
capital/labor relation that seem to elude Parkin's terminology. And
more revolutionary struggles, which might challenge the basic
structure of capitalism, could only with great difficulty be described
as usurpation insofar as their objective is not to "win a greater
share of the resources," but to transform the relations of power
implicated in the production of resources. In short, Parkin's concept
of closure, premised upon an ontology of distributional struggle,
fails to account for the mutual and asymmetrical dependence that
is constitutive of capitalist class relations and reproduced through
the antagonistic practices of classes.

Parkin's voluntarism relates to his second problem, the conception of power itself. Parkin insists that his view of closure is superior
to Marxism insofar as it highlights the analysis of power. He defines

[63]Cf. Marx: "Contradiction of the capitalist mode of production: the workers,
as buyers, are important for the market. But as sellers of their own commodity—
labour-power—the capitalist society tends to keep them down to a minimum price"
(*Capital*, vol. 2, pp. 316f.).

exclusion as "the use of power in a downward direction" and usurpation as "the use of power in an upward direction." But while these formulations quite properly underline the importance of *strategies* of interaction and conflict, they suggest, once again, a voluntarist view of power as a motive and a resource of struggle rather than as an enduring capacity to act. "Power" is thus invoked by Parkin as a general explanation of social struggle rather than as a property of historically specific relationships. Giddens's criticism is thus decisive: "Power is involved everywhere in social life, not only in circumstances of conflict or struggle; although all struggle therefore involves the use or attempted use of power, it is not by any means always struggle *for* power. Parkin's book appears to more than flirt with the idea that all human history is the history of struggles for power; if that is indeed his view, I think it no better or worse than the thesis that all human history is the history of class struggles."[64]

This same problematic of "power struggles" is invoked by Ralf Dahrendorf in his critique of Marxism. Dahrendorf begins by posing a question: "Does Marx understand, by the relations of property or production, the relations of factual control and subordination in the enterprises of industrial production—or merely the authority relations in so far as they are based on the legal title of property?"[65] Dahrendorf answers that Marx entertains a narrow, economistic, and "statutory" concept of class as a legal property relation, and insists that, pace Marx, capitalist ownership "is merely a special case of a more general social force, power."[66] He proceeds to argue that classes should not be understood in terms of relations of production, but as "conflict groups the determinant (or *diferentia specifica*) of which can be found in the participation in or exclusion from authority within any imperatively coordinated associations."[67]

It is power, then, that holds the key to social analysis, a key to which Marxism is oblivious. Dahrendorf, like Parkin, ignores the

[64]Anthony Giddens, "Classes, Capitalism, and the State," *Theory and Society*, no. 9 (1980), 877–94.

[65]Ralf Dahrendorf, *Class and Class Conflict in Industrial Society* (Stanford: Stanford University Press, 1959), p. 21.

[66]Ibid., p. 83.

[67]Ibid., p. 138.

extent to which Marxism, as evidenced by the writings of Marx himself, has persistently addressed questions of power and its contestation. Also like Parkin, he treats power as a substantive social scientific term with explanatory value. Calling social relations relations of power, however, says nothing significant about them, certainly nothing that explains their modus operandi. As we have seen in Chapter 3, all social relations involve social practices and social powers. A theory of power must analyze what *kinds* of powers are distributed by specific social relations, and what is the *nature* of those relations.

Marx's theory of capitalism does precisely this. It analyzes the distribution of powers to capitalists and workers, and understands these powers in terms of the ongoing practices of production and capital accumulation. Marx's theory of capitalist production is a theory of power; and his theory of power is a theory of capitalist production. Poulantzas, writing in another context, defends Marxism against recent post-structuralist critics: "It is not true, as Foucault or Deleuze would have it, that relations of power are, for Marxism, 'in a position of exteriority vis-à-vis other types of relation: namely, economic processes. . . .' The economic process *is* class struggle, *is* therefore relations of power, and not just economic power."[68]

Despite the fact that Dahrendorf cites the following text from Marx, he completely misses its significance: "In each historical epoch, property has developed differently under a set of entirely different social relations. Thus to define property is nothing else than to give an exposition of all the social relations of bourgeois production. To try to give a definition of property as an independent relation, an abstract eternal idea, can be nothing but an illusion of metaphysics or jurisprudence."[69] Marx's point here is that we can only discuss property in terms of the social relations in which it is embedded. It is not that ownership determines the contour of social relations, but that ownership as a legal right takes its significance from the effective relations of production and power. Dahrendorf quite properly rejects the historicist contention

---

[68]Nicos Poulantzas, *State, Power, Socialism* (London: Verso, 1980), p. 36.
[69]Karl Marx, "The Poverty of Philosophy," in Karl Marx and Frederick Engels, *Collected Works*, vol. 6 (New York: International Publishers, 1976), p. 197.

that all social relations are determined by "property relations." But he fails to see that the solution to this problem does not lie in positing the explanatory primacy of "power." It lies in the abandonment of the search for a single foundational explanatory concept and the historically specific analysis of various relations of power and their reproduction.

As we have seen, Parkin and Dahrendorf, in their objections to what they wrongly see as the necessary economic determinism of Marxist theory, have mistakenly insisted on the primacy of power. It is not only the critics of Marxism, however, who have supposed that the concept of power has some foundational explanatory significance. G. A. Cohen, in his formidable *Karl Marx's Theory of History: A Defense*, makes a similar argument in defense of historical materialism. Cohen's intention is to defend the theory of history most notoriously set forth by Marx in his preface to *A Contribution to the Critique of Political Economy*. This thesis is labeled by Cohen the "primacy thesis," and its basic claim is that economic relations, which are "indispensable and independent" of human will, constitute "the real basis, on which rises a legal and political superstructure, and to which correspond definite forms of social consciousness." As Cohen acknowledges, this thesis has been attacked from many quarters, John Plamenatz's criticism being representative: that insofar as economic relations are describable only in legal terms, in terms of ownership, the primacy thesis cannot stand as a causal thesis. Cohen attempts to forestall this criticism by claiming that it is possible to provide nonnormative, "rechtsfrei descriptions of production relations." The concept of power is then advanced to fulfill this role. Marxism is thus construed by Cohen as a general theory of history in which material, nonnormative powers provide the explanation for all social and political relations and their historical transformations. As he puts it, rights "match" powers but are not the same; and "right r is enjoyed because it belongs to a structure of rights, which obtains *because* it secures a matching structure of powers."[70] The right of the capitalist to own means of production is thus causally explained, according to Cohen, by its functionality in securing the nonnormative power of the capitalist to dispose of means of production.

[70]G. A. Cohen, pp. 231–32.

Cohen's discussion relies on certain complexities in the logical grammar of the concepts of "power" and "right," including their nonsynonymity. As we shall see in the next chapter, his determinist version of Marxist explanation has been largely abandoned by contemporary Marxists, who have insisted on the autonomous causal effectivity of noneconomic relations.[71] As Steven Lukes has pointed out, however, Cohen's account of rights and powers, apart from these other difficulties with the primacy thesis, cannot even get off the ground, or rise from the base, so to speak. Lukes convincingly argues that, as we have seen in Chapter 3, social power is essentially normative. "A slave, for example," he writes, "is a slave just because he lacks certain rights, just as a landowner by definition possesses certain rights. Statements attributing powers to occupants of roles such as these are plainly not rechtsfrei, at least where they have or lack these powers in virtue of their roles ... a proper description of the structure ... can scarcely avoid reference to their normatively defined roles."[72] Cohen's argument, Lukes points out, would seem to rest on the philosophically implausible assumption that it is possible to give "thin" behavioral or physicalist descriptions of social conduct. Furthermore, it rests on the equally implausible behavioralist assumption that the specificity of human agency can be read out of the picture. Rather, Lukes insists, "a stable system of enablements and constraints, to be effective, requires that I and relevant others are generally motivated by certain kinds of shared (teleological) reasons for acting and not acting," and these reasons are constitutive of power relations.[73]

Richard Miller, in his recent book *Analyzing Marx*, similarly attempts to vindicate historical materialism by invoking the explanatory primacy of power. Ironically, while participating in the same project as Cohen—the defense of a transhistorical Marxist

[71]For a criticism of Cohen's functionalism, see David Hillel-Ruben, "Review Article: Cohen, Marx, and the Primacy Thesis," *British Journal of Political Science* (1981), 227–34. For a more general critique of Cohen's economic determinism, see Andrew Levine and Erik Olin Wright, "Rationality and the Class Struggle," *New Left Review*, no. 123 (September–October 1980), 47–88.

[72]Steven Lukes, "Can the Base Be Distinguished from the Superstructure?" in David Miller and Larry Siedentop, eds., *The Nature of Political Theory* (Oxford: Clarendon Press, 1983), p. 110.

[73]Ibid., pp. 113–15.

theory of history—Miller begins by criticizing Cohen, setting out "to develop a more political interpretation of Marx, in which power-relations, rather then [sic] technology, and struggles for power, pursued outside of the workplace, typically play a primary role."[74] His analysis does much more, however, than simply establish the centrality of power and of struggles outside of the workplace. For Miller, as for Cohen, power is seen as a substantive explanatory concept; and in rejecting Cohen's argument that ultimately changes in the forces of production (technology) cause social and historical change, he proposes that it is the struggle for power that is the motor of history. "The institutions of a stable society," he writes, "are still means of preserving ruling class control. Basic internal change still occurs because the mode of production as a whole encourages processes that eventually give a social group the ability and the desire to destroy it, and create a new one. But this process of self-destruction can take two forms."[75]

For Miller, then, as for Cohen, modes of production are self-destructive and self-transforming; but for him it is the revolutionary desire and power of subordinate classes, in conflict with dominant classes, which play the determining role in these changes. The power of the dominant class causes its dominance (Miller writes that "the most important features of a relatively stable society are largely explained by the needs and powers of what Marx calls 'the ruling class' "); and the power of the subordinate class determines the destruction of this dominance.[76]

If the argument of this book is correct, then there is certainly nothing wrong with Miller's interest in power, nor with his belief that this concept lies at the heart of Marxian theory. But the belief that power is a primal force, a motor of history, is another matter altogether. For what can it mean to claim that social stability can be explained by the powers of the dominant class, *if we can only understand these powers by analyzing the structural relationships within which they are embedded*? And what can it mean to assert that social transformations can be explained by the needs and powers of subordinate groups, if we can only understand these by

[74]Richard W. Miller, *Analyzing Marx: Morality, Power, and History* (Princeton, N.J.: Princeton University Press, 1984), p. 3.

[75]Ibid., p. 215.

[76]Ibid., p. 206.

analyzing the social circumstances that condition these and the historically specific struggles in which they are developed and articulated? In short, the concept of power cannot function in any primacy thesis for the basic reason that one can only analyze power by analyzing social relationships themselves; power, as Poulantzas has argued, is not something " 'attached to a class-in-itself' understood as a collection of agents, but depends upon, and springs from, a relational system of material places occupied by particular agents."[77]

Furthermore, one suspects that Miller, like Cohen, requires a dubious teleology in order to establish his argument. He writes, for instance, of Marx's view of the "triumph of socialism": "The large-scale unity, discipline, and coordination produced by capitalist work relations gives workers, for the first time, the ability to seize and control the productive forces."[78] But what is this "ability" of which Miller writes? It would require a tremendous leap of faith to conclude that the structural organization of capitalist society actually provides the working class, as a unified class, with the power to seize, let alone to control, the forces of production. Most Marxian theorists would agree, on the contrary, that capitalist society is in fact premised precisely on the exclusion of workers from these powers. It is difficult, in the absence of a commitment to some necessitarian logic, to believe that these powers are somehow immanent in the structure of capitalism. And should the working class ever develop such powers, this would itself require a historically specific explanation, analyzing the means of this power—the forms of organization and ideological commitment—and the conjunctural struggles through which this power was achieved. The concept of power cannot furnish us with the key to the study of historical change because in order to analyze power we must undertake historically specific analyses.

The upshot of this is that power is a purely formal concept, which has explanatory value only when attached to a theory of a historically specific social relationship or society. Outside of such a theory it is simply, in Marx's words, "an abstract, eternal idea." As we have seen in this chapter, the critics of Marxism are wrong

---

[77]Poulantzas, *State*, p. 147.
[78]Miller, p. 207.

to claim that Marxian theory pays insufficient attention to questions of social power and its contestation. Marxian theory operates on the basis of an implicitly realist understanding of power and its operations, and it has produced a wealth of theoretical and empirical investigations into the operations of power in capitalist society. The critics of Marxism are mistaken in proposing that a historicism of power replace a historicism of production. The consequence of this, however, should not be the reversion to tortuous attempts to reinstate Marxist historicism, but the abandonment of all historicisms.

CHAPTER 5

Marxism and the State

Contemporary Marxian theorists have produced an extensive
and significant body of research on class relations which conforms
to the requirements of a realist analysis of power as discussed in
Part I. While Marxian class theory is grounded in an analysis of
economic relations and powers, it does not understand these powers to be narrowly economistic or technical, as merely powers of
disposition over commodities. Instead it views class powers as *social* powers implicated in the practices of production, accumulation,
and class struggle. This is often claimed by Marxists to be what
distinguishes Marxian political economy from marginalist economic theory.[1]

Marxian theory does not, however, provide simply a theory of
the economic relations of capitalism. It also provides an analysis
of the political conditions of class power. Many theorists have
emphasized Marx's own preoccupation, in his early writings, with
the character of the modern state.[2] In fact, it has been argued by
a number of theorists that Marx was first and foremost a political
theorist, despite the preoccupation of his later writing with economic questions. For some this is because of Marx's ongoing concern with the problems of democracy and community.[3] For others

[1]This claim is made by James O'Connor in "What Is Political Economy?" in
David Mermelstein, ed., *Economics: Mainstream Readings and Radical Critiques*
(New York: Random House, 1976).
[2]See Shlomo Avineri, *Karl Marx's Social and Political Thought* (Cambridge:
Cambridge University Press, 1968).
[3]See Paul Thomas, *Karl Marx and the Anarchists* (London: Routledge & Kegan
Paul, 1980).

it is because Marx was the first theorist of proletarian revolution.[4] While these different interpretations often embody different assumptions and conclusions about Marxism as a social theory, they do share a common recognition that the state and political conflict were central to Marx's concerns.

Contemporary Marxian theorists have highlighted this, producing a burgeoning literature on politics and the state, and catalyzing the recent renascence of interest in the state among political scientists. That this literature has been formidable and extremely influential cannot be disputed. It is this fact that prompted Charles Lindblom, in his 1979 presidential address to the American Political Science Association, aphoristically entitled "Another State of Mind," to criticize American political science for its ignorance of radical theory, insisting that "mainstream political science ought to bring it in from the cold."[5] David Easton's recent contribution to a special volume of *Political Theory* on the state of the discipline similarly attests to the importance of Marxian theory.[6] Easton, asked by the editors to remark on the relevance of systems theory to the 1980s, complied with a critique of the writings of Nicos Poulantzas. What better evidence of the vitality of Marxian political theory than the efforts of these elder statesmen of American political science, one to generously and congenially co-opt it into the mainstream, the other to defensively disparage it?

In this chapter I discuss the general contours within which contemporary Marxian theorists have written about the state, paying particular attention to the question of the relationship between class power and state power. My purpose here is not to provide a review of the literature, a task that has been ably performed by authors of a number of recent books.[7] Nor is it to suggest that there is a substantive consensus among Marxists on the state; as Jessop has remarked, Marxian theory evidences "a variety of the-

[4]Louis Althusser, *Lenin and Philosophy and Other Essays* (New York: Monthly Review Press, 1971).

[5]Charles E. Lindblom, "Another State of Mind," *American Political Science Review* 76 (March 1982), 9–21.

[6]David Easton, "The Political System Besieged by the State," *Political Theory* 9 (August 1981), 303–26.

[7]See Bob Jessop, *The Capitalist State: Marxist Theories and Methods* (New York: New York University Press, 1982); and Martin Carnoy, *The State and Political Theory* (Princeton, N.J.: Princeton University Press, 1984).

oretical perspectives which co-exist in an uneasy and unstable relation."[8] It is, rather, to highlight the realist presuppositions of
contemporary Marxian theories of the state and their conformity
with the programmatic of power outlined in Part I.

The Poulantzas-Miliband Debate

The debate conducted in the pages of the *New Left Review*
between Nicos Poulantzas and Ralph Miliband effectively launched
contemporary academic discussion among Marxists on the theory
of the state. The debate centers around the question of the relation
between structure and agency in the understanding of politics, and
it raises as well certain general epistemological questions about the
problem of theorizing about social structures. While it has been
much discussed in the literature,[9] my discussion of the debate will
highlight the implicitly realist position upon which Poulantzas and
Miliband ultimately converge.

While Poulantzas's *Pouvoir Politique et Classes Sociales* was first
published in Paris in 1968, and was subsequently to become the
fulcrum of debate in Anglo-American theory with its publication
in English in 1973 as *Political Power and Social Classes*, it was
Miliband's *The State in Capitalist Society* (1969) that provided the
groundwork of the initial controversy. Miliband's book is perhaps
the first serious effort by an academic Marxist to criticize pluralism,
the dominant approach in political science. His intention, as he
makes clear in his introduction, is to refute the major claims of
pluralist theory—that liberal democratic politics is characterized
by a diffuse distribution of political power and a set of neutral
political institutions that function to reconcile and compromise
interests whose expression is relatively unconstrained.[10] He at-

[8]Jessop, *Capitalist State*, p. xii.
[9]See David Gold, Clarence Lo, and Erik Olin Wright, "Recent Developments
in Marxist Theory of the Capitalist State," *Monthly Review* 27, no. 5 (October
1975), 29–43; no. 6 (November 1975), 36–51.
[10]He writes: "What is wrong with pluralist-democratic theory is not its insistence
on the fact of competition but its claim (very often its implicit assumption) that
the major organized 'interests' in these societies, notably capital and labor, compete
on more or less equal terms, and that none of them is able to achieve a decisive
and permanent advantage in the process of competition" (Ralph Miliband, *The
State in Capitalist Society* [New York: Basic Books, 1969], p. 146).

tempts to do this by empirically establishing the class biases of the state.

Miliband rightly notes that Marx never attempted a systematic analysis of the state, but he contends that nonetheless, "as far as capitalist societies are concerned, his main view of the state is summarized in the famous formulation of the *Communist Manifesto*: 'The executive of the modern state is but a committee for managing the common affairs of the whole bourgeoisie.' "[11] This text provides the foundation of Miliband's inquiry, and it is for this reason that his analysis of the state has been labeled instrumentalist—for Miliband the state is an instrument of class rule, a set of institutions controlled by a more or less unified capitalist class. "In the Marxist scheme," he writes, "the 'ruling class' of capitalist society is that class which owns and controls the means of production and which is able, by virtue of the economic power thus conferred upon it, to use the state as an instrument for the domination of society."[12]

The State in Capitalist Society provides a detailed analysis of state elite recruitment, the connections between business and the state, and the ideological biases of the state bureaucracy, with the intention of empirically demonstrating that the state is controlled by the capitalist class. As Ernesto Laclau has noted, Miliband's account is largely descriptive, failing to specify the nature of these mechanisms of class domination and their connections in any systematic way.[13] Nonetheless, it is worth noting that, however much Miliband leans toward empirical research rather than theoretical specification, his approach to the state is implicitly realist—he suggests that the capitalist class possesses political power by virtue of its structural economic position.

Miliband, however, fails to make the meta-theoretical grounds of his analysis clear, generating an unavoidable confusion. On the one hand, his commitment to empirical analysis, and his method of criticizing pluralist theory through empirical contestation, might suggest that Miliband subscribes to an empiricist theory of scientific

[11]Ibid., p. 5.

[12]Ibid., p. 22.

[13]See Ernesto Laclau, "The Specificity of the Political: The Poulantzas-Miliband Debate,"in his *Politics and Ideology in Marxist Theory* (London: New Left Books, 1977).

explanation. Yet he certainly makes no effort to formulate his hypotheses in deductive-nomological terms and offers no empirical predictions. It is precisely the failure of Marxian political analyses to conform to these standards which makes them the target of empiricist critics like Polsby. On the other hand, while Miliband employs concepts familiar to Marxian theory (like "class," "state," and "ideology"), and while his account presupposes a nonempiricist logic of explanation, he fails to make his own methodological and theoretical commitments sufficiently explicit.

Poulantzas's criticism proceeds from this observation. He writes: "Instead of displacing the epistemological terrain and submitting these ideologies [pluralism—J.I.] to the critique of Marxist science by demonstrating their inadequacy to the real (as Marx does, notably in *Theories of Surplus Value*), Miliband apears to omit this first step. Yet the analysis of modern epistemology shows that it is never possible simply to oppose 'concrete facts' to concepts, but that these must be attacked by other parallel concepts situated in a different problematic."[14] Poulantzas's first criticism, then, is that Miliband has failed to develop Marxian theoretical concepts in his critique of pluralism. More specifically, despite the title of his book, Miliband provides no more than a gestural conceptualization of the state. For Poulantzas this is not simply an epistemological but an ontological problem, for it prevents Miliband from properly grasping the structural character of politics and the state. He asserts:

> Miliband sometimes allows himself to be unduly influenced by the methodological principles of his adversary. How is this manifest? Very briefly, I would say that it is visible in the difficulties that Miliband has in comprehending social classes and the state as *objective structures*, and their relations as an *objective system of regular connections*, a structure and a system whose agents, "men," are in the words of Marx, "bearers" of it—träger. Miliband constantly gives the impression that for him social classes or "groups" are in some way reducible to interpersonal relations.[15]

[14]Nicos Poulantzas, "The Problem of the Capitalist State," *New Left Review*, no. 58 (1969), reprinted in Robin Blackburn, ed., *Ideology in Social Science* (New York: Vintage, 1973), pp. 240–41.
    [15]Ibid., p. 242.

Miliband, in other words, fails to properly theorize the underlying determinants of class power. This is a serious failure, according to Poulantzas, as it results in an inability to grasp the "objective necessity" of class domination and the state's role in reproducing it. Poulantzas continues: "The relation between the bourgeois class and the state is an *objective relation*. This means that if the *function* of the state in a determinate social formation and the *interests* of the dominant class in this formation *coincide*, it is by reason of the system itself: the direct participation of members of the ruling class in the state apparatus is not the *cause*, but the *effect*, and moreover a chance and contingent one, of this objective condition."[16]

Poulantzas's general intention in this criticism is to assert the need for a systematic theory of the structural attributes of the state and of the causal relations between the state and class domination. The implication of Miliband's instrumentalist account of the state is that the character of the state is determined through the contingent interactions of class groups in struggle. Despite the functionalist connotations of Poulantzas's language, his point is to assert the sui generis reality of the state. While for Miliband the state seems to be contingently implicated in the constitution and reproduction of capitalism, for Poulantzas the state-class relation is causally necessary. The capitalist state, as a social structure with its own properties, is necessarily implicated in class domination. It is, as Poulantzas puts it, not simply an effect, but *a cause* of class struggle. It should be apparent, however, that he couches his criticism of Miliband in a heavily structuralist mode, speaking of objective necessities and functions, and referring to individuals and groups as "bearers" of social roles. He derisively labels Miliband's approach a "problematic of the subject," according to which "the agents of a social formation, 'men,' are not considered the bearers of objective instances (as they are for Marx) but as the genetic principle of the level of the social whole."[17] Miliband responded by accusing Poulantzas of a "structural superdeterminism" in which agency and struggle cannot be realistically considered.[18]

It should be clear that this debate is grounded upon two mis-

[16]Ibid., p. 245.
[17]Ibid., p. 242.
[18]Ralph Miliband, "The Capitalist State—Reply to Nicos Poulantzas," *New Left Review*, no. 59 (1970), reprinted in Blackburn.

placed polarities—that between empirical and theoretical analysis, and that between agency and structure. Laclau points out that this does not mean there is simply a difference of emphasis between Miliband and Poulantzas. *The State in Capitalist Society* does not succeed in developing an adequate theory of the capitalist state as a structure with its own logic, and Poulantzas rightly criticizes its scientific weaknesses. The language of his criticism, however, severely overstates his case. As we have seen in Part I, while the analysis of social structure requires us to perform a "methodological epoché," and while in this sense it is possible (and necessary) for us to think of persons as role bearers, this does not occlude the practical significance of human agency, which any concrete historical analysis must take into account. Furthermore, such structural analysis certainly depends on the interpretation of empirical evidence. Poulantzas's verbal commitment to a radical epistemological perspectivism is no more warranted than his dichotomizing of structure and subjectivity, and it only detracts from his critique of Miliband.

All this being said, however, it is important not to overstate the differences between Poulantzas and Miliband. In fact, one can discern in their respective writings a theoretical convergence upon the importance of both class struggle and the state as a sui generis reality. While *The State in Capitalist Society* is primarily concerned with the analysis of the organization of capitalist class power and its exertion upon the state, even this book evidences a number of important structural insights, including the distinction between government and state.[19] And while Poulantzas has always emphasized the structural determinations of class relations, he has also, as we shall see below, insisted upon the importance of strategic objectives and political class struggle.

Realism and the State

In order to write about the state, Poulantzas pointed out in his critique of Miliband, it is necessary to depart from the epistemo-

---

[19]See, for instance, his insistence on the discrepancies between the purposes and the structural consequences of state policy, and his observation that, while the interests of capital are not necessarily the objectives of the state "all other ends are conditioned by, and pass through the prism of, their acceptance of and commitment to the existing economic system" (Miliband, *State*, p. 75).

logical terrain of mainstream social science. Poulantzas's point regarded the necessity of developing specifically Marxian theoretical concepts in the process of criticizing pluralist theory. We can also, however, interpret Poulantzas's point more broadly as a critique not only of pluralist theory but of the meta-theory—empiricism—which has sustained it, insulating it from criticism by preventing the development of alternative theories, particularly those emphasizing the constitutive role of the state in political life. While the concept of the state was a central focus of modern political thought from Hobbes through Weber, many theorists have observed that the advent of behavioralism in political science led to the decline of the state as an object of theoretical inquiry.[20] This is doubly ironic, given the fact that, corresponding to this conceptual eclipse, the real state grew into, among other things, a massive financial supporter of behavioral research. Yet despite (or perhaps precisely because of) this fact, the concept of the state was an early casualty of "scientific rigor." Harold Laswell and Abraham Kaplan wrote in *Power and Society*: "In recent decades a thoroughgoing empiricist philosophy of the sciences has been elaborated... concurring in an insistence on the importance of relating scientific ideas to materials ultimately accessible to direct observation. Adopting this standpoint, the present work analyzes such political abstractions as 'state' and 'sovereignty' in terms of concrete interpersonal relations of influence and control."[21] They continue that "as science," political theory "finds its subject matter in interpersonal relations, not abstract institutions or organizations."[22]

Following this lead David Easton, in *The Political System* and other works, unleashed an assault on the "metaphysical" connotations of the concept of the state.[23] In response to the recent revival of interest in the theory of the state, Easton has reiterated his behavioralist critique. He insists that either the state is the empirical

---

[20]See Alfred Stepan, *The State in Society: Peru in Comparative Perspective* (Princeton, N.J.: Princeton University Press, 1978), pp. 3–4. For a discussion of this, see my "After Empiricism: The Realist Alternative," in Terence Ball, ed., *Idioms of Inquiry: Critique and Renewal in Political Theory* (Albany: State University of New York Press, 1987).

[21]Harold Laswell and Abraham Kaplan, *Power and Society* (New Haven: Yale University Press, 1950), p. xiv.

[22]Ibid., p. xxiv.

[23]See David Easton, *The Political System* (New York: Knopf, 1953).

behaviors of governmental officials "or it is some kind of undefined and undefinable essence, a 'ghost in the machine,' knowable only through its variable manifestations."[24] Easton is here drawing on empiricism's characteristic denial that there are relatively enduring causal mechanisms. As the language of "ghost in the machine" is meant to suggest, all of this writing by Marxists about the state is nothing but "metaphysics," debates about the state's relative autonomy, for instance, being no different from medieval scholastic debates about how many angels can dance on the head of a pin.

Easton here confirms Poulantzas's point—Marxian analysis of the state presupposes a nonempiricist epistemology. But what Easton fails to see is that scientific theory is based precisely on reasoning from empirical phenomena to their causal mechanisms. While we can only know about the state by observing and interpreting the concrete practices and institutions of government and the processes that constitute what Easton calls the "political system," the theoretical concept of the state is necessary in order to *explain* these phenomena. Miliband writes: "It is not very surprising that government and state should often appear as synonymous. For it is the government which speaks on the state's behalf. ... It is these [governmental] institutions in which 'state power' lies and it is through them that this power is wielded in its different manifestations by the people who occupy the leading positions in each of these institutions."[25] The concept thus denotes a historically specific unity among the various processes of legislation, execution, adjudication, and administration within a given territory, implying that, despite a functional division of labor, there is also a coherent set of interests in social and political stability. Thus Poulantzas writes: "The actual relation of the state's institutional powers, which is conceived as a 'separation' of these powers, is in fact fixed in the capitalist state as a mere *distribution* of power, out of the undivided unity of state sovereignty ... this feature of the unity of the capitalist state governs its *centralized* organization."[26] Elsewhere he writes: "The state does not constitute a mere assembly of detachable parts; it exhibits an *apparatus unity* which is normally

[24]Easton, "Political System," p. 316.
[25]Miliband, *State*, pp. 50, 54.
[26]Nicos Poulantzas, *Political Power and Social Classes* (London: New Left Books, 1973), p. 279.

designated by the term centralisation or *centralism*, and which is related to the fissiparous *unity of state power*."[27] Poulantzas's conception of the state as a "factor of unity of the social formation" underscores this in a way little different from the conceptions of Hobbes or Weber.[28]

The concept of the state thus refers to an underlying social structure that is real but not empirical. We cannot "observe" it, though we can experience the activities of its officials. In this respect, we might add, the concept of the state is no different from the concept of a magnetic field—we cannot observe a field, and yet the concept of it has definite scientific meaning, and denotes a hypothetically real structure with real effects. (There are, of course, crucial differences between these concepts; the concept of the state refers to a social structure that exists, in part, in virtue of the concepts and beliefs people have about it, and is thus historically mutable. One of the reasons the debate surrounding the theory of the state is so important is precisely because of its practical implications for the emancipation of people; and one of the most telling limits of Easton's behavioralist position is that, as the title of his essay indicates, he is less concerned with the real state's besieging of society than he is with the challenge the concept of it poses to his theory.)

Contemporary Marxian theorists, in their analysis of the state, thus presuppose a realist conception of scientific explanation, which alone is capable of sustaining the reality of their theoretical object. Many Marxists have begun to acknowledge this reliance on a realist method. Therborn, for instance, insists that Marxian theory of the state is marked by a "profound realism," whereby "theoretical formulations must always be judged ... on the basis of the capacity to grasp the complex and fluid structure of reality."[29]

[27]Nicos Poulantzas, *State, Power, Socialism* (London: Verso, 1980), p. 136.

[28]Hobbes writes: "These are the Rights, which make the Essence of Soveraignty ... for these are incommunicable and inseparable ... a kingdom divided in it selfe cannot stand" (Thomas Hobbes, *Leviathan*, ed. C. B. Macpherson [London: Penguin, 1968], p. 236). Weber writes: "Sovereignty is accepted as the essential attribute of the modern state, conceived as 'unity,' while the acts of its organs are looked upon as instances of the exercise of public duties" (Max Weber, *Economy and Society*, vol. 2, ed. Guenther Roth and Claus Wittich [Berkeley: University of California Press, 1978], p. 652).

[29]Göran Therborn, *What Does the Ruling Class Do When It Rules?* (London: Verso, 1980), p. 18.

And Jessop, in his critical reconstruction of contemporary Marxian theories, argues that an adequate Marxian account of the capitalist state "involves nothing more than a correct application of a realist scientific method to the field of political economy."[30] He discusses at length the methodological difficulties confronting Marxists when they fail to distinguish between underlying structures and political conjunctures, and when they fail to make explicit the level of abstraction at which they are operating. Thus, in criticizing the Marxist-Leninist theory of state monopoly capitalism, Jessop writes: "In place of a specification of the real causal mechanisms that are located beneath the empirically observable level of surface appearances and that generate causal tendencies whose effects are mediated in complex ways and/or are subject to the intervention of countertendencies before being actualised, they either operate wholly on the empirical level . . . or penetrate beneath the surface merely to postulate essential laws that are immediately realised on the surface."[31]

Erik Olin Wright too insists that "it is important to develop a more systematic way of understanding the causal relations between the structural categories of Marxist theory and the level of appearances tapped in empirical investigation."[32] He proposes that Marxian analysis presupposes a number of different "modes of determination." While he invokes realism as a means of clarifying methodological confusions within Marxism, he also argues that it is necessary to make realism explicit in order to legitimize the practice of Marxian social theory in the face of "the hegemony of an empiricist, positivist epistemology in the social sciences."[33]

Given the commitment of contemporary Marxian political theorists to a realist interpretation of the concept of the state, the insistence of some of them that the state possesses no power of its own is, in the least, peculiar. Therborn, for instance, writes that "Marxists are interested in the relationship of classes to state power for a very particular reason. They view the state as a separate material institution, functioning as the nodal point of the relations of power within society. The state as such has no power; it is an

---

[30]Jessop, *Capitalist State*, p. xii.
[31]Ibid., pp. 72–73.
[32]Erik Olin Wright, *Class, Crisis, and the State* (London: Verso, 1979), p. 14.
[33]Ibid., p. 9.

institution where social power is concentrated and exercised."[34] And Poulantzas, who has done more than any other contemporary Marxist to establish the centrality of the state, asserts that the state "is a site and a centre of the exercise of power, but it possesses no power of its own."[35] It is impossible to interpret these claims literally, for if one were to do so the project of a theory of the state would be rendered meaningless. Poulantzas is asserting two things that seem to be incompatible—that the state is a real structure with causal effectivity on class relations, and that the state has "no power of its own."

There are a number of ways of reading the claim that the state has no power of its own. The most damning is that the state is but a surrogate for capitalist class power. Poulantzas's own arguments might support such a reading. As Miliband has noted (and criticized), in one place Poulantzas writes that "when we speak for example of state power . . . we can only mean the power of a determinate class to whose interests (rather than those of other social classes) the state corresponds."[36] Another way of reading the claim is that state power takes its significance from class relations; to say that it has no power as such is simply another way of asserting a basic thesis of Marxian theory, that politics is not autonomous from class structure. Therborn, in the text quoted in the previous paragraph, both refers to state power and claims that the state has no power *as such*. As we have seen, however, Poulantzas is interested in much more than repeating the Marxist thesis about the importance of class relations. His intention is to develop a theory of the "specific internal unity" of the state, which "obeys its own logic" and which is constitutive, and not simply the effect, of class relations. This intention, which is borne out in his various theoretical works, is not compatible with the reductionism implicit in the above, particularly the first, interpretation. The most plausible way of reading his claim that the state lacks its own power is to see it as a denial of an invidious essentialism that would ascribe to the state a univocal, "freestanding" nature. In the text quoted in the previous paragraph, Poulantzas goes on to affirm that the

[34]Therborn, *What Does*, p. 132.

[35]Poulantzas, *State*, p. 132.

[36]Ralph Miliband, "Poulantzas and the Capitalist State," *New Left Review*, no. 82 (November–December 1973), 87.

state is a site, a "strategic field," of the exercise of power, and that political struggles are "inscribed in its framework." The denial that the state has power as such should be read as an insistence that the effects of state power are never certain, however much the state tends to reproduce class relations. Jessop clarifies this when he claims that "the state is a set of political institutions that cannot, *qua* institutional ensemble, exercise power."[37] The powers of the state are always exercised separately, by particular officials, occupying specific institutional roles. Moreover, they are exercised conjuncturally. Political struggles upon, within, and between state institutions will always determine how state power is exercised in, for example, a specific law, policy, or administrative action.

As Miliband has pointed out, it would be much clearer to simply subscribe to a distinction between class power and state power, viewing the latter as "the main and ultimate—but not the only— means whereby class power is assured and maintained."[38] On this view (which, if I am correct, is implicit in the awkward formulations of Therborn and Poulantzas) state power is understood as the various public powers of territorial rule and physical coercion pos- sessed by the specialized agencies of centralized government. Class powers, as we have seen in the previous chapter, are understood as those powers, structural and organizational, which are possessed by economic classes. As Miliband points out, the relationship be- tween state power and class power constitutes the central problem of Marxian political theory.[39] While the writings of contemporary Marxists are only intelligible if we preserve the distinction between state power and class power, they are also only comprehensible if we recognize the centrality of the Marxian interest in the causal relationships that obtain between them. Poulantzas's remark on state power is an insistence upon the futility of any view of the state that fails to analyze its implication in the class relations, and class struggles, with which it is associated.

[37] Jessop, *Capitalist State*, p. 221.
[38] Miliband, "Poulantzas," pp. 87–88. See also Miliband's discussion in his *Marxism and Politics* (Oxford: Oxford University Press, 1977), pp. 54–55, 66– 67.
[39] Miliband, *Marxism*, p. 68.

The Relative Autonomy of the Capitalist State

The concept of relative autonomy has played an important role in recent Marxian political theory, designating the causal relations between class domination and the state. Poulantzas, for instance, drawing upon Marx's analysis of the separation of state and civil society under capitalism, writes of the "characteristic autonomy of the economic and the political" which distinguishes capitalism from feudalism. While the latter was based upon the localized political power of the lords, which was implicated directly in the relations of production, capitalism is based upon a sphere of institutionally separate economic relations that are secured by a legal and coercive order outside of itself. Poulantzas writes of the capitalist state:

> Its fundamental distinctive feature seems to be the fact that it contains no determination of subjects (fixed in the state as "individuals," "citizens," "political persons,") as agents of production; and this was not the case in other types of state. At the same time this class state presents a further specific feature: namely, that political class domination is constantly absent from its institutions. It presents itself as a popular-class state. Its institutions are organized around the principles of the liberty and equality of "individuals" or "political persons." Its legitimacy is no longer founded on the divine will implied by the monarchical principle, but on the ensemble of formally free and equal citizens and on the popular sovereignty and secular responsibility of the state towards the people.... The modern capitalist state thus presents itself as embodying the general interest of the whole society, i.e., as substantiating the will of that "body politic" which is "the nation."[40]

The capitalist class, then, unlike the dominant classes in other modes of production, is not a ruling class.[41] The capitalist does

---

[40]Poulantzas, *Political Power*, p. 123.

[41]While the recognition of this point goes back to Kautsky, C. Wright Mills perceptively remarked on it in *The Power Elite* (Oxford: Oxford University Press, 1956), p. 277. Mills writes: " 'Ruling class' is a badly loaded phrase. 'Class' is an economic term; 'rule' a political one. The phrase, 'ruling class,' thus contains the theory that an economic class rules politically.... Specifically, the phrase 'ruling class,' in its common political connotations, does not allow enough autonomy to the political order and its agents." Richard W. Miller, in his *Analyzing Marx: Morality, Power, and History* (Princeton, N.J.: Princeton University Press, 1984),

rule, so to speak, the production process. But political rule, or territorial control, is ultimately vested in the officials of the state, who act in the name of a generalized interest. The prerogatives of class domination are, as Poulantzas argues, absent from the institutions of the capitalist state. This means that a theory of such a state can in no way be reduced to an analysis of the economic or to any notion of the state as a reflection or expression of the economic. The state is a specific and relatively autonomous structure. As Poulantzas puts it, it is precisely this which "permits us to constitute the political as an autonomous and specific object of science."[42]

Jessop has pointed out that the concept of relative autonomy has served to confuse as much as to clarify theoretical discussion, and he goes so far as to suggest that it should be "abandoned... along with other Althusserian notions."[43] He quotes Poulantzas's response to the question of "how relative is the relative autonomy of the state":

> I cannot reply to this question, since in this form it is utterly absurd. I could have only answered this question, couched in these general terms, if I really had been guilty of structuralism. I can give no general answer—not, as Miliband believes, because I take no account of concrete individuals or of the role of social classes, but precisely because the term "relative" in the expression "relative autonomy" of the state (relative in relation to what or whom?) here refers to the relationship between the state and dominant classes (i.e., relatively autonomous in relation to the dominant classes). In other words, it refers to the class struggle within each social formation and to its corresponding state forms. True, the very principles of Marxist theory

---

attempts to defend a "ruling class" interpretation of Marxism, but he does so without taking any account whatsoever of contemporary Marxian political theory. Miller in fact relies almost exclusively on the one text of Marx—*The Eighteenth Brumaire of Louis Napoleon*—which has been read by most commentators as providing the weakest foundations for such an interpretation; and his offhanded remark about the "increasingly sterile controversy between the so-called 'structuralist' and 'instrumentalist' interpretations" (p. 105) simply indicates, in my view, the limitations of his own argument.

[42] Poulantzas, *Political Power*, p. 29.

[43] Bob Jessop, *Nicos Poulantzas: Marxist Theory and Political Strategy* (New York: St. Martin's, 1985), p. 136. Jessop's account of the logic and genesis of Poulantzas's thought is extremely valuable, and it supports the realist reading I provide here.

lay down the general negative limits of this autonomy. The (capitalist) state, in the long run, can only correspond to the political interests of the dominant class or classes.... Yet, within these limits, the degree, the extent, the forms, etc. (how relative, and how is it relative) of the relative autonomy of the state can only be examined (as I constantly underline throughout my book) with reference to a given capitalist state, and to the precise conjuncture of the corresponding class struggle.[44]

Jessop rightly observes that the concept of relative autonomy functions here to designate both the complex mechanisms of class power and struggle and the ultimate necessity of the reproduction of class domination. He criticizes Poulantzas, saying: "He erred in assuming that somewhere in the state there is something which can somehow *guarantee* bourgeois class domination."[45] But while Poulantzas's language certainly does suggest some notion of such a guarantee ("the general negative limits of this autonomy"), it is also possible to interpret this claim not as an empirical prediction, but as a statement of tendency—that "in the long run" the workings of the state *tend* to reproduce class domination.

On the interpretation of relative autonomy I am suggesting, the state is relatively autonomous in that it is both irreducible to economic relations and importantly determining and determined in relation to them. The economy and the state differ not simply in their personnel, but in their principles of existence and constitutive rationalities. The economy is constituted by a multitude of private institutions (enterprises, corporations, banks) whose rationality is particularism and private profit. The state is constituted by a set of public institutions (executive, parliaments, courts, police, armies, administrative bureaucracies) whose rationality is the provision of internal and external order and "security" and the "general interest." The concept of relative autonomy denotes the structural relation between class relations and the state. Each is a condition of the others' existence, and each is in this sense implicated in the other, while at the same time maintaining its own respective autonomy. Because of this essential and necessary relation between state and class, because the state is what it is in virtue of its rela-

[44]Ibid., pp. 133–34.
[45]Ibid., p. 136.

tionship to class relations, and vice versa, they are only *relatively* autonomous. The concept of relative autonomy thus designates the causal determinations between two social structures, state and relations of production, each of which is characterized by institutional specificity and causal effectivity.

This understanding of the separation under capitalism of the sphere of public power and the sphere of private property does not mean that these spheres are hermetically sealed from each other, but rather than they are distinct and mutually determining. It also does not mean that the economy is strictly "private," in the sense of free of state interventions within it. As Poulantzas insists, the concept of relative autonomy does not denote the liberal, "non-interventionist" state of competitive capitalism, but the more general structural separation of political and economic relations. The continual interfaces of state and economy, and the extensive intervention of the contemporary welfare state in the economy, are in this view "transformed forms" of the relative autonomy of the capitalist state, which is a causal determinant even when it does not intervene, and which maintains its specific autonomy even when it does.[46]

This interpretation of relative autonomy should be distinguished from a number of other recent interpretations. According to Fred Block:

> The basic problem of "relative autonomy" is the conceptualization of the ruling class. Relative autonomy theories assume that the ruling class will respond effectively to the state's abuse of that autonomy. But for the ruling class to be capable of taking such corrective actions, it must have some degree of political cohesion, an understanding of its general interests, and a high degree of political sophistication.... Yet if the ruling class or a segment of it is class conscious, then the degree of autonomy of the state is clearly quite limited. At this point the theory of relative autonomy collapses back into a slightly more sophisticated version of instrumentalism. State policies continue to be seen as a reflection of inputs by a class conscious ruling class.[47]

[46]Poulantzas, *State*, pp. 166–67.
[47]Fred Block, "The Ruling Class Does Not Rule," *Socialist Revolution* 7 (May–June 1977), 6–28.

For Block, relative autonomy thus refers not to a structural relation, but to the relation between state institutions and a concrete group, "the ruling class." In this view the state is relatively autonomous (rather than fully autonomous) because it is ultimately manipulated as an instrument of the capitalist class organized as a ruling class. Block in fact opposes this collapsing of relative autonomy into class instrumentalism. In a more recent essay he suggests that the problem of relative autonomy points to the following questions: "What is the degree to which politics and the state have independent determining effects upon historical outcomes? Can the state or the people who direct the state apparatus be historical subjects?"[48] He answers the second question in the affirmative, and concludes that state managers are historical subjects. What is crucial here is that he interprets the question of relative autonomy as a question of subjectivity and agency, insisting that the objectives of some group, and not a structural relation, lie at its heart. An observation by Laclau is pertinent here:

> From the Poulantzas viewpoint this relative autonomy would be in turn a structural element, that is to say, the result of a particular articulation between the instances corresponding to the mode of production under consideration; in that sense, one more objective determination of the system as a whole. The relative autonomy of the state and its objective determination would be incompatible only if this autonomy were understood as a break in the chain of necessity and the emergence—however relative—of a realm of freedom. But this contraposition only makes sense within a problematic of the subject, which Poulantzas excludes by definition.[49]

As I have remarked, Poulantzas's polarization of structure and agency is unwarranted. But this is equally true in the case of Block. To suggest that the concept of relative autonomy designates the articulation, or causal relationship, between class domination and the state, is not in the least incompatible with the agency of class actors and state officials, both of which exercise their structurally

[48]Fred Block, "Beyond Relative Autonomy: State Managers as Historical Subjects," in Ralph Miliband and John Saville, eds., *The Socialist Register 1980* (London: Merlin Press, 1980), p. 227.
[49]Laclau, 1977, p. 65.

determined powers conjuncturally, within the framework of their particular definitions of reality. The concept of relative autonomy, however, marks not a moment where structural determination ends and agency begins; it marks the structural delimitation of state power and class power.

Miliband, in *Marxism and Politics*, provides a more subtle interpretation of the concept. According to him, relative autonomy refers to the "structural constraints which do beset any government working within the context of a particular mode of production."[50] On this view the concept does not mark the free will of a historical subject; it marks a relationship of structural determination, more specifically, the structural economic limits upon state action. This interpretation is closer to the one we are proposing. It suffers, however, from a one-sided emphasis on the structural determination of the state rather than on the determination of economic relations *by* the state. Miliband notes this in a more recent essay: "There has been considerable discussion among Marxists and others about the nature of the constraints and pressures which cause the state to serve the needs of capital—notably whether these constraints and pressures were 'structural' and impersonal, or produced by a ruling class armed with an arsenal of formidable weapons and resources. But beyond the differences that were expressed in these discussions, there was also a fundamental measure of agreement that the state *was* decisively constrained by forces *external to it*."[51] Miliband correctly insists upon the importance of the causal effectivity of the state. But astonishingly, he completely ignores a body of work within the Marxian tradition, particularly that of Poulantzas, which addresses precisely this point. And in doing so he endorses Theda Skocpol's claim that Marxists have not adequately considered "what states are in their own right."[52] As we shall see in the next section, the analysis of the state's role, as an autonomous institutional structure, in constituting and re-

---

[50]Miliband, *Marxism*, pp. 73–74. He writes: "A capitalist economy has its own 'rationality' to which any government and state must sooner or later submit, and usually sooner."

[51]Ralph Miliband, "State Power and Class Interests," *New Left Review*, no. 138 (March–April 1983), 58–59.

[52]Theda Skocpol, *States and Social Revolutions* (Cambridge: Cambridge University Press, 1979), p. 29.

producing class domination, has been an important theme in recent Marxian writing. The concept of relative autonomy, in this regard, is best construed as denoting the *mutual* determinations between class relations and the state.

The State as a Determinant of Class Relations

Marxian theorists have focused on a number of ways in which the capitalist state secures the conditions of capital accumulation and maintains the domination of capital. These state functions, or *effects* of state power, have as their not necessarily intended consequence the tendential reproduction of class relations. We emphasize the unintentional nature of these reproductive functions insofar as most of the theorists we will discuss posit no teleology, or purposive mechanism, which pursues these consequences. The effects are tendential in that the theory of the state posits no guarantee that the state will actually reproduce class relations; it only posits that the state tends to have this effect because of its specific mode of operation. Thus, despite the interest of certain recent Marxists in functionalist explanation, the explanatory schema I will outline below is not to be understood in functionalist terms.[53] Insofar as we employ the language of "functions," there is no implication of teleology or iron-clad necessity; the functions of the state are simply those things the state does, the typical effects of state power.

The first function emphasized by Marxian theorists, and the most obvious, is the state's narrowly legal function. The capitalist state provides a uniform set of standards, a rationalized code of civil law, which makes capitalist activity possible, both by defining private property rights (contracts, torts, liability, inheritance, etc.) and

[53]On functional explanation and Marxism, see G. A. Cohen, *Karl Marx's Theory of History: A Defense* (Princeton, N.J.: Princeton University Press, 1978). For criticisms, see David Hillel-Ruben, "Review Article: Cohen, Marx, and the Primacy Thesis," *British Journal of Political Science* (1981), 227–34; and James Noble, "Marxian Functionalism," in Terence Ball and James Farr, eds., *After Marx* (Cambridge: Cambridge University Press, 1984). As Noble argues, the language of "function" in Marxism is best understood as referring to structural consequences; and "the typical explanandum of a functional explanation is a structural tendency" (p. 113).

by regulating their exercise. Whether this is accomplished by means of statute (e.g., England's enclosure laws) or constitutional guarantee (e.g., the U.S. Constitution's provisions on "due process" and their interpretation by the Supreme Court), the legal functions of the state are an absolutely essential precondition of capitalism.[54] As the so-called "capital derivation" school, inspired by Eugeny Pashukanis, has emphasized, this not only involves the definition of rights over objects; it also involves the constitution of individuals as bearers of private rights capable of engaging in market transactions.[55] And as Philip Corrigan has pointed out (with regard to English capitalism, but also to capitalism more generally): "The 'rights' which are naturalized by the 1780's or so (and sanctified by the Law) depend entirely upon the destruction and suppression of other rights and the withering away of duties"—particularly the precapitalist norms of reciprocity that obtained in peasant and artisan communities.[56]

This brings us to the second function of the capitalist state emphasized by recent theorists: the repressive function. As with all all states, of course, this has to do with its monopoly of the institutionalized means of violence. Legal guarantees of private property, for example, are reinforced by the state's coercive power. The state has historically performed this function in uprooting squatters, enforcing the lockout of strikers and limiting the freedoms of picketers, and enforcing debts and foreclosures.[57] The state's repressive functions are not limited, however, to the enforcement of civil law; they extend to the more global and political realm as well. Here we must take account of the extensive

---

[54]For an overview, see Colin Sumner, "The Rule of Law and Civil Rights in Contemporary Marxist Theory," *Kapitalistate* 9 (1981), 63–92. On American law, see Arthur Selwyn Miller, *The Supreme Court and American Capitalism* (New York: Free Press, 1968). See also Karl Klare, "Labor Law and the Liberal Political Imagination,"*Socialist Review*, no. 61 (March–April 1982), 45–71.

[55]See Eugeny B. Pashukanis, *Law and Marxism: A General Theory* (London: Ink Links, 1978); John Holloway and Sol Piccioto, eds., *State and Capital: A Marxist Debate* (Austin: University of Texas Press, 1978); and Jessop, *Capitalist State*, pp. 78–141.

[56]Philip Corrigan, "Towards a History of State Formation in Early Modern England," in Philip Corrigan, ed., *Capitalism, State Formation, and Marxist Theory* (London: Quartet Books, 1980), p. 41.

[57]See Alan Wolfe, *The Seamy Side of Democracy* (New York: David McKay, 1973).

network of policing and "national security" institutions that operate to keep "subversives" under surveillance and to regulate the activities of left-wing groups.[58] What we might call manifest class repression has been a far from negligible feature of the history of capitalist politics. But the repressive operations of the state clearly go beyond the suppression of anticapitalist activities and include the more general function of securing "public order," which, however unintentionally, has the effect of maintaining the subordination of the working class. After all, food riots are a disturbance of the peace, but layoffs are the result of the "orderly" workings of the market.[59]

Of course the capitalist state, particularly in its democratic form, is premised, unlike other types of state, on the existence of some form of constitution regulating its exercise of coercive power and providing individual subjects/citizens with legal guarantees (freedoms of expression, organization) and the institutional means of recourse in the event of their violation (the courts). As Poulantzas argues, however, it would be a mistake to polarize the operations of law and violence: "In every State, law is an integral part of the repressive order and of the organization of violence. By issuing rules and passing laws, the State establishes an initial field of injunctions, prohibitions and censorship, and thus institutes the practical terrain and object of violence. Furthermore, law organizes the conditions for physical repression, designating its modalities and structuring the devices by means of which it is exercised. In this sense, law is *the code of organized public violence.*"[60]

Furthermore, Poulantzas points out that the capitalist state, unlike its historical predecessors, possesses not only a monopoly of violence, but a monopoly of war. The institutions of contemporary "national security"— military establishments, administrative bureaucracies, intelligence agencies—function not so much to inhibit anticapitalist political activity as to inhibit *any* political activity. Poulantzas, in his final book, *State, Power, Socialism,* argued at

[58]See Frank Donner, *The Age of Surveillance: The Aims and Methods of America's Political Intelligence System* (New York: Vintage, 1981). E. P. Thompson has reflected on this in his *Writing by Candlelight* (London: Merlin Press, 1980).

[59]See Richard Cloward and Frances Fox Piven, *Poor Peoples' Movements* (New York: Pantheon, 1977).

[60]Poulantzas, *State*, p. 77.

length that a new form of capitalist politics, which he called authoritarian statism, was emerging. Characterized by the decline of parliaments, political parties, and public debate, and the ascendancy of administrative bureaucracies and official secrecy, this form of politics is one in which the supremacy of institutions of repression and "national security" produces a historically novel form of depoliticization whose by-product is, obviously, an even greater difficulty in mobilizing popular opposition to capitalism. And while this type of state does not, by and large, directly exercise its coercive power to suppress socialist politics, a number of recent theorists have argued that the use of military power by advanced capitalist states in the Third World to support corporate mobility and anticommunist dictators serves to weaken labor movements and socialist politics.[61]

Third, on the Marxian view the capitalist state performs an ideological role. This can be seen best by examining the juridico-political function of bourgeois law. Capitalism, as we have seen, is based on the structural separation of the economic and the political. The political sphere here appears as a realm of human equality and the common good. Describing bourgeois law, Poulantzas observes "All trace of class domination is systematically absent from its language."[62] This is true both of private law, where persons are classified as equal bearers of private rights, and of public law, where persons are classified as equal subjects/citizens of the state. The state is thus a plebiscitary structure that tends to relegate all particulars to the realm of the private and to assimilate all intermediary loyalties to the obligation to the unitary state. The consequence of this is what Poulantzas has called the "isolation effect."[63] The effect of bourgeois law, in other words, is to conceal from workers the class nature of their situations by "interpellating" them, constituting their identities as individual citizens, members

[61] See Noam Chomsky, *Towards a New Cold War* (New York: Pantheon, 1982); Mike Davis, "Nuclear Imperialism and Extended Deterrence," in E. P. Thompson et al., *Exterminism and Cold War* (London: Verso, 1982); and James F. Petras and Morris H. Morley, "Imperialism and Intervention in the Third World: U.S. Foreign Policy and Central America," in Ralph Miliband and John Saville, eds., *The Socialist Register 1982* (London: Merlin Press, 1982).

[62] Poulantzas, *Political Power*, p. 214.

[63] Ibid., p. 130.

of a "national community." This concealment is not construed by Poulantzas as either deception or misperception. Rather, it is the lived experience of workers and capitalists that they are bearers of legal private property rights (whether they own means of production or labor power), that they engage in formally free contracts, that they compete with one another on the basis of legal equality, that there are no traditional bonds between them, and that they possess political rights.[64] Isolation, or what Poulantzas later calls "individualization," is thus constitutive of the reality of classes; but it coexists with another reality, the reality of class domination. It is thus not legal equality in abstraction that is highlighted by the theory of the isolation effect, but the effects of this equality within the capitalist mode of production.

The isolation effect, as Poulantzas discusses it, involves three specific processes: (1) the isolation of individuals through private law, as bearers of legal rights; (2) the isolation of individuals through public law, as formally equal subjects/citizens; and (3) the "reconstitution" or "representation" of the unity of individuals so isolated. "This means," Poulantzas writes, "that the state represents the unity of an isolation effect which is, because of the role of the ideological, largely its own effect."[65] The political consequence of this is what Poulantzas calls the disorganization or disunification of the working class. He writes: "This ideology of individualization not only serves to mask and obscure class relations (the capitalist State never presents itself as a class State), but also plays an active part in the divisions and isolation (individualization) of the popular masses."[66] Class, absent from the language of the state, becomes relegated to the realm of the private, and workers assume the public identity of citizens, free and equal, protected by the state. Thus, the organization of a working-class "public" becomes limited; and workers tend to pursue their corporate interests, reproducing the

[64]See Louis Althusser, "Ideology and Ideological State Apparatuses," in his *Lenin*; see also Göran Therborn, *The Ideology of Power and the Power of Ideology* (London: Verso, 1980).

[65]Poulantzas, *Political Power*, p. 134. For a discussion of this with reference to the history of political thought, see my "Was John Locke a Bourgeois Theorist? A Critical Appraisal of Macpherson and Tully," *Canadian Journal of Political and Social Theory* (Fall 1987).

[66]Poulantzas, *State*, p. 66.

separation of public and private that shapes their identities. The consequence, of course, is a weakening of what we have called the "organizational capacities" of the working class, particularly as regards the formation of a socialist political movement. This constraint, it must be emphasized, is not understood as the result of either physical repression or legal prohibition. Rather, it is the effect of the ideological operation of the state and its "repressive tolerance."[67]

In this regard, it should be noted that while this characteristic can be discerned in all forms of capitalist states by virtue of the separation of the economic and the political, it is only in the democratic form of the capitalist state that these characteristics are fully realized. For Poulantzas, like Marx, the democratic state is the characteristic, or normal, form of the capitalist state.[68] The democratic state embodies the complete institutional separation of the economic and the political, insofar as all persons are considered bearers not only of private rights, but of public rights of citizenship as well. Here the state fully constitutes the unity of society, acting universally and impartially through parliamentary and representative institutions, and responding to the demands of a populace formally free and equal to express their preferences and to influence, albeit indirectly, the course of state policy.

Thus the conventional notion of pluralism operates quite characteristically here. Robert Dahl writes: "Democratic politics is merely the chaff, it is the surface manifestation, representing superficial conflicts. Prior to politics, beneath it, enveloping it, restricting it, conditioning it, is the underlying consensus among a predominant portion of the politically active members."[69] But this "underlying consensus," in the Marxian view, is itself an effect of

---

[67]The notion of "repressive tolerance" comes from Herbert Marcuse's "Repressive Tolerance," in Robert Paul Wolff, ed., *A Critique of Pure Tolerance* (Boston: Beacon Press, 1969). Paul Thomas has recurred to this notion in his "Alien Politics," in Ball and Farr.

[68]See Karl Marx, "Contribution to the Critique of Hegel's Philosophy of Law," in Karl Marx and Frederick Engels, *Collected Works*, vol. 3 (New York: International Publishers, 1976), pp. 30–31, on "the political republic" as "the most developed form of the abstract state" and "the negation of this estrangement within its own sphere."

[69]Robert A. Dahl, *A Preface to Democratic Theory* (Chicago: University of Chicago Press, 1956), p. 132.

an underlying structure—the capitalist state. Pluralistic bargaining over economistic demands takes place under the rubric of a legal framework under which all are formally equal citizens with a formally equal voice in government. This framework not only facilitates pluralism, but encourages it by dispersing the political organization of classes. The German theorist Claus Offe has noted a crucial feature of pluralist politics, one that has been lauded by many of the more conservative defenders of pluralism: "The pluralistic system of organized interests excludes from the process of consensus formation all articulations of demands that are general in nature and not associated with any status group."[70] According to Poulantzas, this is substantially because of the ideological effects of the capitalist state, which itself poses as the embodiment of the general interest.

Recent theorists of the capitalist state, particularly Poulantzas, thus view it as an inclusive political structure that extends political and social rights to the working classes. In this they draw their inspiration from Marx, who in "On the Jewish Question" wrote about the franchise: "The *property qualification* is the last *political* form in which private property is recognized. But the political suppression of private property not only does not abolish private property; it actually presupposes its existence.... Far from abolishing these effective differences [of wealth, property, power—J.I.] it only exists insofar as they are presupposed; it is conscious of being a *political state* and it manifests a *universality* only in opposition to these elements."[71]

The argument that T. H. Marshall, Reinhard Bendix, and Ralf Dahrendorf have leveled against Marxism—that social democracy, in extending rights to the working classes, insulates the state from class inequality and therefore invalidates the Marxian theory of the state—is thus based on a thorough misunderstanding of both Marx and contemporary Marxists.[72] Indeed, Bendix's discussion

---

[70]Claus Offe, "Political Authority and Class Structures," in Paul Connerton, ed., *Critical Sociology: Selected Readings* (Harmondsworth, Middlesex: Penguin, 1976), p. 404.

[71]Karl Marx, "On the Jewish Question," in Robert C. Tucker, ed., *The Marx-Engels Reader*, 1st ed. (New York: Norton, 1972), p. 31.

[72]See T. H. Marshall, *Class, Citizenship, and Social Development* (New York: Doubleday, 1964); Ralf Dahrendorf, *Class and Class Conflict in Industrial Society*

of the "civic incorporation of the lower classes" in nineteenth-century Europe is perfectly compatible with the concept of the isolation effect. Bendix writes: "In the nation-state each citizen stands in a direct relation to the sovereign authority of the country. ... Therefore, a core element of nation-building is the codification of the rights and duties of all adults who are classified as citizens. ... The constitution of the modern nation-state is typically the fountainhead of the rights of citizenship, and these rights are a token of nationwide equality. Politics itself has become nationwide, and the lower classes now have the opportunity of active participation."[73]

It is, of course, the articulation of these political rights with class domination, and the ideological effect of these rights in reproducing this domination, which is the central point of the Marxian criticism of capitalist democracy. It is ironic that Bendix uses the word *token* to describe these rights, because in the Marxian view these rights are a token of political equality, whose symbolic significance exceeds their real effectivity as means of working-class empowerment. It is important to emphasize, however, that the great majority of contemporary Marxian theorists acknowledge the genuine importance of political democracy, which they understand both as a supremely valuable product of popular struggle and as an absolutely necessary precondition of socialism. Poulantzas concludes his final book with: "One thing is certain: socialism will be democratic or it will not be at all."[74]

Contemporary Marxian political theorists, in discussing the capitalist state, thus acknowledge its typically democratic character. It has often been noted by critics of Marxism that the working class does not act politically as a unified class and does not vote as a class. It is undeniable that this constitutes something of an anomaly for classical Marxism. Despite the subtlety of some of the analyses of Marx (and, we might add, of Lenin) on the subject of the complex mechanisms of class domination, classical Marxism displayed a general optimism about the imminence of a mass-based socialist working-class movement. This optimism, as is historically

---

(Stanford: Stanford University Press, 1959); and Reinhard Bendix, *Nation-Building and Citizenship* (Berkeley: University of California Press, 1977).

[73]Bendix, pp. 89–90.

[74]Poulantzas, *State*, p. 265.

obvious, has been dashed in the twentieth century, as national working classes have been successfully (though not unproblematically) incorporated into the structure of capitalist democracy. Contemporary Marxian theorists have attempted to explain this anomaly, both through revised theories of the accumulation process and, in the case of Poulantzas, through an analysis of the political and ideological mechanisms of incorporation.

Thus, while democracy as a form of capitalist state, in providing the working classes with the vote, offers them real opportunities for socialist politics through its relatively open and peaceful institutionalization of conflict, it also serves as a barrier to such a politics, as a structural constraint. In one sense Marxian theorists might agree with Seymour Martin Lipset's argument that elections are the arena of "the democratic class struggle."[75] But as Poulantzas has emphasized, while capitalist democracy is based on the existence of a subordinate working class, it does not give the working class as such the vote—it gives the vote to individual members of the working class as individuals, *despite* their membership in the working class. In Marx's words, it manifests a universality only in opposition to the asymmetries of private life.[76]

Rather than interpreting the capitalist state as a structure that represses an imminent class-majoritarian movement for socialism, contemporary Marxian theorists have tried to explain why such a movement is not imminent. Poulantzas's formulations about the state and its ideological effects are attempts to understand how it is possible that class domination, class struggle, and the periodic economic crises that capitalism generates have not led to a socialist transformation of capitalism. Marxian theorists have confronted the reality of reform and have acknowledged the role democratic institutions, through their forms of law and representative mechanisms, have played in the structuration of reform. These reforms are, however, reforms *of* capitalism, not its negation. In expanding the umbrella of political and social rights, the capitalist state has

---

[75]Seymour Martin Lipset, "Elections: The Expression of Democratic Class Struggle," in his *Political Man: The Social Bases of Politics* (New York: Doubleday Anchor, 1963). For a Marxian discussion, see Bob Jessop, "Capitalism and Democracy: The Best Possible Shell?" in G. Littlejohn, ed., *Power and the State* (London: Croom Helm, 1978).

[76]See Thomas, in Ball and Farr.

at the same time reinforced the separation of production and politics, which is the hallmark of capitalism as a mode of production. Marxist theorists have not only highlighted the way the state is a determinant of class relations, functioning to reproduce them over time, they have also described the structural constraints impinging upon the state, limiting it as a potential means of socialist transformation and sustaining a class bias in its public policies.

Capitalism and the Determination of the State

As we have seen, for many Marxian theorists the capitalist state must be understood as truly a "superstructure" in a radically nonreductionist sense. That is, it is a relatively autonomous structure of centralized political power which, far from standing in a mechanical relation of exteriority, "has always, in different forms, been present in the constitution and reproduction of the relations of production."[77] If Marxian theorists have emphasized the effectivity of state power, however, they have also highlighted its *limits*. The state is a political structure, concerned with territorial rule and order, but it is not an economic structure. In the Marxian view the capitalist state rules and secures the conditions of existence of a set of economic practices, capitalist production and accumulation, which are institutionally distinct from itself. The class relations of capitalist production, and the domination of capital, thus impose crucial limitations on the capitalist state, limitations that are particularly felt by social democratic and socialist governments attempting to reform or challenge the power of capital. Marxian theorists have placed great emphasis on these limits.

The first limit is that the capitalist state does not engage directly in economically productive activities, and as such does not produce its own sources of revenue. It is thus limited by the private accumulation process and depends on the successful production and circulation of commodities and the accumulation and reinvestment of capital. What Claus Offe calls "problems of economic stability" are thus significant constraints on state policy. Offe and Volker Ronge write:

[77]Poulantzas, *State*, p. 17.

Since the state *depends* on a process of accumulation which is beyond its power to *organize*, every occupant of state power is interested in promoting those conditions most conducive to accumulation. This interest does not result from alliance of a particular government with particular classes also interested in accumulation, nor does it result from any political power of the capitalist class which "puts pressure" on the incumbents of state power to pursue its class interest. Rather, it does result from an *institutional self-interest* of the state which is conditioned by the fact that the state is *denied* the power to control the flow of those resources which are indispensable for the *use* of state power.[78]

Economic prosperity, as generated through private accumulation, is thus a constraint upon the state insofar as it is a necessary condition of state revenues and thus of political stability itself. Lindblom has called this the "privileged position of business." He writes: "Because public functions in the market system rest in the hands of businessmen, it follows that jobs, prices, production, growth, the standard of living, and the economic security of every-one all rest in their hands. Consequently, government officials can-not be indifferent to how well business performs its functions."[79] As Claus Offe and Helmut Wiesenthal point out, this privileged position of the capitalist class, which is directly grounded in the powers of economic possession discussed in Chapter 4, translates into a special relationship between business and the state:

Communications of business associations with the state differ in that they are less visible publicly (because there is a lesser need to mobilize the support of external allies), more technical (because the insight into the political "desirability," that is, factual indispensability, can be presupposed as already agreed upon), more universal (because business associations can speak in the name of all those interests that require for their fulfillment a healthy and continuous rate of accu-mulation, which from the point of view of capital and the state is true of virtually everybody), and negative (because, given the fact that the government has to consider as desirable what is in fact

[78]See Claus Offe and Volker Ronge, "Theses on the Theory of the State," *New German Critique*, no. 6 (Fall 1975), 137–47.
[79]Charles E. Lindblom, *Politics and Markets* (New York: Harper Colophon, 1977), p. 172.

desirable for capital, the only thing that remains to be done is to warn government against imprudent, "unrealistic," and otherwise inopportune decisions and measures).[80]

This privileged position, it must be emphasized, is conceived of as a structural constraint upon capitalist states. While it provides the political organizations of capital with privileged access to the state, and in general enhances the organizational capacities of the capitalist class, it does not mean that the state is incapable of acting against the politically expressed preferences of capital. Nor does it mean that every policy pursued by the state is undertaken with an eye toward short-term economic prosperity. It simply, but crucially, means that successful capital accumulation is an essential policy consideration due to the state's dependence on economic prosperity for revenues and stability. State interventions in the economy (macroeconomic policy, health and safety regulations, etc.) always run the risk of overstepping "system limits," of discouraging or otherwise inhibiting investment, and of generating economic instability. The experience of the Mitterrand government in France is a particularly graphic example of this structural constraint upon state policy, which has recently been felt in one form or another by the governments of all the advanced capitalist societies.[81] Wright refers to this constraint as the "limits of functional compatibility": governmental policies designed to bring about certain objectives—like Mitterrand's reduction in the work week or his redistributionary programs—prove themselves to be dysfunctional to the accumulation process, producing an investment crisis that undermines the policies.[82] This functional limitation does not work itself out in a mysterious system-adaptive fashion; it is manifested in a situation

[80]Claus Offe and Helmut Wiesenthal, "Two Logics of Collective Action: Theoretical Notes on Social Class and Organizational Form," in Maurice Zeitlin, ed., *Political Power and Social Theory* (Greenwich, Conn.: JAI Press, 1979), p. 86.

[81]See George Ross and Jane Jenson, "Crisis and France's 'Third Way': Genesis, Implementation, and Contradictions of a Left Strategy out of Economic Crisis," *Studies in Political Economy*, no. 11 (Summer 1983), 71–103, and Mark Kesselman, "Capitalist Austerity versus Socialist 'Rigeur': Does It Make a Difference? The Case of France," *New Political Science*, no. 12 (Summer 1983), 37–56. On this problem, see also Andrew Martin, "Is Democratic Control of Capitalist Economies Possible?" in Leon Lindberg et al., *Stress and Contradiction in Modern Capitalism* (Lexington, Mass.: D. C. Heath, 1975).

[82]Wright, *Class*, pp. 19–21.

of economic instability that generates a fiscal crisis of the state and, consequently, a decline in popular support for the government. Policies that were initially popular become unpopular as they come up against the structural imperatives of the accumulation process and the structural interests of capital.

As Offe and Ronge are quick to point out, however, this special interest or privileged position of the capitalist class does not appear as a special or privileged interest: "[It] does not directly mean guarding the general interests of a particular class, but guarding the general interests of all classes on the basis of capitalist exchange relationships."[83] Przeworski explains how this is so:

> Since profit is the necessary condition of universal expansion, capitalists appear within capitalist societies as the bearers of universal interest. Their present interests happen to coincide with the future interests of anyone in the society: the larger the profits they appropriate, the greater the capacity of the entire society to improve the future conditions of material life. Demands on the part of any other group to improve their current conditions of life appear as inimical to the realization of the interests of the entire society in the future. Under capitalism conflicts over wages and profits appear as a trade-off between the present and the future. Capitalists are in a unique position by virtue of the organization of the capitalist system of production: their interests appear as universal, while the interests of all other groups appear as particularistic.[84]

The structural privileging of capital, then, not only serves as a constraint on even the most radical governmental programs (I do not mean to suggest that Mitterrand's program was the most radical, although some of his initial domestic policies did attempt to challenge the investment power of French capital, particularly of the banks), undermining them through the limits of functional compatibility, but it also serves to cast in a negative light any potential programs that challenge the power of capital. Within the context of a capitalist economy, any such policies are taken to

---

[83]Offe and Ronge, p. 142.

[84]Adam Przeworski, "Proletariat into a Class: The Process of Class Formation from Karl Kautsky's 'The Class Struggle' to Recent Controversies," *Politics and Society* 7 (1977), 350.

"efficiency" of capital and labor markets and undermine the long-term growth and prosperity of society as a whole.

As Marxian theorists have emphasized, however, if the structure of capitalist production limits the scope of state intervention, it also generates pressures on the state to intervene in social life. One of the most basic claims of the Marxian tradition is that capital accumulation is not a stable and unproblematic process of linear growth, but a contradictory one—a dynamic process that generates inherent class antagonisms, its very success tending to undermine it and produce economic crises. According to classical Marxian political economy, this is due to a basic contradiction between use value and exchange value under capitalism—the fact that individual capitalists typically produce as much as they can in order to make a profit, and then must realize this profit through the circulation of commodities on the market.[85] The anarchy of production is thus, for Marxism, a major cause of economic crises of realization or profitability.

Contemporary Marxian theorists, however, have also emphasized the importance of a number of other "defects" of the capitalist market— various externalities and maldistributions—which, while not the products of crisis tendencies, do confront the state as "social problems" to be processed and resolved. These social problems are sometimes manifested diffusely, in the form of social disequilibrium (demographic and industrial shifts, unemployment, pollution), discontent, or lawlessness. And sometimes they are manifested directly in social and political struggles, as explicit political demands for state action and proposals for public policy.[86] State intervention thus becomes imperative, particularly in times of economic crisis when the problem of "business confidence" is diminished by the manifest inability of the market to promote prosperity.

The capitalist state is thus caught in something of a dilemma— it is constrained to respect the privileged position of capital as the source of investment and accumulation, *and* it is constrained to

[85]See Paul Sweezy, *The Theory of Capitalist Development* (New York: Monthly Review Books, 1942); and Ernest Mandel, *Marxist Economic Theory*, vol. 1 (New York: Monthly Review Press, 1971).

[86]See Claus Offe, "The Theory of the Capitalist State and the Problem of Policy Formation," in Lindberg.

intervene to remedy the problems of the capitalist market produced by the manner in which capital accumulation takes place. As Offe points out, "These two strategies thwart and paralyze each other." He has argued that this situation generates what he calls "a crisis of crisis management," whereby state institutions, organizationally unprepared to secure crisis-free economic growth through regulatory and planning mechanisms, fail to "solve" the problems of the private economy and in fact reproduce them within the state itself. "State regulation," he writes, "has a self-obstructing character... this inability results from the self-contradictory imperatives of state policy: while it must organize the dysfunctional social consequences of private production, state policy is not supposed to infringe on the primacy of private production."[87]

James O'Connor, in his influential book *The Fiscal Crisis of the State*, has similarly argued that the capitalist state is prone to debilitating fiscal crises: "The capitalist state must try to fulfill two basic and often mutually contradictory functions—accumulation and legitimization.... This means that the state must try to maintain or create the conditions in which profitable capital accumulation is possible. However, the state also must try to maintain or create the conditions for social harmony."[88] O'Connor and others point out that the consequence of these contradictory imperatives toward intervention is that the state itself becomes the site of struggle over a whole series of distributional and more generally economic questions— infrastructural spending, educational and other social capital expenses, transfer payments, and systems of taxation. The state both assumes a responsibility for these conditions of capitalism, which cannot be secured through the market, and it suffers a structural liability that persistently limits its ability to raise revenues and administer programs effectively. Marxian theorists have pioneered the study of the "governability crisis" that has beset the contemporary capitalist state, focusing on both the structural

---

[87]Claus Offe, " 'Crisis of Crisis Management': Elements of a Political Crisis Theory," in Claus Offe, *Contradictions of the Welfare State* (Cambridge, Mass.: MIT Press, 1984), p. 61.

[88]James O'Connor, *The Fiscal Crisis of the State* (New York: St. Martin's, 1973), p. 6. See also his "The Fiscal Crisis of the State Revisited: A Look at Economic Crisis and Reagan's Budget Policy," *Kapitalistate* 9 (1981), 41–62.

contradictions of capitalism as a mode of production and the privileged position the capitalist state accords private capital in the formation of public policy.[89]

Class Struggle, Political Conflict, and the State

As we saw in Chapter 4, while the Marxian analysis of class emphasizes the importance of structural determinations, it does not reduce class agents to the status of mere "effects" of a structure. Rather, the specific cultural and organizational practices and forms of power developed by classes are viewed as central to the analysis of capitalism. Similarly, although contemporary Marxists have analyzed the state as a real "objective" structure, and formulated theories regarding its relative autonomy from class relations, in doing so they have not supposed that the state is "above" human practice. Rather, they have, however implicitly, viewed it as both the medium and the effect of political struggle. As Gösta Esping-Andersen, Roger Friedland, and Erik Olin Wright have argued, "The state is simultaneously a product, an object, and a determinant of class conflict."[90]

Most of the concern of this chapter has been with the state as a *determinant* of class conflict; as a structure of centralized political power, as a source of law and public policy, and as a principal determinant of social identity in capitalist society, the state plays a crucial role in shaping and constraining the organization and exercise of political power on the part of classes and other social groups. The state is also, as most political theorists would acknowledge, an *object* of class conflict; as the sovereign power, the "factor of cohesion" of the social formation, the state is the primary means of achieving social and political objectives, which political organizations strive to influence, occupy, and control. Finally, the state is a *product* of political conflict; as a system of institutions,

---

[89]See Claus Offe, " 'Ungovernablity': The Renaissance of Conservative Theories of Crisis," in Offe, *Contradictions*. See also Jürgen Habermas, *Legitimation Crisis* (Boston: Beacon Press, 1975); and Alan Wolfe, *The Limits of Legitimacy* (New York: Free Press, 1977).

[90]Gösta Esping-Andersen, Roger Friedland, and Erik Olin Wright, "Modes of Class Struggle and the Capitalist State," *Kapitalistate* 4–5 (1976).

rather than a thing, the state changes over time in response to the pressures and demands placed upon it, as well as to the attempts of groups and organizations to alter its structure. (Poulantzas, for instance, writes of the state as a "specific material condensation of a relationship of forces among classes and class fractions," suggesting both that the institutions of the state bear the imprint of previous struggles and that they shape present and future struggles, which take place not only outside but within the state.)[91]

It is important to recognize, then, that what we might call the *compromise* function of the state, its role in serving as an arena of political conflict and in granting concessions to the working classes, occupies an important place in Marxian political theory.[92] This is true in particular in the case of Poulantzas, despite the criticism frequently leveled at his "hyperstructuralism." He writes:

> Thus, in its relations to the field of class struggle, the capitalist state's relative autonomy depends on the characteristics peculiar to the economic and political class struggle in the capitalist mode of production and in a capitalist formation. This must be understood in the general sense of the relations between the structures and the field of the class struggle. In this sense the state sets the *limits* within which the class struggle affects it; *the play of its institutions allows and makes possible* this relative autonomy from the dominant classes and fractions. The *variations and modalities* of this relative autonomy depend upon the concrete relation between social forces in the field of political class struggle; in particular they depend upon the *political struggle of the dominated classes*.[93]

In other words, the state sets limits on the political struggle, which in turn transforms the state itself. The variations and modalities of the state's relative autonomy from the dominant class are determined by class struggle and political organization. At times cap-

[91]Poulantzas, *State*, p. 129.

[92]Adam Przeworski, "Material Bases of Consent: Economics and Politics in a Hegemonic System," in Zeitlin; also Adam Przeworski and Michael Wallerstein, "The Structure of Class Conflict in Democratic Capitalist Societies," *American Political Science Review* 76 (June 1982), 215–38, and Joshua Cohen and Joel Rogers, *On Democracy* (London: Penguin, 1984). For a historical overview of the question of class compromise, see Adam Przeworski, "Social Democracy as a Historical Phenomenon," *New Left Review*, no. 122 (1980), 27–58.

[93]Poulantzas, *Political Power*, p. 289.

italists may be better organized and placed to influence the state; at times the working classes may be so situated. Poulantzas points out that this can only be analyzed at the level of a concrete conjuncture within a specific social formation. Once again, it is essential to distinguish the different levels of abstraction at which theory is pitched, and to insist that general propositions about the state's structural autonomy must always be complemented by a more concrete assessment of the political situation at hand. As Poulantzas's text makes clear, what we have called the organizational capacities of classes—as embodied particularly in business associations, trade unions, and political parties—play a crucial role in determining the outcomes of such political struggles. Poulantzas, particularly in his later writings, increasingly gravitated toward a strategic concept of political power, urging that "the political power of a class, its capacity to realize its political interests, depends not only on its class place (and determination) with regard to other classes, but also on the position and strategy it displays in relation to them—on what I have called opponent strategy."[94]

Poulantzas also makes clear, however, that this specific autonomy, its modalities and variations, is made possible by the "play" of the institutions of the capitalist state. "All these variations," he writes, "occur within the limits of the relative autonomy constitutive of the capitalist type of state."[95] In other words, it is the structural separation of the the economic and the political that makes the modalities of the exercise of state power possible. This makes the state in no case, no matter how politically weak and disorganized the working class, a mere instrument of capital. And it makes it equally in no case, no matter how politically organized and influential the working class, a neutral instrument of a potential socialist transformation.[96]

It is in this light that we should note the remarkable revival of interest in Antonio Gramsci on the part of Western Marxists, and in particular the attention his concept of "hegemony" has received.[97] For Gramsci this concept designated the "intellectual and

---

[94]Poulantzas, *State*, p. 147.

[95]Poulantzas, *Political Power*, p. 287.

[96]On this point see Leo Panitch, "Trade Unions and the Capitalist State," *New Left Review*, no. 125 (1981), 21–43.

[97]See Perry Anderson, "The Antinomies of Antonio Gramsci," *New Left Review*,

moral leadership" a social group exercised within society. As Jessop points out, the concept has often been used by Marxists in two different senses. In the first sense, the concept refers to the structural, particularly the ideological, determination of class domination; in this sense, the capitalist class is hegemonic insofar as its structural power involves a blend of coercion and consent, being neither a simple imposition upon a recalcitrant subordinate nor an unconstrained, freely accepted capacity. In the second sense, the concept refers directly to the class struggle itself, to the stance adopted by classes in relation to other classes, the organizational capacities they have developed and the political projects they are capable of initiating.[98] Chantal Mouffe writes: "Hegemony, which always has its basis, for Gramsci, in 'the decisive function exercised by the leading group in the decisive nucleus of economic activity,' operates principally in civil society via the articulation of the interests of the fundamental class to those of its allies in order to form a collective will, a unified political subject."[99]

In this second sense hegemony refers to the political weight and influence class groups and organizations are able to conjuncturally assert. Colin Leys, for instance, has recently written of the historical failure of British manufacturing capital to become hegemonic, and of the relative strength of British financial and multinational capital, both of which have contributed to the rise of Thatcherism and the policy of deindustrialization.[100] And Mike Davis has argued that the hegemony of a hyperentrepreneurial fraction of capital, based in the Sun Belt and California, has contributed to the rise of the New Right and Reaganism in the United States.[101] In this sense of

no. 100 (November 1976–January 1977); Chantal Mouffe, ed., *Gramsci and Marxist Theory* (London: Routledge & Kegan Paul, 1979); Christine Buci-Glucksmann, *Gramsci and the State* (London: Lawrence and Wishart, 1980); Anne Showstack Sassoon, *Approaches to Gramsci* (London: Writers and Readers Publishing Cooperative, 1982); John Hoffman, *The Gramscian Challenge: Coercion and Consent in Marxist Political Theory* (Oxford: Blackwell, 1984); and Carl Boggs, *The Two Revolutions: Gramsci and the Dilemmas of Western Marxism* (Boston: South End Press, 1984).

[98]Jessop, *Nicos Poulantzas*, p. 139.

[99]Chantal Mouffe, "Introduction: Gramsci Today," in Mouffe, p. 10.

[100]Colin Leys, "Thatcherism and British Manufacturing: A Question of Hegemony," *New Left Review*, no. 151 (May–June 1985), 5–25. On this point see also Frank Longstreth, "The City, Industry, and the State," in Colin Crouch, ed., *State and Economy in Contemporary Capitalism* (London: Croom Helm, 1979).

[101]Mike Davis, "The New Right's Road to Power," *New Left Review*, no. 128

hegemony it is possible to conceive of the working class becoming hegemonic within capitalist society, insofar as its members are capable of mobilizing mass popular support for a socialist project and of developing the institutional means (unions, neighborhood, local, and enterprise councils, political parties and coalitions) to support it. Gramsci, of course, envisioned just such a possibility in the following, much-quoted discussion of the foundation of working-class hegemony:

> A third moment is that in which one becomes aware that one's own corporate interests, in their present and future development, transcend the corporate limits of the purely economic class, and can and must become the interests of other subordinate groups too. This is the most purely political phase, and marks the decisive passage from the structure to the sphere of the superstructures; it is the phase in which previously germinated ideologies become "party," come into confrontation and conflict, until only one of them, or at least a single combination of them, tends to prevail, to gain the upper hand, to propagate itself throughout society, bringing about not only a unison of economic and political claims, but also intellectual and moral unity ...on a "universal" plane, and thus creating the hegemony of a fundamental social group over a series of subordinate groups.[102]

Of course this does not mean that all working-class political struggle is hegemonic, and it certainly should not be taken as a guarantee of the historical "necessity" of the emergence of a mass socialist, working-class politics. But it does indicate the importance of political and ideological struggle within Marxian theory and practice. And it also points toward a necessary precondition of socialism that has been acknowledged by most contemporary Marxian theorists—the always problematic and contested construction, through persuasion and struggle, of a democratic movement that, in the struggle against capitalism, recognizes the indispensability, on moral and strategic grounds, of political diversity and mass support.

(July–August 1981), 28–49, and "The Political Economy of Late Imperial America," *New Left Review*, no. 143 (January–February 1984), 6–38.

[102]Antonio Gramsci, "The Modern Prince," in Geoffrey Nowell Smith and Quentin Hoare, eds., *Selections from the Prison Notebooks* (New York: International Publishers, 1971), pp. 181–82.

This strategic program, clearly associated with some variant of Eurocommunism and with the abandonment of Leninism, follows quite logically from the sort of analysis of the state we have sketched above. In this view capitalist democracy is not a sham or a "class dictatorship."[103] Rather, it is a specific constellation of class power and state power that, while premised upon the domination of capital, also affords genuine opportunities for anticapitalist political struggle, and institutionalizes the results of such struggle. In this sense it is relatively autonomous; but in thinking about the autonomy of the state, Marxists have also insisted on the *relativity* of this autonomy. As we began this chapter, it is fitting to end with Miliband and Poulantzas.

Miliband, in *Marxism and Politics*, concludes by raising the following question: "Let it be supposed . . . that a left-wing and communist-led government, backed by an electoral and parliamentary majority, did decide to carry through far-reaching anti-capitalist measures. . . . What then?" He suggests that a protracted struggle would ensue both inside and outside of the state, and that such measures would invariably lead to capital disinvestment, economic instability, and serious economic hardship for large numbers of workers and citizens. The economic constraints on the capitalist state, in other words, would limit what even the most committed socialist government could accomplish, producing both economic deterioration and popular animosity toward the government. Miliband thus concludes that "the government has only one major resource, namely its popular support. But this support, expressed at the polls, has to be sustained through extremely difficult times, and it has to be mobilized . . . [and] must lead to a vast extension of democratic participation in all areas of civil life."[104] In other words, working-class organizational power must be cultivated and popular support deepened so that it can be sustained in the times of economic hardship that will invariably befall any socialist government.

---

[103]For criticism of the concept of "dictatorship of the proletariat," see Ralph Miliband, "Constitutionalism and Revolution: Notes on Eurocommunism," in Ralph Miliband and John Saville, eds., *The Socialist Register 1978* (New York: Monthly Review Press, 1978); and Roy Medvedev, *Leninism and Western Marxism* (London: Verso, 1979).

[104]Miliband, *Marxism*, pp. 183–90.

Similarly Poulantzas, in his last book, *State, Power, Socialism*, writes of "the extension and deepening of political freedom and the institutions of representative democracy ... combined with the unfurling of forms of direct democracy and the mushrooming of self-management bodies,"[105] envisioning these developments as part of a socialist movement-building strategy. Like Miliband, he sees these as necessary as a "guarantee against the reaction of the enemy," thinking primarily of the problems of economic destabilization, but also of the possibility and the danger of political repression. But he also sees them as necessary in a more fundamental sense, insofar as they are essential to the creation of a socialist identity, to the establishment of forms of solidarity in the absence of which the prospects of governmental power are hopeless. The democratization of the state and of society, in this view, is necessary to counteract not only the class power of capital, but also the ideological effects of state power, which Poulantzas has called the "isolation effect."

Political struggle, as a means of controlling the state and influencing public policy, and as a means of transforming its operations, is thus at the center of recent Marxian theories of the state. Skocpol is thus simply incorrect when she accuses Marxian theorists, particularly Poulantzas, of "political functionalism." She writes:

> Poulantzian theory predicts functional outcomes of state policies and interventions. ... Poulantzas is saying that no matter what, the state functions automatically to stabilize and reproduce the capitalist system ... [he] wants us to believe that the state and politics always do just what needs to be done to stabilize capitalist society and keep the economy going. If this were really true, then state structures, state interventions, and political conflicts would not really be worth studying in any detail, and politics as such would have no explanatory importance.[106]

This is a gross mischaracterization, for the point of recent Marxian theorizing has been precisely to insist upon the sui generis reality

---

[105]Poulantzas, *State*, p. 256.

[106]Theda Skocpol, "Political Response to Capitalist Crisis: Neo-Marxist Theories of the State and the Case of the New Deal," *Politics and Society* 10 (1980), 172–73, 182.

of politics and the state. As we have argued, this theorizing rests upon implicitly realist presuppositions; and insofar as it is interested in characterizing structures, it eschews the canons of empiricism and speaks of tendencies, not regularities. For Poulantzas, Miliband, and others, the capitalist state, for reasons having to do with its internal characteristics and its structural relationship to the economy, tends to reproduce the domination of capital. But in social life nothing happens "automatically," and the state certainly provides no historical guarantees to capital. One searches in vain in the writings of Poulantzas, even his original critique of Miliband, which most bears the traces of functionalist language, for the suggestion that "the state and politics always do just what needs to be done to stabilize capitalist society." As we have seen, in the Marxian view politics does not do anything; rather, politics is *practiced* by class collectivities, who define their interests, organize themselves around these interests, and struggle in pursuit of them.

There are certainly criticisms one might level against Marxist political theory. Skocpol in her own research has indicated some of them. But before we can engage in a critical assessment of the merits of Marxism we must exorcize the specters of empiricism, abandon the language of predictions and functional necessities, and take seriously both the critical revisions contemporary Marxists have made within the Marxist corpus and the substantial contribution they have made to political analysis.

CHAPTER 6

Power and the
Limits of Marxism

The major burden of my argument has thus far been methodological. As I have argued, the prevailing way of thinking about power in political science suffers from serious weaknesses, and a realist interpretation of power provides us with a plausible alternative that goes beyond the confines of the usual debate, transcending the constraints of empiricism. I have also argued that Marxian theory, speaking broadly, presupposes such a realist perspective. As such, it is eminently scientific and deserves to be taken seriously by all of those who identify themselves as practitioners of social scientific analysis. Such methodological arguments are crucially important, given both the general methodological orientation of contemporary social and political theory and the more specific hold empiricist methodologies have had upon social science.

I harbor no illusions, however, about the force of such methodological arguments, which are in themselves relatively ineffective and have required, if the history of contemporary social science is any guide, powerful institutional support if they are to take hold. There are many reasons, most of them far from methodological, for the subaltern status of Marxism within the social scientific community, and however important methodology has been as an ideological buffer for mainstream social science, it would be a serious mistake to imagine that a methodological analysis such as this book could decisively challenge the situation. Furthermore, on theoretical grounds alone it is far from clear that Marxism, however scientific it is, is truly a *valid* science. A satisfactory treatment of this issue would require another volume. And yet the present book would be grossly unsatisfactory if we failed to address it.

In what follows, then, I will attempt to provide some tentative, and programmatic, answers to the question of the validity of Marxism, concluding that, however insufficient, Marxism is a necessary condition of our understanding of power in contemporary society. The comments that follow should be understood as reflections on Marxism as a problematic in the most literal sense—on the genuine *problems* of Marxism as a theory and practice of power. Such a critical attitude is necessary in the pursuit of scientific knowledge and it is indispensable for the continued flourishing of Marxian theory. Although Marxian theory has its limits, the recognition of this need not lead us to abandon it. In this light, while the reflections below suggest certain problems for Marxism, they are equally critical of those contemporary critics who have rejected Marxism in toto. We can only agree with the observation of Anthony Giddens, that, whatever its limitations, "Marx's analysis of the mechanisms of capitalist production...remains the necessary core of any attempt to come to terms with the massive transformations that have swept through the world since the eighteenth century."[1]

Pluralism and Ideology

Pluralist theorists like Dahl and Polsby have never taken Marxism very seriously, except insofar as it seemed to them to represent a manifestly unscientific, and thus clearly illegitimate, intellectual enterprise. As we have seen, this view of Marxism is mistaken. The mistake, however, has persisted by virtue of a deeper mistake, the commitment to philosophical empiricism. This of course was not simply an intellectual mistake, however much it was this; the institutionalization of disciplines and the bureaucratization of the university, corporation, and state certainly played important roles in the historical formation of this commitment, providing powerful inducements to discard any trace of "metaphysics" and to under-

---

[1] Anthony Giddens, *A Contemporary Critique of Historical Materialism* (Berkeley: University of California Press, 1981), p. 1.

take what Mills has called abstracted empiricist research.[2] As we
have seen, methodological empiricism has played a crucial role in
delegitimizing radical political science. It should thus not be surprising that it has played a corresponding role in fortifying pluralist
theory. Empiricism in political science provided a scientific ideal
toward which political theorists could aspire. And behavioralists,
like Dahl and Polsby, seemed to practice political science according
to this ideal. In this sense empiricism can be seen as an ideology—
a regulative norm of political research. But it can also be seen as
an ideology in a more fundamental sense—as a norm that has
mystified social scientific research, providing both a methodological
buttress for mainstream political science and misconceiving its actual foundations.

There is certainly a pluralist theory of power. And yet, if my
argument is correct, the methodological debate among political
scientists about the concept of power, a debate stimulated by pluralist theorists like Dahl, has produced nothing in the way of substantive theory. Polsby himself admits that "the study of
community power has contributed little or nothing in the way of
knowledge."[3] The debate, of course, has had important effects,
blocking the development of alternatives to pluralist theory and
consequently providing methodological justification for pluralism.
But it has not issued in any theoretical analyses of power that
actually conform to the empiricist standards it prescribed. This is
remarkable, and it has proved difficult for many commentators,
who have imagined that Dahl's analysis of New Haven, for instance, looked only at the "first face of power."[4] Dahl's analysis
in fact examined many things, being infinitely richer than the methodological arguments that have subserved it. And it also failed to
look at many things relevant to the study of power in cities like
New Haven. But what should be clear to anyone who has read
Dahl's methodological articles on power is that *Who Governs?* is

[2] C. Wright Mills, *The Sociological Imagination* (Oxford: Oxford University
Press, 1959). For a recent account of this, see Peter T. Manicas, *A History and
Philosophy of Social Science* (Oxford: Blackwell, 1987).
[3] Nelson R. Polsby, *Community Power and Political Theory*, 2d ed. (New Haven:
Yale University Press, 1980), p. xi.
[4] See Andrew Cox et al., *Power in Capitalist Society: Theory, Explanations, and
Cases* (New York: St. Martin's, 1985).

not an "operationalization" of the method these articles prescribe.[5]
The interpretation of counterfactuals, and the more general deductive-nomological analysis that supports it, play virtually no role
in Dahl's discussion; and insofar as he talks about power, for
instance in his discussions of Mayor Richard Lee, the term is used
in the loosest of senses, being vaguely substitutable for the word
influence.

In fact, while the book is undeniably a masterful case study, it
is considered a classic in contemporary political science because it
purports to illustrate certain general features of liberal democratic
politics. Yet although it certainly does articulate certain generalizations about the nature (dare we say structure?) of liberal democracy, it clearly does not do so with any of the rigor or formality
required by empiricism. Pluralist theorists have had no trouble
articulating their theory, but when they do so they sound remark-
ably like the "metaphysicians" they criticize, making categorical
claims and providing existential rather than conditional explanations. Polsby summarizes the characteristics of liberal democracy
highlighted by pluralist theory: "Dispersion of power among many
rather than a few participants in decision-making; competition or
conflict among political leaders; specialization of leaders to relatively restricted sets of issue areas; bargaining rather than hierarchical decision-making; elections in which suffrage is relatively
widespread as a major determinant of participation in key decisions; bases of influence over decisions are relatively dispersed
rather than closely held...."[6]

Dahl's work is similarly characterized by existential claims about
the nature of democracy. In fact none of his major theoretical
works, from his *Polyarchy* to his recent *Dilemmas of Pluralist
Democracy*, represents the kind of search for behavioral regularities
trumpeted by behavioralism. Rather, they involve the analysis, in
general terms, of what Dahl has called the "institutional conditions" of pluralist democracy.[7] I would contend that pluralism is
an implicitly realist theory of political power, a theory distinguished

---

[5]See Peter Morriss, "Power in New Haven: A Reassessment of 'Who Governs?' "
British Journal of Political Science, no. 2 (October 1972), 457–65.

[6]Polsby, *Community Power*, p. 154.

[7]Robert A. Dahl, *Polyarchy* (New Haven: Yale University Press, 1971), and
Dilemmas of Pluralist Democracy (New Haven: Yale University Press, 1982).

by three general claims: (1) the political institutions of liberal democracies are relatively open, public, and responsive to the pressures brought upon them; (2) they are therefore neutral as regards
the interests that can be articulated and the policies that can be
adopted; and (3) under these institutional conditions there tends
to be a plurality of competing groups and a dispersal of political
influence among them.

Once we pierce the empiricist illusions that have helped sustain
pluralist theory, we can see that these sorts of claims are formally
no different from the competing claims of Marxian theory. Pluralism can then stand or fall on its own substantive merits, not on
the basis of specious methodological supports. On these grounds
it has something to recommend itself. It provides a plausible empirical description of the workings of liberal democratic politics,
and it is certainly the case that, in its emphasis on political het-
erogeneity, it appears more adequate than any theory positing an
immanent polarization of society. Simply theories of elite manipulation, and historicist versions of class conflict, are not borne out
by any sort of empirical evidence; and it would certainly not be
inaccurate to view pluralist theory as postwar liberalism's self-
consciousness of its own susceptibility to reform, and as the trium-
phalist response to the shattering of socialist optimism regarding
the prospects for revolution.

If the events of the mid-twentieth century threw a monkey
wrench into the expectations of Marxism, however, it would seem
that the current self-proclaimed crisis of postwar liberal democracy,
dating back to the political explosions of the 1960s, have dealt a
similarly harsh blow to pluralist theory. And while, as we have
seen, contemporary Marxian political theory has reequilibrated
itself in the face of the theoretical anomalies posed by the liberal
democratic containment of socialism, it is not at all clear that
pluralist theory is capable of a similar resuscitation. Just as the
political turbulence of the sixties challenged the pluralist belief in
the penetrability of the state, and in its ability to aggregate interests
and smoothly process political demands, the economic crisis of the
seventies and eighties has posed an even more fundamental challenge to a basic premise of pluralist theory—the autonomy of the
state from society, and the consequent lack of any need for the
analysis of political power to take account of the structure of so-

ciety. Pluralist theory never denied the existence of social and economic inequalities; it simply took them as a given, which required
no explanation and which could not be assumed to have any determinacy in the formation of public policy. The so-called "governability crisis" of liberal democracy has severely damaged these
beliefs, highlighting both the centrality of class conflict between
labor and capital in political life and the severe economic and
institutional constraints under which the liberal democratic state
operates. In the face of these developments pluralist theory has
experienced a serious identity crisis. Lindblom, as we have already
seen, has not only suggested that the political science mainstream
acknowledge the relevance of Marxian analysis. He has also, in his
Politics and Markets, initiated a strategic retreat among pluralist
theorists, providing an analysis of liberal democratic politics that
substantially confirms the Marxian analysis of the constraints class
power and capital accumulation exert on public policy. And even
Dahl, in his two most recent books, has publicly proclaimed his
"democratic socialism," arguing that there are serious structural
impediments to the democratic operation of the state in advanced
capitalist societies.[8]

In the face of this crisis of pluralist theory (and practice) the
influence of Marxian theory has grown enormously. Unlike plu-
ralists, Marxian theorists have always maintained that the structure
of class power and the dynamics of capital accumulation play a
determining role in the politics of capitalist democracies. As we
have seen, while they have carefully avoided the catastrophism and
historicism that burdened earlier versions of Marxism, contemporary Marxists have emphasized the fragility of class compromise
and the centrality of the antagonistic interests underlying such com-
promises. And in analyzing these antagonisms, Marxists have always insisted upon both the importance of working-class forms of

[8]Charles E. Lindblom, *Politics and Markets* (New York: Harper Torchbooks,
1977); Dahl, *Dilemmas,* and *A Preface to Economic Democracy* (Berkeley: University of California Press, 1984). For a discussion of this strategic retreat and its
limits, see John Manley, "Neopluralism: A Class Analysis of Pluralism I and II,"
American Political Science Review 77 (June 1983), 368–83. Also indicative of the
crisis of pluralism is the proliferation of writings on corporatism and the political
economy of the state. See Leo Panitch, "Recent Theorizations of Corporatism:
Reflections on a Growth Industry," *British Journal of Sociology* 21 (1980), 159–
87.

economic and political power and the decisive structural and organizational advantages accruing to capital in the arena of class struggle. Marxian theory would seem indispensable to the understanding of power and the state in advanced capitalist societies and, in its emphasis on the structural determinations of the state, its explanatory power far surpasses that of its major pluralist rival. The defense of Marxism against its pluralist critics is certainly a necessary task, one hardly exhausted by these all-too-brief comments. Necessary though it is to point out the advantages of Marxism, however, it is also necessary to point out the serious challenges confronting it. This has, as we shall see, not only a theoretical significance, but a practical significance as well.

Militarism, Bureaucracy, and the State

Pluralism has been the main theoretical competitor of Marxism, but it has by no means been the only one. A number of contemporary theorists have developed an understanding of the contemporary state that is critical of both pluralism and Marxism. Taking as their point of reference the cold war antagonism between the United States and the Soviet Union, and its ensuing "balance of terror," these theorists have argued that the primary characteristic of contemporary politics is what might be called state militarism. Against pluralist theory, these theorists contend that political debate and priorities, in both liberal democratic and authoritarian communist states, revolve around the military confrontation of the superpowers; and they thus argue that the legal guarantees of political openness and competition characteristic of liberal democracies are suffocated in practice by a combination of political repression, bureaucratic machination, and ideological conformity. Insofar as these theorists emphasize the structural constraints impinging on the state and the effective limitation of political alternatives, they share with Marxists a common objection to pluralism. This approach, however, is also highly critical of Marxism, insisting that the categories of class analysis are insufficient (if not irrelevant) to the understanding of contemporary statist politics.

Mills's *The Power Elite* is probably the most prominent and influential representative of this approach in contemporary social theory. Mills's analysis was arguably the major casualty of the behavioralist analysis of power. Dahl's "A Critique of the Ruling Elite Model," we may recall, was a methodological critique of Mills. It is important to see that Mills's analysis of power here is implicitly realist, and that the argument I developed in Part I to justify Marxism serves equally to reestablish its validity. Mills's purpose in *The Power Elite* is to provide an account of the structure of contemporary politics. The power elite, as he defines it, comprises those individuals who "come to occupy positions in American society from which they can look down upon, so to speak, and by their decisions mightily affect, the everyday worlds of ordinary men and women."[9] Mills is primarily interested in these structural positions within the major institutions of society, and how power is distributed by them; he is only secondarily, when at all, interested in the way the agents who occupy these positions exercise their power on specific occasions. "These hierarchies of state and corporation and army," Mills writes, "constitute the means of power." And while he acknowledges that the power elite located within these institutions is not omnipotent, and does not make all decisions of relevance to the society, he argues that it is through these institutions that significant social power is exercised. He writes: "Not all power, it is true, is anchored in and exercised by means of these institutions, but only within and through them can power be more or less continuous and important."[10] Finally, Mills does not argue that the power elite is a monolithic, cohesive historical agent; rather, he writes of "the uneasy coincidence of economic, military, and political power," suggesting that it is not a single set of objectives, but a set of shared institutional interests that constitutes the unity of this elite.[11]

For Mills these shared interests clearly revolve around the postwar militarization of society: "Insofar as the structural clue to the power elite today lies in the enlarged and military state, that clue becomes evident in the military ascendancy.... The seemingly permanent military threat places a premium on the military and upon their control of men, materiel, money, and power; virtually all

[9]C. Wright Mills, *The Power Elite* (Oxford: Oxford University Press, 1956), p. 3.
[10]Ibid., p. 9.
[11]Ibid., pp. 269–97.

political and economic actions are now judged in terms of military definitions of reality."[12] The structural consequence of this, for Mills, is the rationalization of three major institutions—large corporations, the political executive, and the military establishment—each of which has become both increasingly bureaucratic and increasingly interlocked with the other two. And the thread that binds them together is what Mills calls "the permanent war economy," which is based on the production and reproduction simultaneously of private profit, political stalemate, and a frightening combination of national emergency and national security.

For Mills these realities serve to call into serious question the basic premises of Marxian political theory. This is because, according to Mills, the division between capital and labor has been effectively supplanted by the division between the power elite and the powerless mass of ordinary individuals. Mills does not deny the existence of the former division; but the thrust of his argument is that this division has been rendered politically innocuous. Mills provides a number of reasons for this. First, the capitalist class has been largely incorporated within the power elite, where its interests have become parasitic upon state action and the strength of the military establishment at home and abroad. It is in this light that Mills rejects the concept of a "ruling class":

> "Ruling class" is a badly loaded phrase. "Class" is an economic term; "rule" is a political one. The phrase, "ruling class," thus contains the theory that an economic class rules politically.... Specifically, the phrase "ruling class," in its common political connotations, does not allow enough autonomy to the political order and its agents, and it says nothing about the military as such. It should be clear to the reader by now that we do not accept as adequate the simple view that high economic men unilaterally make all decisions of national consequence. We hold that such a simple view of "economic determinism" must be elaborated by "political determinism" and "military determinism"; that the higher agents of each of these three domains now often have a noticeable degree of autonomy; and that only in the often intricate ways of coalition do they make up and carry through the most important decisions. Those are the major reasons we prefer "power elite" to "ruling class" as a characterizing

[12]Ibid., p. 275.

phrase for the higher circles when we consider them in terms of power.[13]

For Mills it is the ascendancy of the military, in terms of both personnel and justifying ideology, which is at the heart of the distribution of power in contemporary society, and the interests of capital are important only insofar as they are connected with this fact. According to Mills the major division with respect to the distribution of power in society is the division between the super-power blocs; and it is this fact of international relations that accounts for the military posturing of states and the consequent militarization of societies. "On each side of the world-split running through central Europe and around the Asiatic rimlands," Mills writes, "there is an ever-increasing interlocking of economic, military, and political structures."[14]

Second, Mills highlights the decline of the working class as a historical agent, providing a number of explanations for this political reality: divisions within the working class; the growth of a new white-collar managerial stratum, which takes the edge off class conflict; the growth of consumerism; and the consolidation of the union movement and its incorporation into the state.[15]

But for Mills what is unquestionably the most problematic feature of Marxism is something it shares with many of its liberal opponents—a historical optimism that has rested upon "the happy assumption of the inherent relation of reason and freedom."[16] The major argument of *The Power Elite* is simply that the bipolar division of the world, and the "unprecedented situation" of a balance of terror and of societies organizing themselves around the pursuit of World War III, has led to *a decline of politics*, what Marcuse has elsewhere called the closure of the political universe.[17] According to Mills, contemporary society has become a "mass society" where a national consensus on the importance of "national

[13]Ibid., p. 277.

[14]Ibid., p. 8.

[15]See Irving Louis Horowitz, C. *Wright Mills: An American Utopian* (New York: Free Press, 1983).

[16]Mills, *Sociological*, p. 166.

[17]Herbert Marcuse, *One-Dimensional Man* (Boston: Beacon Press, 1964). For a penetrating discussion of Marcuse on these issues, see Douglas Kellner, *Herbert Marcuse and the Crisis of Marxism* (Berkeley: University of California Press, 1984).

security" sublimates political controversy, and where the masses of individuals have become figurative "cheerful robots," quiescent in their powerlessness and secure in the insecurity the power elite reproduces daily. "The ultimate problem of freedom," writes Mills, "is the problem of the cheerful robot, and it arises in this form today because today it has become evident to us that all men do not naturally want to be free; that all men are not willing or not able, as the case may be, to exert themselves to acquire the reason that freedom requires."[18] For Mills, the mechanisms of mass society tend to suffocate any forms of radical historical agency and oppositional politics.

Mills's analysis of the national security state has stimulated a number of important studies of the subject. Richard Barnet has written at length on the national security establishment and on the rationality of national security managers; Seymour Melman and Gordon Adams have researched the connections constituting the "iron triangle" of military contracting; Noam Chomsky has explored the role of the mass media in creating a national consensus on militarism; and Frank Donner has produced an important study of the operations of intelligence agencies in restricting the scope of public debate and in harassing political dissidents.[19] Perhaps the most important recent work in this genre has been E. P. Thompson's "Notes on Exterminism, the Last Stage of Civilization." Thompson has been one of the most influential Marxist historians of the postwar world. But this essay, as the title suggests, is intended to indicate the limits of Marxism in the face of contemporary militarism and the threat of nuclear extermination. The title, of course, refers to Lenin's classic essay *Imperialism: The Highest Stage of Capitalism*; but as Thompson's title suggests, it is something he calls "exterminism," not imperialism or capitalism, which is the object of his criticism, and unlike Lenin, Thompson does not

---

[18]Mills, *Sociological*, p. 175.

[19]Richard J. Barnet, *Intervention and Revolution* (New York: New American Library, 1968), and *Roots of War* (New York: Atheneum, 1972); Seymour Melman, *Pentagon Capitalism: The Political Economy of War* (New York: McGraw-Hill, 1970); Gordon Adams, *The Iron Triangle* (New Brunswick, N.J.: Transactions, 1982); Noam Chomsky, *Towards a New Cold War* (New York: Pantheon, 1982), and Frank Donner, *The Age of Surveillance: The Aims and Methods of America's Political Intelligence System* (New York: Vintage, 1981).

see this as the darkness before the dawn of human emacipation, but rather as the possible harbinger of the *literal* end of human history. According to Thompson, exterminism is a historically novel form of social structure that has transmuted, if not transcended, both capitalism and communism:

> Exterminism is a configuration...whose institutional base is the weapons system, and the entire economic, scientific, political, and ideological support system—the social system which researches it, "chooses" it, produces it, polices it, justifies it, and maintains it in being...the inertial thrust towards war (or collision) arises from bases deeply enstructured within the opposed powers. We tend to evade this conclusion by employing concepts which delimit the problem: we speak (as I have done) of the "military-industrial complex," or of the military "sector" or "interest" or the arms "lobby." This suggests that the evil is confined in a known and limited place: it may threaten to push forward, but it can be restrained: contamination does not extend throughout the whole societal body.[20]

Marxist theory, according to Thompson, is insufficient to the task of understanding this configuration for two basic reasons: (1) the theory of capitalism and imperialism places too much emphasis on questions of economic interests and class antagonisms and fails to account for the specificity of military interests and military technologies; and (2) it has proven unable to account for the fact that this "inertia" toward geopolitical expansion and collision is not confined to capitalist states, but rather is characteristic of communistic states as well. "We must acknowledge," says Thompson, "not one but two imperial formations, however different their origin and character."[21]

The first thing that should be said of such criticisms of Marxism is that they are most powerful when viewed as objections to that strand of reductionism that has unquestionably been pervasive in the history of Marxism. Mills, for instance, in criticizing the idea of a ruling class, quite explicitly linked it to a "labor metaphysic" within Marxism, according to which the subordination of industrial

---

[20]E. P. Thompson, "Notes on Exterminism, the Last Stage of Civilization," in Thompson et al., *Exterminism and Cold War* (London: Verso, 1982), pp. 20–21.
[21]Ibid., p. 3.

workers and their eventual liberation constitutes the central drama of human history (a narrative clearly traceable to the language of *The Communist Manifesto*, among many other of Marx and Engels's texts).[22] One can detect traces of this metaphysic even in the Althusserian claim that the economy is "determinant in the last instance," language clearly suggesting the secondary character of nonclass relations.[23] Such an essentialist version of Marxism not only insists upon rigidly adhering to the theory of imperialism as a sufficient explanation of contemporary international politics; it also practices a kind of *theoretical* imperialism, supposing that the categories of Marxian class analysis can lay claim to a special explanatory power, requiring the supplementation of no other concepts or considerations.

The analyses of Mills and Thompson are certainly sufficient to call this view into question. Not simply the historical outcome of the Russian Revolution, but the entire history of the twentieth century, from the two world wars to the dropping of the atomic bombs at Hiroshima and Nagasaki to the interventions in Vietnam and Afghanistan, casts doubt upon any notion of the secondary character of statism and militarism. And the language of "determination in the last instance," however imaginatively revisionist, is simply a way of adding new epicycles, dogmatically saving the appearances of historical materialism. Poulantzas, I believe, came to recognize this. Asked in an interview if Marxian theory is capable of grappling with the specificity of the state and politics, he replied: "I will answer this question very simply because we could discuss it for years. It is very simple. One must know whether one remains within a Marxist framework or not; and if one does one accepts the determinant role of the economic in the very complex sense. . . . I am not absolutely sure myself that I am right to be a Marxist; one is never sure. But if one is Marxist, the determinant role of relations of production, in the very complex sense, must mean something."[24]

This response has a rather dogmatic ring to it—to be a Marxist

---

[22]C. Wright Mills, *The Marxists* (New York: Dell, 1962).

[23]See Ted Benton, *The Rise and Fall of Structural Marxism: Althusser and His Influence* (New York: St. Martin's, 1984).

[24]Nico Poulantzas, "Political Parties and the Crisis of Marxism," *Socialist Review*, no. 48 (November–December 1979), 68.

is to believe certain propositions that, however problematic, must be true if Marxism is to be true. Poulantzas, in his final book, however, provides a different way of thinking about this. Arguing that Marxism must play a decisive role in explaining the development of authoritarian communism in the Soviet Union and elsewhere, he asserts: "I say merely a 'decisive' role because Marxism alone cannot explain everything."[25] He here seems to indicate that, while the theoretical concepts of Marxism properly highlight the importance of certain (primarily economic) determinants, there are other determinants of social reality that require Marxian theory to be supplemented with other theories.

As we have seen, contemporary Marxists have produced a thoroughly nonreductionist analysis of class relations and class politics; and they have also begun to acknowledge the need to supplement class analysis and to provide serious accounts of the realities of the contemporary national security state. Poulantzas's theory of "authoritarian statism," for instance, is in many respects quite similar to Mills's analysis in its emphasis on the convergence of state and economy, the rise of administrative state bureaucracies and official secrecy, and the decline of parliaments, political parties, and ideological conflict.[26] In fact, the concept of the "isolation effect" has some interesting affinities with Mills's notion of "mass society," both of which suggest a citizenry that has been rendered politically inert by the primarily ideological operations of the state. Miliband has undertaken a critique of Soviet military interventionism, suggesting that what Mills called "crackpot realism"—the military definition of reality—is as characteristic of Soviet-type states as it is of capitalist ones, and that the class character of capitalist states is therefore not a sufficient condition of contemporary militarism.[27] *Exterminism and Cold War*, in which E. P. Thompson's essay on exterminism appears, represents a promising example of the openness of Marxian theory to these issues, observing of the issue of nuclear confrontation and of the antinuclear movement: "This entirely unprecedented situation demands a reworking of the prin-

[25]Nicos Poulantzas, *State, Power, Socialism* (London: Verso, 1978), p. 23.
[26]Ibid., pp. 203–51.
[27]Ralph Miliband, "Military Intervention and Socialist Internationalism," in Ralph Miliband and John Saville, eds., *The Socialist Register 1980* (London: Merlin Press, 1980).

cipal traditions of socialist thought...a rethinking of values as well as of analyses."[28] Fred Halliday's *The Making of the Second Cold War* is probably the most sustained attempt to integrate a Marxian analysis of forms of national and international capital accumulation and class conflict with an analysis of the specificity of interstate politics and the arms race.[29]

Even the most conscientious efforts to open up Marxism, however, sometimes bear the traces of a lingering reductionism. See, for instance, Perry Anderson's characterization of the current nuclear confrontation between the superpowers: "It is the awful, but intelligible product of precisely that global class struggle whose understanding gave birth to historical materialism—a conflict founded on the ceaseless determination of major capitalist states to stifle every attempt to build socialism, from the Russian to the Vietnamese, the Central European to the Central American revolutions, and the deformities the resistance to it has wrought within them. The potential outcome of this conflict transcends the opposition between capital and labor: but its actual springs remain tightly coiled within it."[30] The language here indicates that the workings of capitalism are a sufficient condition of this military confrontation, suggesting not only that the militarism of capitalist states is caused mainly by their "ceaseless determination...to stifle every attempt to build socialism," but that the militarism of "socialist states" like the Soviet Union is merely a consequence of "deformities" wrought within them by capitalism. Such a formulation seems to deny the theoretical and practical importance of nonclass relations and powers, considering them at very best derivative of a more fundamental antagonism, and it seems at odds with the generally open and exploratory character of much of the recent Marxian writing on these issues. What these attempts to extend and redefine Marxian theory acknowledge is the autonomous power of the state as an institutional actor both in domestic and international relations, and its irreducibility to class relations. They illustrate in practice that the continued revitalization of Marx-

---

[28]Thompson et al., *Exterminism*, p. vii.
[29]Fred Halliday, *The Making of the Second Cold War* (London: Verso, 1983).
[30]Perry Anderson, *In the Tracks of Historical Materialism* (Chicago: University of Chicago Press, 1984), pp. 95–96.

ian theory requires a movement beyond class analysis and an openness to alternative theories of state bureaucratism, militarism, and international politics.

It is also important, however, to emphasize that this need for supplementation extends in both directions. If a Marxian version of class reductionism is inadequate to the realities of contemporary statist politics, this is not to recommend a new form of reductionism in its stead. Although we can certainly understand his passion and his concern, when Thompson writes that "what is known as the 'Cold War' is the central human fracture, the absolute pole of power, the fulcrum upon which power turns, in the world," we can only observe that this exaggeration, however rhetorically justifiable, is still an exaggeration.[31] As Thompson himself remarks, there are two imperial formations *whose origin and character differ*. But certainly these differences are theoretically as well as practically significant. However insufficient Marxian theory is with regard to understanding these matters, it is certainly necessary.

First, while capitalist imperialism is not the only cause of the cold war, it must be reckoned as a crucial one, one that expresses one of the important differences between the superpower blocs. As Mike Davis, Fred Halliday, and others have emphasized, American militarism, and the capitalist militarism it subserves more generally, is determined in crucial ways by the imperatives of continuous, profitable capital accumulation.[32] Not only multinational corporate foreign investment, but the entire system of military expenditures plays a role in the capitalist economies very different from the role it plays in communist ones; and, as the Medvedevs have argued, it generates an independent dynamic toward expansion that is arguably absent in communist states.[33]

Second, as Poulantzas observes of the national security state in capitalist societies: "The authoritarian statism of the contemporary State is terrifyingly real. But in spite of this (or rather because of it), the State remains a clay-footed colossus, fleeing ahead on treach-

[31]Thompson et al., *Exterminism*, p. 3.
[32]See Mike Davis, "Nuclear Imperialism and Extended Deterrence," and Fred Halliday, "The Sources of the New Cold War," in Thompson et al., *Exterminism*.
[33]Roy Medvedev and Zhores Medvedev, "The U.S. and the Arms Race," in Thompson et al., *Exterminism*.

erous ground; it should be remembered that wild animals are most dangerous when they are wounded."[34] What he means to call attention to here is the existence of contradictions within advanced capitalist societies that pose the possibility of undermining the political consensus, contradictions that indicate "the structural limits that mark all capitalist States." The most important of these for him is, of course, the antagonism between capital and labor, and the economic instability this engenders in capitalist society, an instability that permeates not only civil society, but the state itself. One might extend this argument and suggest that similar sorts of contradictions exist in communist states. Here Marxism has yet to prove its ability to provide plausible theoretical explanations. But it is certainly possible to argue that, insofar as communist societies are structured by their own relations of production, Marxism might play a role in laying bare these relations of domination and subordination.[35]

Post-Marxism and the New Social Movements

It is not only with regard to the questions of statism and militarism that Marxian theory is faced with a critical challenge. The postwar political settlement in the advanced capitalist societies has seen the emergence of a number of what have been called "new social movements"—the feminist, civil rights, peace, and ecological movements. While the antagonisms these movements express are certainly not historically new, their specific grievances and organizational forms bear the mark of postwar social and political developments: the disruption of the nuclear family by mass media and mass consumerism and the increased participation of women in the labor market in the case of feminism; national and international demographic shifts in the case of civil rights; the militarization of society and the nuclear arms race in the case of peace; and haphazard regional economic development, and the growth of

---

[34]Poulantzas, "Political Parties," p. 205.
[35]See, for example, Roy Medvedev, *On Socialist Democracy* (New York: Norton, 1972) and, more recently, Rudolph Bahro, *The Alternative in Eastern Europe* (London: New Left Books, 1978).

chemical, pharmaceutical, and nuclear power industries in the case of ecology.

These movements have provided a challenge to the structure of power in contemporary capitalist societies. And while they articulate a plurality of grievances, they also challenge the pluralist claim that the democratic state is a neutral arbiter of social antagonisms. As Frederico Stame has pointed out, these movements "enter into conflict with the modes of political participation that have come about in conjunction with the activities of state intervention. ... [They] are often outside of the circuits of legitimation of the institutional apparatuses of the state; have often challenged its forms of political representation and have constituted, if not the only, certainly a very important medium of political transformation in advanced Western societies."[36]

It is also clear, however, that the antagonisms these movements articulate are not class antagonisms, and that they point toward nonclass relations of power. Insofar as this is true, they also provide Marxism with a serious challenge—how to deal with these phenomena without somehow reducing them to derivations of class relations. A number of Marxian theorists have responded to this challenge by abandoning Marxism altogether. Barry Hindess and Paul Hirst, for example, drawing on Michel Foucault's critique of modern epistemology in general and Marxism in particular, have rejected the reductionism that they see at the heart of the Marxian paradigm.[37] In their critical analysis of basic Marxian categories they have incisively exposed a lingering essentialism. One can certainly discern in contemporary Marxism the language of the primacy of class antagonisms and economic determinants, and of politics as the "expression" and "representation" of class interests, even in those theorists, like Althusser and Poulantzas, most anxious to expunge any trace of reductionism from Marxism. The fact is

---

[36]Frederico Stame, "The Crisis of the Left and New Social Identities," *Telos*, no. 60 (Summer 1984), 8–9. See also Jean L. Cohen and Andrew Arato, "The German Green Party: A Movement between Fundamentalism and Modernism," *Dissent* (Summer 1984), 327–32.

[37]For Foucault's critique, see the essays in his *Power/Knowledge* (New York: Pantheon, 1980). The critical literature on Foucault is immense, but see particularly Peter Dews, "Power and Subjectivity in Foucault," *New Left Review*, no. 144 (March–April 1984), 72–95.

that even though contemporary Marxists have abandoned historical teleology and any belief in the necessity of social transformation, their analyses of power in contemporary society have
dwelled almost exclusively on questions of class relations. Erik
Wright accurately articulates the attitude of contemporary realist
Marxism, responding to Giddens's critique of Marxian class
reductionism:

> Many, perhaps most, contemporary Marxist theorists accept much
> of this argument. In general there is a recognition that at least ethnic
> and sexual domination are not simply reflexes of class domination,
> and some Marxists would add inter-state domination as well. How
> much autonomy such relations have and precisely how their artic-
> ulation with the class system should be understood are, of course,
> matters of considerable disagreement. While tendencies towards
> functional reductionism continue in the Marxist tradition, it is never-
> theless the case that the thrust of much contemporary Marxist think-
> ing has been against attempts at intrasocial class reductionism.
>   Where Marxists would tend to disagree with Giddens is in the
> implication that such irreducibility of sex or ethnicity or nationality
> to class implies that these various forms of domination/exploitation
> are of potentially equal status in defining the differences between or
> dynamics within societies. Most Marxists would continue to argue
> for a general primacy of class, even if other relations are not simple
> reflections of class.[38]

This formulation indicates the seriousness contemporary realist
Marxism is prepared to accord nonclass relations, but Wright's
continued insistence on the primacy of class also marks an important limit of this Marxism. While explicitly rejecting reductionism,
the language of primacy serves to indicate the secondary importance of nonclass struggles. Wright attempts to defend this position,
and though he concedes a great deal to the causal pluralist view I
propose below, his defense relies ultimately on the reintroduction
of a teleology into the argument. "While it may be the case," he
writes, "that different forms of domination reciprocally condition
each other... Marxists have generally argued that only class

[38]Erik Olin Wright, "Giddens' Critique of Marxism," *New Left Review*, no.
138 (March–April 1983), 22–23.

relations have an internal logic of development, a logic which generates systematic tendencies for a trajectory of transformation of the class structure. This trajectory has a general directionality ... "[39] Ultimately, then, class powers and class struggles are viewed as the basic causes of historical transformation, and the working class is viewed as the necessary center of any radical historical agency.

But not only have contemporary Marxists like Wright demonstrated the absence of any such "directionality" in contemporary capitalist societies; insofar as there have been challenges to the structure of these societies, neither have they issued exclusively from the agency of the working class. Hindess and Hirst, in criticizing this lingering class essentialism within Marxism, starkly pose the problem: "The choice for Marxism is clear: Either we effectively reduce political and ideological phenomena to class interests determined elsewhere (basically in the economy).... Or we must face up to the real autonomy of political and ideological phenomena."[40] There own analyses, however, have gone beyond the necessary critique of this reductionism. First, in rejecting any kind of historical teleology (a teleology, it should be repeated, which has been substantially dismissed by contemporary Marxists, despite occasional lapses), they fall back on the discourse analysis of French poststructuralism, with its distinctly idealist overtones.[41] Thus, they write of theory: "What is specified in theoretical discourse can only be conceived through that form of discourse ... it cannot be conceived extra-discursively. The question of the 'reality of the external world' is not the issue. It is not a question of whether objects exist when we do not speak of them. Objects of discourse do not exist. The entities discourse refers to are constituted in and by it."[42]

In asserting the above, Hindess and Hirst are trying to undermine any claim Marxism might have to a grounding in reality, and to insist that the "truth" of Marxism derives from nothing more than its own will-to-power. They continue: "The discursive primacy accorded to economic relations in Marxism and more generally in

---

[39]Ibid., p. 24.

[40]Barry Hindess, "Classes and Politics in Marxist Theory," in Gary Littlejohn et al., *Power and the State* (London: Croom Helm, 1978), p. 96.

[41]See Anderson, *In the Tracks*, pp. 32–55.

[42]Barry Hindess and Paul Hirst, *Mode of Production and Social Formation* (London: Macmillan, 1977), p. 208.

socialist discourse cannot be conceived as an effect of the onto-logical structure of reality. On the contrary it is an effect of a definite political ideology and a definite political objective, namely, the objective of a socialist transformation of capitalist relations of pro-duction."[43] Hindess and Hirst rightly point out the practical and theoretical limitations of the primacy thesis (particularly its te-leogical implications, and its rhetorical devaluation of nonclass struggles), but they fail to consider whether these limitations are truly a necessary consequence of epistemological realism, and whether it is possible to reconstruct Marxism while abandoning this thesis. For them the alternatives are clear: a Marxian reduc-tionism or an agnostic idealism. On this view Marxism represents a dangerous effort on the part of one discourse—a working-class discourse— to imperialize other discourses that have no necessary relation of subordination to it. This is what leads Hindess and Hirst to their much-discussed thesis of the "necessary non-correspond-ence"—the absolute autonomy—of social relations. On this view the new social movements each mark an autonomous discourse (feminism, racial empowerment, ecology) and embody the attempts of separate groups (women, oppressed races, ecologists) to advance their own discursively defined interests, interests that are not in any sense pregiven by any structural relations, but which are con-stituted in the course of historically contingent struggle.[44]

Ernesto Laclau and Chantal Mouffe have extended this argument in their 1985 book *Hegemony and Socialist Strategy*, which they describe as "situated in a post-Marxist terrain." Their book is an incisive critique of a class essentialism that, they argue, is located at the heart of the history of Marxian theory and practice, an essentialism called into question by the political events and horrors of the twentieth century: "What is now in crisis is a whole con-ception of socialism which rests upon the ontological centrality of the working class, upon the role of Revolution, with a capital 'r,'

[43] Anthony Cutler, Barry Hindess, Paul Hirst, and Athar Hussain, *Marx's 'Cap-ital' and Capitalism Today*, vol. 1 (London: Routledge & Kegan Paul, 1977), quoted in Alex Callinicos, *Is There a Future for Marxism?* (Atlantic Highlands, N.J.: Humanities Press, 1982), p. 173.

[44] For a polemical critique, see Philip Corrigan and Derek Sayer, "Hindess and Hirst: A Critical Review," in Ralph Miliband and John Saville, eds., *The Socialist Register 1978* (London: Merlin Press, 1978), pp. 194–214.

as the founding moment in the transition from one type of society to another, and upon the illusory prospect of a perfectly unitary and homogenous collective will that will render pointless the moment of politics. The plural and multifarious character of contemporary struggles has finally dissolved the last foundation for that political imaginary."[45]

Like Hindess and Hirst, Laclau and Mouffe emphasize the discursive constitution of social reality and deny the existence of any single underlying antagonism or principle of historical transformation. They argue that the great error of Marxism is the belief, which they attribute even to contemporary nonteleological Marxists, that society can be conceived of as a "sutured," or perfectly ordered, whole, governed by a single principle and organized in such a way that the identities of social agents are fixed by social structure. Laclau and Mouffe propose instead that society is a historically open system of relations, that social identities are not fixed, and that they are constructed through a discursive process they call "articulation." In this view there is no reason to believe that social antagonisms will necessarily resolve themselves into class antagonisms, and even less to believe that questions of class power occupy a special place in either theoretical analysis or historical practice. Laclau and Mouffe thus insist that the various forms of social power and struggle, and the connections between them, must "be defined in terms of new theoretical categories whose status . . . constitutes a problem."[46]

Although Laclau and Mouffe share with Hindess and Hirst an aversion to forms of Marxian reductionism, they dissent from them on a key point—the necessary noncorrespondence of various social identities and relations. Laclau and Mouffe reject the proposition that these identities and relations—class, gender, race—are absolutely autonomous: "Were the decentring operation to be concluded at this point, we would only have managed to affirm a new form of fixity: that of the various decentred subject positions. If these themselves are not fixed, it is clear that a logic of detotalization cannot simply affirm the separation of different struggles

[45]Ernesto Laclau and Chantal Mouffe, *Hegemony and Socialist Strategy: Towards a Radical Democratic Politics* (London: Verso, 1985), p. 2.
[46]Ibid., p. 86.

and demands, and that their articulation cannot just be conceived as the linkage of dissimilar and fully constituted elements."[47] In other words, just as it is mistaken to believe that the relation between these struggles is fixed, all of them being expressions of class struggle, it is equally mistaken to believe that they are fixed in the hermetic purity of their autonomy. For Laclau and Mouffe, *hegemony* refers to that "articulatory" practice whereby connections are established between these struggles, and common identities forged among the individuals occupying these social positions. In their view political intervention ultimately determines the relation between the various subject positions.

Laclau and Mouffe's argument represents the most tenacious and self-critical attempt to articulate a post-Marxian position capable of acknowledging the irreducible significance of nonclass relations and struggles. Their critique of that strand of historicism within the Marxian tradition, traces of which can be discerned even in contemporary nonteleological theorists, is convincing. If by post-Marxism we mean nothing more than a critical surmounting of the theoretical and practical dangers posed by such a historicism, then their argument is well taken. There are, however, two difficulties with their argument—one methodological, one substantive—which suggest the limits of such a post-Marxism. In short, Laclau and Mouffe fail to recognize the genuine virtues of Marxism as a *realist* social theory and the indispensability of the kind of structural account of the causal relations between various relations of power that a sufficiently modest Marxism is capable of providing.

The first difficulty is a real ambiguity about the nature of causality in social life. Laclau and Mouffe, in criticizing forms of Marxist determinism, consistently counterpose a naturalistic and a discursive understanding of social life, suggesting that a causal analysis of social relations is incompatible with a recognition of their historically contested and contingent character. They make this most explicit in an interview discussing their argument, and it is worth quoting them at length:

In a causal relation of the physical-natural type, we have a relationship among events which is meaningless. But in social life any event

[47]Ibid., p. 87.

has a meaning. . . . to understand a social event, we do not appeal to any type of physical causality but we have to understand its meaning—the ensemble of its signifying relations. In this sense the concept of discourse is as large as the concept of social life. . . . To have politics we need to have choice, that is, a situation whose outcome is open and depends on the struggle between antagonistic forces. This is compatible with a discursive conception of social antagonisms, but not with a causalist one.[48]

Here they envision only two, polar, possibilities—either a kind of Marxist behaviorism or the abandonment of scientific, causal analysis. What they fail to see, of course, is that a realist understanding of causality is perfectly compatible with the openness of the world, and that a realist concept of social structure is premised upon a duality, rather than a dual*ism*, of structure and agency. In insisting upon the discursive character of social identity, and in acknowledging the discursive character of theory itself, they seem to come close to what Bhaskar has called the "epistemic fallacy"—the belief that our theoretical apparatuses constitute the world.[49] It is unclear in their account precisely how determining our discourses—Marxism, feminism, democracy—are in shaping social identities and actions, or, conversely, whether there are also real structural determinants operative in social life, determinants that both set limits and provide enablements to our social and political activity, including our discursive interventions. They convincingly argue, for instance, that there is no necessary correspondence between working-class economic position and political identity. But this hinges on the meaning of "necessary." If we mean by this "predictable" or "inevitable," then their point is unexceptionable. But if we mean by this "causal" or "determinate," then things become more complicated. Laclau and Mouffe would surely agree that discursive and pedagogic activity is determinate. But the real question is whether they would concede that there are other causally effective determinants of working-class political subjectivity. Workers may certainly subscribe to a variety of political ideologies

---

[48]Ernesto Laclau and Chantal Mouffe, "Recasting Marxism: Hegemony and New Political Movements," *Socialist Review* 12 (November–December 1982), 97.

[49]Roy Bhaskar, *A Realist Theory of Science*, 2d ed. (Atlantic Highlands, N.J.: Humanities Press, 1978), pp. 36–38.

and are certainly not necessarily socialist; but does their structural position as workers play no role in shaping these identities? Are the identities of workers infinitely malleable?

There are places in their argument where Laclau and Mouffe sound almost Humean, contending, for instance, that "we are dealing here with contingent relations whose nature we have to determine," and labeling as "essentialist" not only variants of historical determinism, but any view of social reality as being fixed or structured.[50] Workers may not necessarily be socialists, but they are workers, however they might subjectively interpret this fact; and is there anything about their being workers that makes the possibility of their identifying as socialists more likely than the possibility of their identifying as chickens? More specifically, is there anything about the reality of their class position which makes them more or less liable to certain political appeals than others, and which empowers or limits them in the pursuit of these interests (which we have called, in Chapter 3, subjective interests)? In short, do Laclau and Mouffe go too far, rejecting not simply implausible and reductionist variants of Marxian theory, but the project of a theoretical analysis of social life itself? It is not clear that they do. They write about "structural limits" operating upon "articulatory" practices, and they acknowledge that social identities are not infinitely malleable, suggesting that social structure plays some determining role. They even equivocate, criticizing the concept of "a causal relation of the physical-natural type," but implying with this qualification of "causal" that there may be some other appropriate concept of causality. But this is a serious problem in their argument, as it is in the writing of all those post-Marxists who bear the influence of another reductionism, that of French post-structuralism and its characteristically idealist "exorbitation of language."[51]

This relates to their second difficulty: a lack of clarity about the force of their rejection of a totalizing theory of power. It is clear that in their view Marxism, at least in its "actually existing" forms, represents such a theory insofar as it posits the primacy of class relations and class struggles. But does the rejection of a primacy thesis entail the repudiation of any attempt to uncover the con-

---

[50]Laclau and Mouffe, *Hegemony*, p. 96.
[51]The phrase is Perry Anderson's, *In the Tracks*, p. 40.

nection between various social relations and their antagonisms? Laclau and Mouffe acknowledge that there is no necessary separation between, say, the operations of sexism and racism; and they claim that it is perfectly possible that connections between these can be highlighted by a "hegemonic" discourse, and that this can contribute to the formation of common meanings and projects between women and subordinate racial groups. But are these connections simply a function of the intervention of political discourses, or are there real, structural connections between the operations of racism and sexism, connections that are both the object of critical theoretical analysis and the "ground" of possible practical political unity?

What these critical comments mean to suggest is that the necessary abandonment of a kind of Marxist reductionism should not be confused with the unwarranted abandonment of theoretical analysis; and that, however inadequate the Althusserian concept of a "mode of production," a determinist analysis of structure should not give way to an equally indeterminist analysis of agency. Rather, what is called for is a complementarity in the analysis of the various social relations and powers and the various forms of agency obtaining in society. This requires an analysis of class relations and class agency; but it also requires an analysis of the many other irreducible relations and struggles, both in their specifity and in their connection to one another. Laclau and Mouffe, in arguing that "power is never foundational," make a similar point: "The problem of power cannot, therefore, be posed in terms of the search for *the* class or *the* dominant sector which constitutes the centre of a hegemonic formation, given that, by definition, such a centre will always elude us. But it is equally wrong to propose as an alternative either pluralism or the total diffusion of power within the social, as this would blind the analysis to the presence of nodal points and to the partial concentrations of power existing in every concrete social formation."[52]

This conceptualization of power is perfectly compatible with the realist view developed in Part I; and the discussion of Marxism in Part II can be seen as an analysis of one nodal point of power in contemporary capitalist societies—classes and their economic and

[52]Laclau and Mouffe, *Hegemony*, p. 142.

political constitution. There is nothing in this discussion requiring that this relation has any "absolute validity, in the sense of defining a space or structural moment which could not in its turn be subverted."[53] There are certainly other relations, and there is no way of knowing a priori which will assume paramount political significance at a given historical moment. The effort of post-Marxist theory to highlight the importance of nonclass relations constitutes an indispensable contribution to contemporary political theory. Such a view, however, does not require the abandonment of causal analysis, but rather the realist understanding of causality that alone is capable of sustaining the reality of nonclass relations. Further, such a view is in no way incompatible with the efforts of contemporary Marxists to discover, in Wright's words, "how much autonomy such relations have and precisely how their articulation with the class system should be understood."[54]

Whatever criticisms we have leveled at post-Marxist analysis, it should almost go without saying that this problematic has much more to recommend it than recent attempts to reassert Marxian orthodoxy. Ellen Wood, for instance, writes, in response to recent Marxian attempts to accommodate the reality of new social movements, that "class struggle is the nucleus of Marxism. This is so in two inseparable senses: it is the class struggle that for Marxism explains the dynamic of history, and it is the abolition of classes, the obverse or end-product of class struggle, that is the ultimate objective of the revolutionary process. . . . The inseparable unity of this view of history and this revolutionary objective is what above all distinguishes Marxism from other conceptions of social transformation, and without it there is no Marxism."[55]

This is really no argument at all, simply an assertion of received "truths"; and however true it is that the basic principle of historical materialism is that class domination is "the root of social and political oppression," this does not make this principle true. Wood's formulation, positing a single foundational source of social

[53]Ibid., p. 143.

[54]Wright, "Giddens' Critique," p. 22.

[55]Ellen Meiksins Wood, "Marxism without Class Struggle?" in Ralph Miliband and John Saville, eds., *The Socialist Register 1983* (London: Merlin Press, 1983). See also her *The Retreat from Class* (London: Verso, 1986), which came out as this book was going to press.

antagonism and teleologically anthropomorphizing the historical process, is a perfect example of the kind of historical thinking post-Marxism has criticized. My disagreement with Laclau and Mouffe, however, turns on the accuracy of Wood's description. Agreeing that without this historical teleology there is no Marxism, they have chosen to abandon Marxism. If the rejection of historicism is treason, after all, then make the most of it. In making this break, it should be pointed out, they have not repudiated their belief in the importance of class domination nor their commitment to socialism; what they have done is repudiate the historical primacy this question has assumed within Marxism.[56] The real question, however, is whether or not it is possible to reconstruct, and to continue to revitalize, a nonhistoricist Marxism. Whether it is possible for Marxism to maintain its integrity by sacrificing some of its theoretical and practical ambition, and whether it is possible to remain committed to Marxian categories and still respect the theoretical and practical reality of nonclass relations—these are the central challenges of contemporary Marxian political theory. Such challenges should be cause for neither self-righteousness nor defensiveness on the part of Marxian theorists; they demand instead a serious rethinking of perspectives and an openness to a causal pluralism. Neither should it be cause for despair. Ted Benton has aptly reflected on the serious challenges confronting Marxism: "Nonetheless I see no *other* intellectual tradition with a comparable scope in the human sciences or with a comparable richness of resources, and none of the challenges so far offered to Marxism seem to me to be fatal."[57]

Marxism and the Limits of Power

I have attempted to argue thus far that while Marxian theory provides an analysis of the relations of class power under capital-

---

[56]Laclau and Mouffe write: "Of course, every project for radical democracy implies a socialist dimension, as it is necessary to put an end to capitalist relations of production, which are at the root of numerous relations of subordination; but socialism is *one* of the components of a project for radical democracy, not vice versa" (*Hegemony*, p. 178).

[57]Benton, *Rise and Fall*, p. 227.

ism, it does not provide a sufficient analysis of power in capitalist societies (let alone noncapitalist societies); and that the plausibility of Marxian theory rests on its ability to jettison all remaining vestiges of historicism and to acknowledge both the plurality of relations and struggles in society and the absence of a single, historically fixed locus of human domination and emancipation. The body of Marxian theory we discussed in the previous chapters is based on such an acknowledgment and represents an attempt to meet some of the challenges confronting Marxism. As Laclau and Mouffe put it, such an acknowledgment requires abandoning an entire, long-standing conception of socialism. This conception rests upon two basic beliefs. The first is that all antagonisms in capitalist society will ultimately ("in the last instance?") resolve themselves into class antagonism, and that the consequence of this will be a mass, majoritarian working-class movement against capitalism and for socialism. Whatever currency this belief has had within certain strains of twentieth-century Marxism, contemporary Marxian political theorists have largely rejected it and played an important role in analyzing its deficiencies: a naive and historicist view of the ultimate transparency and necessity of objective interests, a reductionist understanding of nonclass relations and struggles, and a blindness to the real and persistent problem of constructing such a movement, unifying diverse constituencies, balancing competing claims, and sustaining ideological commitments.

The second belief upon which this conception of socialism rests is equally naive and entirely *unrealistic*: the belief in the possibility, indeed the necessity, of the ultimate reconciliation of all social antagonisms. The most powerful, but by no means the only statement of this belief is none other than Marx's claim, in his *Paris Manuscripts*, that communism is "the *genuine* resolution of the conflict between man and nature, and between man and man—the true resolution of the strife between existence and essence, between objectification and self-confirmation, between freedom and necessity, between the individual and the species.... Communism is the riddle of history solved, and it knows itself to be this solution."[58]

---

[58]Karl Marx, "Private Property and Communism," in Robert C. Tucker, ed., *The Marx-Engels Reader*, 1st ed. (New York: Norton, 1972), p. 70. Leszek Kolakowski has argued that this formulation bore the seeds of Stalinist totalitarianism. While we wish to call attention to the limits and ambiguity of Marx's view here,

The primary focus of this book has been on developing a realist understanding of social power and making clear that Marxian theory presupposes such an understanding. Such a view cuts against empiricist critics of Marxism; but it also decisively cuts against any historicist efforts to defend Marxism. On the view we have developed, power must always be understood in terms of the specific relations in which it is embedded; this view does not lend itself to any form of reductionism. Furthermore, on this view power is intrinsically hermeneutic and is chronically negotiated and renegotiated in the course of its exercise by diverse, socially situated agents; this view cuts against any notion of power as located in a single, unambiguous source or center, as well as against any notion of an ultimately monolithic unity either for or against the status quo. On methodological as well as substantive grounds, then, we have good reason to reject any variant of Marxian historicism (we have not even considered the practical consequences of such historicism, but the record of twentieth-century historical experience could only further indicate its dangers); and that version I have reconstructed in Chapters 4 and 5 is noticeably shorn of any traces of such a historicism.

There is, however, another argument to be made, an argument concerning how we think about the future, about what Marx called "human emancipation." For not only must we acknowledge the limits of Marxism, particularly in its historicist variants, as an analysis of power, recognizing the need for other forms of analysis (like feminism); we must also acknowledge that connected to this analytical limitation is a dangerous and invidious strand of *utopianism* that has characterized the history of Marxism. This resides in its failure to take seriously enough the problem of the *limits of power*. This utopianism can be traced to a number of features of Marx's own corpus: the historicist optimism of his early writings, his belief that "human emancipation" would transcend the separation of state and society, transcending the problem of "bourgeois right," and his various remarks about the dictatorship of the proletariat (as well as Engels's comments on the "withering away of

---

Kolakowski's interpretation would seem to embody the same kind of teleology of which he accuses Marx. See his exchange with Mihailo Markovic, "Stalinism and Marxism," in Robert C. Tucker, ed., *Stalinism: Essays in Historical Interpretation* (New York: Norton, 1977).

the state"). Side by side, of course, we must place with these Marx's early defenses of freedom of speech, his acknowledgment that the liberties comprising liberal democracy "represents a great progress," his decentralist and antistatist remarks about the Paris Commune, and his gradualist strategic remarks about "the birthmarks of the old society" in his *Critique of the Gotha Programme*. Marx's own theoretical and practical legacy on the question of the organization of power in postcapitalist society is ambiguous.[59] And despite all that can be said in favor of his anti-utopianism, and of his yeomanlike assurances that the working class has "no ready-made utopias to introduce *par décret du peuple*,"[60] one must adjudge Marx's reticence to articulate an explicit visionary program if not a "blueprint" a great and tragic failure, particularly in the light of the subsequent history of Marxism.[61]

The revitalization of Marxian theory rests not only on its willingness to take seriously the importance of nonclass relations and struggles, but also on its ability to make good the promise of Marx's critique of capitalist domination, and to articulate a genuine ethical-political theory of the means and ends of socialist transformation. In accomplishing this we must pay close attention to the deficiencies of Marxian thought, beginning with the thought of Marx himself.

---

[59]See Frederic Bender, "The Ambiguity of Marx's Concepts of 'Proletarian Dictatorship' and 'Transition to Communism,'" *History of Political Thought* 2 (Winter 1981). On the democratic character of Marx's thought, see Paul Thomas, *Karl Marx and the Anarchists* (London: Routledge & Kegan Paul, 1980), and Alan Gilbert, *Marx's Politics: Communists and Citizens* (New Brunswick, N.J.: Rutgers University Press, 1981).

[60]Karl Marx, "The Civil War in France," in Tucker, *Marx-Engels Reader*, p. 558.

[61]Perry Anderson has observed of Marxian theory, from the vantage point of the failures and disappointments of twentieth-century Marxism: "It remains true that little or none of this work has touched on the actualization of a tangible socialist future.... Yet it is quite clear that without serious exploration and mapping of it, any political advance beyond parliamentary capitalism will continue to be blocked. No working-class or popular bloc in a Western society will ever make a leap in the dark, at this point in history, let alone into the grey on grey of an Eastern society of the type that exists today" (*In the Tracks*, p. 99). Norman Geras makes a similar point, observing of Marxism's characteristic disavowal of moral argument, a disavowal at odds with its own ethical presuppositions: "Marxists should not any longer continue to propagate the aboriginal confusion and self-contradiction in this area, but must openly take responsibility for their own ethical positions, spell them out, defend and refine them" ("The Controversy about Marx and Justice," *New Left Review*, no. 150 [March–April 1985], 85).

But we must also take seriously the lessons of historical experience. And the greatest lesson of twentieth-century history is that the revolutionary belief in an ultimate harmonious kingdom of ends—what Albert Camus called "totality"—is likely to result not in the transcendence of power and the mere "administration of things," but on the contrary, in a system of domination whose ultimate consequence is the administration of repression.[62] Any emancipatory political theory must begin from the premise of human difference. What follows from this is the reality and ubiquity of social power and its chronic contestation, and the necessity of developing new ways of organizing it.

Marx's own historical optimism—which he shared with virtually every nineteenth-century thinker of note, from Mill to Tocqueville to Comte—rested on the belief that the abolition of capitalism would result in the abolition of all forms of social and historical constraint, and in the emancipation of genuinely *human powers*. All individuals would be free to express themselves as they desired; as Marx put it: "Society regulates the general production and thus makes it possible for me to do one thing today and another tomorrow, to hunt in the morning, fish in the afternoon, rear cattle in the evening, criticise after dinner, just as I have a mind, without ever becoming hunter, fisherman, shepherd, or critic."[63] But as should be obvious, the key unexamined premise in this vision is that "society regulates." What does this mean? What is the nature of the social decision-making process, and of the associated production process? Marx's formulation illustrates that, in envisioning an emancipated future, we cannot avoid the realities of a social division of labor and of a corresponding *social distribution of power*. Marx, of course, did write at length about the importance of democracy, and particularly in his discussions of the transition between capitalism and socialism/communism, he indicated the centrality of both power and its organization. But there is also a very powerful utopian strain in Marx's writings, evidenced in the text quoted in this paragraph, particularly insofar as Marx tended to view the problem of social and political power as a problem of

[62]Albert Camus, *The Rebel: An Essay on Man in Revolt* (New York: Vintage, 1956).
[63]Marx, "The German Ideology," in Tucker, *Marx-Engels Reader*, p. 124.

the transition to communism rather than as a problem of its very constitution.

Marx's vision of communist society seems to be based on a thoroughly unrealistic view of the ultimate independence of each individual, free of all constraints of associated living and of what Dewey called "conjoint behavior"; it is also, as Carmen Sirianni argues, based on a questionable view of human nature.[64] Marx, the same Marx who wrote that "the individual is a being only in and through society," suggests in his writings on communism that social identity per se is an obstacle to human freedom, and that the communist individual will have no social identity, only a "human identity." But, it must be asked, what is the content of this human identity? What is being fully human if it is not the identification with certain specific practices and their social value, and the continued successful pursuit of them? Marx himself, in his fragment "The Power of Money in Bourgeois Society," gestures at this when he writes: "Assume man to be man and his relationship to the world to be a human one: then you can exchange love only for love, trust for trust, etc.... If you want to enjoy art, you must be an artistically cultivated person; if you want to exercise influence over other people, you must be a person with a stimulating and encouraging effect on other people. Everyone of your relations to man and to nature must be a specific expression, corresponding to the object of your will, of your real life."[65]

Marx suggests, plausibly, that individuals will differ in their interests and their talents, and that their identities will be shaped by these varying interests and talents. On this premise communism would be an alternative organization of society where, given the abolition of private property in the means of production and a break in the connection between money and individual fulfillment, individuals would have a greater possibility of expressing their individuality and of pursuing their specific interests. As Marx recognizes here, this is not a vision of existential bliss, but rather of

[64]Carmen Sirianni, "Production and Power in a Classless Society: A Critical Analysis of the Utopian Dimensions of Marxist Theory," *Socialist Review*, no. 59 (September–October 1981), 33–82. Sirianni has analyzed the concrete difficulties of constructing democratic socialist practices and institutions in his *Workers Control and Socialist Democracy: The Soviet Experience* (London: Verso, 1982).

[65]Marx, in Tucker, *Marx-Engels Reader*, p. 83.

existential opportunity and choice: "If you love without evoking love in return—that is, if your loving as loving does not produce reciprocal love; if through a living expression of yourself as a loving person you do not make yourself a loved person, then your love is impotent—a misfortune." One might even go further; this is a vision of socially articulated and socially structured human differences. In his discussions of communism Marx tends to speak exclusively of preindustrial forms of (primarily nonproductive) pursuit— reading, art, love. But there is every reason to believe that these will not be the only forms of social identity in an emancipated society. Occupational differences, regional differences, and differences of political opinion will not cease to exist.[66] A critical social and political theory must not only expose and criticize those relations of domination that currently exist, it must also articulate new ways of organizing social power. In the course of doing so, it must incorporate a number of important lessons.

First, a critical theory must acknowledge the important human value of political democracy.[67] As contemporary Marxian theorists like Poulantzas and Miliband have argued, drawing upon that democratic tradition within Marxism tracing back to Marx himself, it is no longer possible to view democracy as a bourgeois illusion. Such a view oversimplifies to the point of absurdity the way in which capitalist democracy operates. But it also denigrates the real historical significance of political democracy, as evidenced both by

[66]Reinhold Niebuhr, while quite sympathetic to Marxism in the 1930s, describing it as "a true enough interpretation of what the industrial worker feels about society and history, to have become the accepted social and political philosophy of all self-conscious and politically intelligent industrial workers," was nonetheless critical of the Marxian view of communism. He writes: "The hope that the internal enemies will all be destroyed and that the new society will create only men who will be in perfect accord with the collective will of society, and will not seek personal advantage in the social process, is romantic in its interpretation of the possibilities of human nature and in its mystical glorification of the anticipated automatic mutuality in the communist society...there can never be a perfect mutuality of interest between individuals who perform different functions in society" (*Moral Man and Immoral Society* [New York: Scribner's, 1932], pp. 194–95).

[67]For discussion, see Steven Lukes's criticism of Marxism, "Can a Marxist Believe in Human Rights?" *Praxis International* 1 (January 1982), 334–45, and two rejoinders in defense of Marxism: Drucilla Cornell, "Should a Marxist Believe in Rights?" and William L. McBride: "Rights and the Marxian Tradition," both in *Praxis International* (April 1984), 45–74. See also Timothy O'Hagan, *The End of Law?* (Oxford: Blackwell, 1984).

the consequences of its absence elsewhere and by its importance in the struggles of workers and other oppressed groups within capitalist societies. Rosa Luxemburg's critique of the political practice of Bolshevism was on target: "Socialist democracy is not something which begins only in the promised land after the foundations of socialist democracy are created; it does not come from some sort of Christmas present for the worthy people who, in the interim, have loyally supported a handful of socialist dictators. Socialist democracy begins simultaneously with the beginnings of the destruction of class rule and the construction of socialism." She insists: "The only way to rebirth is the school of public life itself, the most unlimited, the broadest democracy and public opinion."[68]

Camus echoed Luxemburg's sentiment more than thirty years later, criticizing a dangerous tendency within twentieth-century revolutionary Marxist thought: "From a justifiable and healthy distrust of the way that bourgeois democracy prostituted freedom, people came to distrust freedom itself. At best, it was postponed to the end of time, with the request that meanwhile it be not talked about."[69] The problem of course, is one that Camus perceived— that this notion of an end of time or, in Luxemburg's words, a "promised land," is nothing but a utopian mystification, however well intentioned. It rests on an act of faith, with "history" simply usurping the role of God. There is no reason to make such a leap of faith, and political theory, after all, relies on reason.[70] This

[68]Rosa Luxemburg, "The Russian Revolution," in Mary-Alice Waters, ed., *Rosa Luxemburg Speaks* (New York: Pathfinder Press, 1970), pp. 365–95.

[69]Albert Camus, "Bread and Freedom," in his *Resistance, Rebellion, and Death* (New York: Knopf, 1960), p. 91.

[70]It is worth noting, in this era of resurgent cold war ideology, that Camus, while critical of revolutionary historicism, was also well aware of the dangers of bourgeois historicism. He articulated this most clearly in his essay "Why Spain?" in Camus, *Resistance*. It is also worth noting that, in his unpublished "In Defense of the Rebel," Camus made very clear his hostility toward the cold war ideological use of his critique of revolution in *The Rebel*: "It is certainly possible to allow oneself to speak of this subject irresponsibly. Today everyone would like to take credit for the revolution without paying the price, or wear his revolt in his buttonhole while true revolt is without adornment.... I have concluded—and it is this alone which must be discussed—that, in order to reject organized terror and the police, revolution needs to keep intact the spirit of rebellion which has given birth to it, as rebellion needs a revolutionary development in order to find substance and truth. Each, finally, is the limit of the other" (quoted in David Sprintzen, *Revolt, Dialogue, and Community: An Interpretative and Critical Study of the*

recognition of the necessity of political freedom is related, of course, to the problem of the relationship between means and ends in the construction of socialism.[71] But it is also related to the need to decisively repudiate any notion of an *absolute end* of history.

Human beings, in all of their individual and relational complexity, must be the premise of any vision of an emancipated society. Not only will power be implicated in any social division of labor, but more specifically, it must be assumed that there will of necessity exist institutionally distinct forms of political power. These may be in important respects different from the bureaucratic states we have come to know; they may support different, socialist, relations of production and distribution, and they may be both more responsive and more participatory. But they will perform the necessary function of setting social priorities, mediating social differences, and regulating social conduct.[72] In the language of John Dewey, the problems of the public will not disappear in a postcapitalist society:

> Thus the problem of discovering the state is not a problem for theoretical inquirers engaged solely in surveying institutions which already exist. It is a practical problem of human beings living in association with one another, of mankind generically. It is a complex problem. It demands power to perceive and recognize the consequences of the behavior of individuals joined in groups and to trace them to their sources and origin. It involves selection of persons to

---

Thought of Albert Camus [unpublished]. My understanding of the issues discussed in this chapter is informed by this account, as well as by conversations with its author).

[71]On this issue, see Svetozar Stojanovic, *In Search of Democracy in Socialism: History and Party Consciousness* (New York: Prometheus, 1981).

[72]On the deficiency of traditional Marxian views of central planning, the indispensability of markets, and the necessary complexity of a socialist economy, see Alec Nove, *The Economics of Feasible Socialism* (London: Allen & Unwin, 1983). More generally, see Raymond Williams, "Towards Many Socialisms," *Socialist Review* 16 (January–February 1986), 45–66. See also Branko Horvat, Mihailo Markovic, and Rudi Supek, eds., *Self-Governing Socialism*, 2 vols. (New York: International Arts and Sciences Press, 1975); and Mihailo Markovic and Gajo Petrovic, eds., *Praxis: Yugoslav Essays in the Philosophy and Methodology of the Social Sciences* (Dortrecht, Holland: D. Reidel, 1979). For a discussion of the Praxis group in Yugoslavia, and their efforts to deal with some of these practical problems, see David A. Crocker, *Praxis and Democratic Socialism* (Atlantic Highlands, N.J.: Humanities Press, 1983).

serve as representatives of the interests created by these perceived consequences and to define the functions which they shall possess and employ. It requires the institution of a government such that those having the reknown and power which goes with the exercise of these functions shall employ them for the public and not turn them to their own private interest.[73]

Democratic rights—of free speech, assembly, suffrage—are certainly not a sufficient guarantee of the responsible exercise of public power; in fact, no political institutions can provide such a guarantee, which can be secured, if at all, only by the practical vigilance and participation of free individuals and groups. But these rights are clearly a necessary condition of such accountability, as they are of the more general popular empowerment Marxian theory has always purported to articulate. As we have seen, most contemporary Marxian theorists have recognized this and subscribe to a broadly democratic socialist line on this issue. But perhaps the most interesting recent Marxian treatment of this issue is Roy Medvedev's 1981 book *Leninism and Western Socialism*, which provides a sweeping critique of the failure of orthodox Marxism, particularly in its Bolshevist variant, to take seriously the question of democratic rights.[74] It is worth noting that such a view of the indispensability of political democracy does not involve an uncritical celebration of the virtues of parliamentarism, nor does it involve viewing socialism as a "mere extension of bourgeois democracy."[75] It is quite compatible with the kind of critique of capitalist democracy I outlined in Chapter 5 and understands serious political struggles, including extraparliamentary ones, to be a necessary ingredient of a strategy of social transformation. But it also acknowledges the real value of parliamentary institutions

[73]John Dewey, *The Public and Its Problems* (Chicago: Swallow Press, 1927), p. 32. For an interpretation that stresses Dewey's radicalism, see Peter T. Manicas, "John Dewey and the Political State," *Transactions of the Charles S. Peirce Society* 15 (Spring 1982), 133–58.

[74]Roy Medvedev, *Leninism and Western Socialism* (London: Verso, 1981).

[75]The dismissive language is Ellen Wood's, in her "Marxism," p. 267. Callinicos is equally dismissive of a socialist political strategy based on working through and transforming the institutions of the capitalist democratic state. He derisively writes of Poulantzas: "It is a melancholy sight: the most influential Marxist political theorist of the last decade collapsing into liberal platitudes" (*Is There a Future*, p. 216).

and envisions the problem of emancipation as concerning the deepening and transforming, not the abolition, of these institutions, which, however insufficient, would seem to be a necessary condition of socialist democracy.

Second, a critical theory must confront the danger state militarism poses, both to peace and to the possibility of the emancipation of human beings. War may be, as Randolph Bourne facetiously quipped, the health of the state; but war, and the preparation for it, is a fatal plague upon the democratic body politic.[76] Questions of the military powers of states, and the regulation of interstate relations, must be taken very seriously by those undertaking a critique of the contemporary distribution of power in society. However desirable, it seems unlikely that nationalism or substitute forms of territorial identification will completely disappear in a postcapitalist world. To avoid addressing these problems is not to make them go away; it is only to be forced to deal with them later, and in ways that all too frequently tend to reproduce them in their worst incarnations.

Finally, a critical theory must be based on a theoretical and practical *pluralism.* By pluralism here I do not mean a noncommittal eclecticism.[77] Nor do I mean a celebration of liberal democratic institutions and a blindness to the necessity of political struggle and movement building in order to transcend existing forms of domination.[78] By pluralism I mean a sincere recognition that there are many forms of domination, and many forms of struggle against them, none of which occupies a position of his-

[76]Randolph Bourne, "The State," in Olaf Hansen, ed., *Selected Writings 1911–1918* (New York: Urizen Books, 1977), pp. 355–95.

[77]Cox et al., for example, exemplify the worst kind of tolerance when they advocate a "principled eclecticism [that] entails...the development of a critical awareness of one's own values and a willingness to learn from the insights of others ...keeping an open mind to the insights which competing theories offer and recognizing that some concepts are likely to remain essentially contested" (*Power,* p. 39). I have criticized this in my "Power in Capitalist Society," *Contemporary Sociology* 15 (September 1986), 766–67.

[78]Dahl, *Dilemmas,* writes about both "pluralist democracy" and "democratic socialism," but one might argue that he is at least liable to the second criticism. Michael Walzer's *Spheres of Justice: A Defense of Pluralism and Equality* (New York: Basic Books, 1983) provides a more radical understanding of a socialist pluralism, though it too lacks a strategic analysis of the structural obstacles standing in the way of such a vision.

torical privilege and each of which warrants respect and critical support. One important implication of this is that the term "post-capitalist society" is itself an inadequate way to designate the character of an emancipated society, insofar as it refers only to the transformation of class relations and says nothing about those other relations standing in the way of greater human freedom. Any form of theoretical or practical reductionism will tend to produce only a hopeless and politically ineffective sectarianism; and it will also tend to reproduce those forms of domination that are viewed as somehow less essential. But this "respect and critical support" should not be taken as an excuse for a kind of "repressive tolerance" among radical groups. First, the word *critical* indicates the necessity of subjecting all organizations and movements to questioning on both strategic and tactical issues. Second, insofar as the various forms of domination in society are interconnected, the struggle against them must be similarly interdependent. And an emancipated society must reflect this interdependence, neither eliminating class domination at the expense of gender domination, for example, nor vice versa. Needless to say, the precise forms of this pluralism can be worked out only in practice.[79]

Political theory can play a crucial role in examining and demystifying the various forms of domination that exist in society. That is why the sorts of methodological and substantive arguments I have developed in this book are so important. But as Marx wrote of philosophy, and of theory more generally, it is only "the head of emancipation." Equally indispensable for emancipation is a heart, and the heart of emancipation is the practical dedication of extraordinary and more ordinary people to cast off the frustrating fetters of domination and to create new forms of social power. This project may be more complicated than the Marxian tradition has imagined. But in pursuing it Marxian theory and practice can play an indispensable role in providing a critique of the historical constitution of class domination in capitalist society, and a vision of a "free association of producers." It may not be too simplistic to suggest that the revitalization of the contemporary

[79]For an account of such a pluralist political strategy, see Michael Rustin, *For a Pluralist Socialism* (London: Verso, 1985).

movements struggling against domination in the Western world depends on integrating such a critique. And it is equally clear that such an encounter with these movements may be just what is needed to sustain the continued revitalization of Marxism.

Index

Library of Congress Cataloging-in-Publication Data

Isaac, Jeffrey C., 1957–
    Power and Marxist theory.

    Includes index.
    1. Power (Social sciences)   2. Communism and society.   3. Marx, Karl,
1818–1883.   I. Title.
JC330.I84   1987   303.3'3   87–6690
ISBN 0–8014–1934–4 (alk. paper)